Reforming Farm Policy

Toward a National Agenda

Reforming Farm Policy

Toward a National Agenda

Willard W. Cochrane
C. Ford Runge

Iowa State University Press / Ames

For Our Pioneering Families
Who Helped Build Rural America

Willard W. Cochrane is a professor emeritus and C. Ford Runge is a professor in the Department of Agricultural and Applied Economics at the University of Minnesota. Both are affiliates of the Center for International Food and Agricultural Policy at the University of Minnesota.

Authorization to photocopy items for internal or personal use, or the internal or personal use of specific clients, is granted by Iowa State University Press, provided that the base fee of $.10 per copy is paid directly to the Copyright Clearance Center, 27 Congress Street, Salem, MA 01970. For those organizations that have been granted a photocopy license by CCC, a separate system of payments has been arranged. The fee code for users of the Transactional Reporting Service is 0-8138-0448-5/92 $.10.

⊗ Printed on acid-free paper in the United States of America

First edition, 1992
Second printing, 1993

Library of Congress Cataloging-in-Publication Data

Cochrane, Willard Wesley
    Reforming farm policy: toward a national agenda / Willard W. Cochrane, C. Ford Runge. — 1st ed.
        p.   cm.
    Includes index.
    ISBN 0-8138-0448-5
    1. Agriculture and state — United States. I. Runge, C. Ford (Carlisle Ford)
II. Title.
HD1761.C62 1992
338.1'873 — dc20   92-11113

CONTENTS

PREFACE

The pattern of ideas, concerned with farm policy reform, that takes shape in this volume did not emerge full blown in an instantaneous revelation. For Cochrane the development of these ideas occurred over a long period of time and along a tortuous route; it occurred as the resource concentration process in farming made some of his earlier policy ideas obsolete, and successive farm bills turned farm policy into the domain of a relatively few large to very large farmers while ignoring the developmental needs of rural America and the environmental needs of the nation. For Runge, the development of these farm policy ideas took a different route; he began with an international perspective and discovered over time how the domestic farm programs of the United States operated to place roadblocks in the way of an open international trading system and thereby impeded the exports of farm products from the United States, as well as ignored the needs of the rural poor and the environmental needs of the nation. These different intellectual paths of the co authors converged in the writing of this book, and through many hours of discussion, idea development, and compromise, a farm policy reform package emerged.

Many people and institutions assisted us in the writing of this book. John Schnittker and Robert Paarlberg read early drafts of many chapters and encouraged us to proceed with the project, and made suggestions for strengthening the presentation. Two seminars sponsored by the Department of Agricultural and Applied Economics at the University of Minnesota enabled us to present our policy reform ideas to a large group of our professional peers as well as some farm and agri-business leaders. In these seminars, and the discussions that followed, we received some friendly but sharp criticism which helped us to tighten our arguments and to avoid certain conceptual pitfalls. Discussions with the staff of the Food and Agricultural Policy Research Institute (FAPRI), Abner Womack and Ken Bailey of the University of Missouri and William Meyers and Patrick Westhoff of Iowa State University preparatory to the modelling of our proposals by FAPRI enabled us to fine tune and sharpen those proposals. And the quantitative estimates of the impacts of our proposals were produced by FAPRI and are presented in Chapter 9.

Professor Jerry Hammond of the University of Minnesota helped us develop a set of dairy proposals consistent with our overall reform package. Tom Stinson assisted us in thinking about rural development issues. Louise Letnes, Departmental Librarian, helped us on numerous occasions to locate hard-to-find information and documents which we required. Laura Bipes, Administrative Director, ironed out several financial and logistic problems for us. Laurie Erdman, a graduate assistant, read the entire manuscript with the objective of eradicating errors, employing a consistent note system and bringing data up-to-date wherever possible; she also developed the tabular material at the end of Chapter 6 comparing the principal features of the Cochrane/Runge proposals with the features of the 1985 and 1990 farm legislation. Judy Berdahl, our secretary, typed and retyped the many drafts of the manuscript and helped two very independent co-authors work as a team.

The Department of Agricultural and Applied Economics at the University of Minnesota and the University Center for International Food and Agricultural Policy provided the congenial and stimulating atmosphere in which to write this book, as well as the necessary physical facilities. The Northwest Area Foundation of St. Paul, Minnesota, provided general support for the project. A grant from the First Bank Systems, Inc. Minneapolis, Minnesota, provided a part of the funding support for this book writing project.

Many people and institutions provided valuable assistance in the writing of this book, as noted above, but ultimately Cochrane and Runge wrote it. Thus, the ideas and proposals contained in the book are solely the responsibility of the authors, as are any errors of logic or fact that may be found in it.

April 1992   Willard W. Cochrane
                                                                    C. Ford Runge

Reforming Farm Policy

Toward a National Agenda

1 An Introduction to the Policy Problem

It is the basic premise of this book that current farm policy badly needs reforming. In particular, the commodity programs which form the core of the policy are out-of-date, and out-of-sync with the modern farm economy. They help those farmers most that need it least, provide little or no help to those people in rural areas living in poverty, ignore the special problems of part-time farmers, create obstacles to the movement of farm products in international trade, and provide no lasting solution to the chronic problem of overproduction.

It was not always thus. In the 1930s, the Great Depression years, when the programs were conceived, the vast majority of farmers were medium-sized farmers, and almost all were in financial trouble as the result of disastrously low farm prices. The programs were designed to deal with the common problems of this broad group of farmers. And they largely succeeded.

Following World War II the farming landscape began to change and change rapidly. Two technological revolutions swept over American agriculture: the first mechanical, the second chemical-biological. The more aggressive, innovative farmers were quick to adopt these new technologies, to reduce their unit costs, and to prosper economically. As a result, they sought to expand their operations. The laggard farmers, on the other hand, were slow to adopt these new technologies, were slow to get their unit costs down and sustained financial losses. As a result, they went out of business in a continuing stream that widened in the 1980s when farm prices sagged. The land and productive resources from these failed operations enabled the aggressive, innovative farmers to expand their operations.

In the 1950s, 1960s, and 1970s, the farming landscape in America underwent a profound change that has never been fully appreciated. The total number of farms declined dramatically. The bulk of the productive resources and the output of those resources were concentrated into the hands of a few hundred thousand large to very large farmers. A new and

3

large group of part-time farmers emerged for whom farming became a sideline to other employment. Over that long period the resource concentration process continued unabated as each year a few thousand unsuccessful farmers went out of business and their resources were gobbled up by their hard driving, innovative neighbors.

The farm depression of the 1980s also caused a large number of farmers, who made the wrong investment decisions in the 1970s, to fail and go out of business. The resource concentration process was thus given added force. As a result, the size distribution of farms had become highly skewed by 1989: roughly 300,000 large to very large farms produced about 75 percent of the total national farm product;[1] perhaps another 300,000 farms—medium to small farms—produced about 15 percent of the total product; and another 1.5 million or more part-time farmers, trying to earn a few dollars from farming, produced some 10 percent of the total product (USDA/ERS 1991). The commercial farming sector in the 1990s is thus basically comprised of a few hundred thousand very large and very efficient farms. Many, if not most of these farms, are family proprietorships; but they are a far cry, in terms of capital investment, from the medium-size family farms of the 1930s.

Over this same long period the details of the farm programs changed almost every year. They became increasingly complex in terms of new features and options as the Congress and successive administrations tried to meet the diverse needs of program participants. But the basic program design never changed. Programs were designed along commodity lines. Producers were provided price or income support based on the number of units of a specific commodity produced by them. Excess production capacity was dealt with on a yearly basis through voluntary production controls (i.e., by paying individual farmers to take some of their land out of production). Surplus stocks acquired by government in price-supported operations were disposed of outside commercial channels, in part through relief schemes in the domestic market, but mainly through foreign food assistance. When domestic prices were supported above world levels, exports were maintained or increased by means of export subsidies. This is the basic farm program that took shape in the 1930s, and is still with us today.

A Social Contract?

It is sometimes argued that a "Social Contract" exists between society and agriculture in the United States in which society has made a commitment to protect farm prices and incomes, and agriculture has made a commitment to produce an abundant supply of food for society.[2] This formulation of the contract may be more explicit than, in fact, ever existed. Certainly, the representatives of agriculture and society never sat down around a negotiating table and hammered out a formal contract. But politicians for most of the twentieth century have praised farmers for their willingness to produce bountifully and promised them, in return, that their prices and incomes would be protected. Thus, some sort of an implicit contract has existed.

In a recent essay Robert L. Paarlberg (1990) examined the notion of such a contract, observing that it dated at least to the Great Depression. Precisely because of its Depression era origins, Paarlberg noted that it did not create a "balanced exchange." The original contract was struck at a time of acute disadvantage for the farm sector, and was written to provide one-way policy benefits for agriculture.

First, the farm sector got a unique *price-support* guarantee, established in the 1933 Agricultural Adjustment Act. The most important U.S. farm commodities would have their minimum price set not in the economic marketplace, but the political marketplace, by the U.S. Congress and the U.S. Department of Agriculture. Second, it would be farmers, or the designated representatives of farmers, who would exercise sovereignty over this political marketplace. Commodity price support legislation would be the job of the agriculture committees of Congress, historically controlled by farm districts. The implementation of farm legislation would be the job of the Department of Agriculture, whose budget was determined by these agricultural committees. At the local level it would mostly be farmers themselves, or former farmers, or the relatives of farmers, who would have the final operational word over how their own sector of the economy would be governed. In effect, such sectoral support, devised and conducted by and for farmers, guaranteed that they would be "supported by society, yet governed by farmers."

These guarantees made some sense during the Great Depression, when the U.S. agricultural sector was clearly in need of societal support, and when it functioned largely separately from the rest of society. But from today's vantage point, farming is no longer a relatively disadvantaged sector. Wealth per person in the U.S. farm sector is now substantially *higher* than in the nonfarm sector. Even the average income of farm households is higher (by about 20 percent in 1988), compared to nonfarm households (Kalbacher and Brooks 1990).

Farm consolidation resulting from modern agricultural technology means that for every farmer in the U.S. agricultural sector today, there are six or seven nonfarmers, working in industries either upstream or downstream from the farm. Roughly 85 percent of all U.S. agricultural economic activity actually takes place off the farm. Farm families themselves now earn nearly half of their income through activities off of farms, so that the assumption that farmers are somehow separate from the rest of us also has to be set aside.

In short, Paarlberg concludes that

> The set of guarantees that farming originally received from the rest of society during the Great Depression is no longer necessary or appropriate, either to the enhanced prosperity of farmers, or to the altered role and structure of farming within our society.
>
> Yet these guarantees have mostly remained in place. The contract has never really been re-written; farming has remained a politically privileged economic activity (Paarlberg 1990, p. 4).

Like Paarlberg we believe that farm policy badly needs to be reformed. It is no longer compatible with the structure of farming, with the needs of rural America, with the environmental needs of the nation or with the foreign trade needs of both agriculture and the national economy. Since, however, there is some validity to the social contract argument we will not propose later in this book that *all programs* providing income protection to farmers and price stability to the food and farm sectors be terminated. As the title of the book suggest, it deals with farm policy reform—how to eliminate certain programs, add certain programs, and change and modify certain programs to make them compatible with the needs of the food, farm, and rural sectors of the economy in the 1990s.

Farm Policy and Macroeconomic Policies

The authors recognize the dominant role of macroeconomic policies— monetary policy, fiscal policy, and exchange rate policy—in determining the level of national economic activity. That these macro-economic policies are of overriding importance in determining the degree of prosperity in the farm and rural sectors is well understood. The tight monetary policy pursued in the late 1970s and early 1980s to curb the inflationary spiral in the United States, for example, proved to be devastating for the farm sector in the first half of the 1980s. And no one knows where the inept fiscal policies of the federal government in the decade of the 1980s will ultimately lead. The inter-relations of macro-economic policies with farm prosperity and depression are discussed in an historical context in Chapter 3.

But this book does not deal with the substance of and the impact of macroeconomic policies. This book deals with the substance of and the impact of policies and programs undertaken to deal directly with the problems of the food, farm, and rural sectors. The expertise of the authors lies in this latter area, and problems, both acute and chronic, abound in this latter area. Policy reforms are needed in the food, farm, and rural sectors regardless of the level of national economic activity and to this need we address ourselves in this book.

A Reader's Guide

Chapter 2 provides a perspective for the policy analysis that follows. It describes the images of the farm sector, which serve to confuse the policy issues, and the policy and political realities that confront the nation. In this chapter we also formulate a set of principles to provide guidance and direction to the analysis that follows: first in the appraisal of current policies and second in the development of a farm policy reform package. From where do these principles emerge? They emerge from or are a reflection of the beliefs and values of society. Thus, much of the chapter is concerned with giving these principles substantive content and operational meaning.

In Chapters 3, 4, and 5 we present an appraisal of the current farm policy in the setting of an interdependent world agricultural economy, a highly dynamic and efficient domestic agricultural production plant, but one in which the bulk of the production resources are concentrated in a few hundred thousand large to very large farms. In this appraisal the shortcomings of the current farm policy far outweigh its positive aspects. We conclude that the current policy needs reform.

On the basis of our appraisal of current farm policy in Chapters 3, 4, and 5 and the decision principles formulated in Chapter 2, we develop our version of a desirable farm policy in Chapter 6. In this formulation we will be as program specific as space allows, because we want the reader to have a clear grasp of the content of this policy. And our formulation will be broad because we believe that farm policy has many facets and should not be viewed simply as a collection of commodity programs. But we recognize that the policy product of any two other analysts could be somewhat different from ours because their belief and value systems are different, leading to different judgments. Further, we recognize that the political process in Washington in which policies are hammered out will produce a farm policy different from the one that we articulate. Nonetheless, we believe that the logic of the process that we present, and the farm policy product that we have produced, can have an influence on the real world of farm policy development. We believe this because we believe that we are talking sense about a policy that is consistent with the goals and ideals of American society.

In Chapters 7 and 8 we will develop the logical consequences of the policy set forth in Chapter 6. We do this first with respect to its economic and social consequences on the domestic scene. Second, we trace out its consequences in the international arena. On balance, we would expect these consequences to be favorable. But there will be some negative consequences for certain groups. It is important to understand and recognize who will be hurt, and under what circumstances, as well as to understand the nature and magnitude of the benefits.

In Chapter 9, with help from the Food and Agricultural Policy Research Institute at the University of Missouri and at Iowa State University, we present quantitative estimates of key variables (e.g., prices, incomes, quantities, trade volumes, government costs) over a five year period under the assumption that our policy proposals were operative. Of course, many assumptions must be made in such an econometric analysis: the state of the economy, foreign trade institutions and technological developments, for example. But such is the case in any econometric analysis that takes the form of a projection. Nonetheless, such quantitative projections do help the reader to gain a view of what could happen to key economic variables given the operation of the proposed policy. This is especially true if the analysis includes a base line projection from which estimates under the policy proposal may be judged.

In Chapter 10 we appraise the policy proposal in terms of real world politics. Does it have any chance of gaining political support and becoming government policy? If so, what kind of a political coalition will be needed to provide that political support? And where must the leadership come from to build that coalition?

Chapter 11 will summarize the arguments presented by the authors in the form of a closing argument.

About the Authors

It is somewhat unusual for authors to include autobiographical sketches in the text of their volume, but we do so because we believe that Gunnar Myrdal was correct when he argued in his important work *An American Dilemma: The Negro Problem and Modern Democracy* (page 1043):

> Valuations will, when driven underground, hinder observation and inference from becoming truly objective. This can be avoided only by making the valuations explicit. *There is no other device for excluding biases in social sciences than to face the valuations and to introduce them as explicitly stated, specific and concretized value premises.*

We have tried to do this by laying our valuations on the table for all to see.

Willard W. Cochrane, (1914–): My father died suddenly in the spring of 1926 less than two months before my twelfth birthday. My life in a secure, conservative, modestly prosperous California ranch family thus ended abruptly. The next few years were difficult ones for my mother and me; we survived, but just barely. And in those days, there was no social security net to provide help in the event of a family catastrophe. The onset of the Great Depression in 1929 did not help matters, although my mother held onto a rather low paying clerical job during the worst of those years.

In 1931 I graduated from high school and tried to find a job. But there were no jobs to be found in Los Angeles where we lived. After a few months of making the rounds to employment agencies, a friend of a friend gave me a job working in a furniture factory that made relatively simple items such as card tables. With the exception of the foreman, the owner worked all "teenage" boys on a piece work basis. No matter how hard you worked, you could not earn over $12 per week. When your productivity increased, the owner cut the piece rate. After a few months of that, another friend of a friend hired me as a messenger for a printing concern. So for about six months, I rode a bicycle in downtown Los Angeles as a messenger boy. Then I decided to go back to school; "There must be better ways to earn a living than riding a bicycle in heavy traffic," I reasoned.

I enrolled in Los Angeles Junior College partly to study and partly to run on the track team. I could do this in 1932 because my mother still had her job that paid in the neighborhood of $80 a month. But I got lucky this time; I got a job as a part-time janitor at a nearby junior high school which provided me with money to attend college. My track career never led to stardom, but my grades did begin to improve. And they improved enough so that I could transfer to the University of California at Berkeley in 1934. At Berkeley I earned my room and board working for various fraternities and private boarding houses, and earned some ready cash working for the National Youth Administration. This was my first meeting with a New Deal depression agency. I also discovered the rather new curriculum, agricultural economics, which I selected as my major. I took all the bread and butter courses in agricultural economics—marketing, farm management, farm finance, and statistics—in the hopes that they would lead to a job after graduation. I also received a full immersion in classical economic theory of which *The Principles of Economics* (8th edition) by Alfred Marshall served as the Bible. But I learned not one thing about why we were in the midst of a terrible depression (which I had witnessed first hand) or anything about how we might emerge from it.

I did not give consideration to doing graduate work until late in my senior year. The one prestigious midwestern school to which I applied turned down my application. This is not surprising because my undergraduate grades were rather uneven: very good in my major field, in history and in the biological sciences, but rather poor in such areas as accounting and the physical sciences. But through the auspices of my undergraduate advisor, E. C. Voorhies, I was granted a fellowship at Montana State College in a master's degree program initiated that year, 1937.

This was one of the best things that ever happened to me. Montana State College in 1937 was an exciting place. I did not learn much economics at MSC, but I learned a lot about Great Plains agriculture and its problems in the 1930s. I also got a first-hand look at the operation of New Deal farm programs in a serious problem area. The aura of M. L. Wilson still clung to the place and everyone from undergraduate students to senior faculty was focusing on the problems of Montana agriculture and how to deal with them.

Armed with a fresh master's degree, I moved on to the University of Minnesota in the fall of 1938. At the U of M, I shifted back from a problem solver to a student learner. From F. M. Garver, I learned what were the strong and the weak points of classical theory. From a bright young professor, Francis Boddy, the whole world of monopolistic competition and oligopoly was laid open to me. And from Warren Waite on the farm campus, I began to see how statistics could be used to estimate various economic relationships (e.g., demand curves). In those days it was called price analysis; now it is called econometrics.

But I tarried only a year at Minnesota. In the spring of 1939, I was offered a job at the grand salary of $2,000 per year in the Cooperative Research and Service Division of the Farm Credit Administration. I jumped at the opportunity. Here was a chance to earn some real money, and $2,000 per year in 1939 was real money. My first assignment was not much fun— taking a census of defunct cooperatives. But I soon began meeting some exciting people: Patrick O'Donnell in my own agency just down from Harvard, Harry Trelogan from the central office of the Farm Credit Administration and preceding me by a year from Minnesota, Mordicai Ezekiel and Louis Bean from the office of the secretary of agriculture and Carl C. Taylor, a stimulating sociologist from the old Bureau of Agricultural Economics (BAE). Buzzing with new ideas and unhappy with my job in the Agency for Cooperatives, I took off for Harvard in January 1941 with the promise of funding assistance from John D. Black as a carrot and my draft board breathing down my back as a push.

Harvard was all I had hoped for and more—exciting student colleagues, exciting teachers and exciting course work. Many things happened to me and around me between January 1941 and January 1942, the latter month in which I took and passed the preliminary examination for the Ph.D. degree and took off to join the navy. But I shall mention only three which bear on my intellectual growth and development. First, I discovered Kenneth Boulding's new book *Economic Analysis* published in March of 1941 which made the many subtle relationships of classical economic theory clear to me (and to many other graduate students of that era) for the first time. Second, from Alvin Hansen and his assistant, Paul Samuelson, I learned the Keynesian system, with its American adaptations, which Keynes had hidden behind the colorful writing of the *General Theory*. Third, from Charles Howard McIlwain, the finest teacher that crossed my path in my graduate career, I gained an understanding and appreciation of the growth of political thought in Western civilization. Finally, I should mention that in all this I had the backing of a powerful figure, John D. Black, who did deliver on his promise to find me funding assistance; I received a Littauer fellowship in the summer of 1941. Harvard was a wonderful adventure in ideas and people.

In late January 1942, I dashed off to join the navy, only to discover that the paperwork would take another three months. After a brief stint in the navy, some part of which was productive, but most of which was spent in hospitals, I was discharged, honorably, in the spring of 1943. After another six months of kicking around in veteran's hospitals and spending a little time with the War Food Administration in Denver, I was back in Washington in a junior staff capacity to the chief of the Bureau of Agricultural Economics (BAE). In this capacity, I had time to produce a doctoral dissertation defining and measuring a concept of high level food consumption in the United States (which branded me as a consumption economist for a time), while doing odd jobs for the office of the chief. In this latter role, I had the opportunity to meet and work with all the major staff members of the BAE, and become involved in a large planning exercise which later took the title of "What Peace Can Mean to American Farmers." Here working under the general leadership of H. R. Tolley and directly with Bushrod Allin, James Maddox and James Cavin, as well as consulting with O. V. Wells and Mordicai Ezekiel, I completed my training and apprenticeship as an agricultural economist.

My role in all this was to work with the commodity specialists and production people to bring forth an internally consistent set of estimates, to bring the latest thinking on national employment policy (i.e., the Keynesian system) to the leaders of the project, and to prepare draft after draft of the final reports. After working nearly two years on this project with the BAE leadership named above, I emerged as a full fledged New Deal liberal. But this, of course, represented no basic change in my economic and social outlook—all of my training and experience from Montana State through Harvard University was leading in that direction. The BAE experience simply solidified my ideological outlook.

What were the beliefs and values of a New Deal Liberal in 1945–46, as I viewed it? First, we believed that productive, successful members of society had an obligation, a duty, to lend a helping hand to the poor, down-trodden members of society. Second, we believed that, although private charity was nice, the state had an obligation to take action to assist the poor and the down-trodden. Third, we believed that politicians and leaders in society, working with experts like ourselves could fashion the action programs that could successfully assist the poor and down-trodden to become productive citizens. And we believed these points fervently. Further, these beliefs squared perfectly with the paramount value in my system of values; namely, the "Golden Rule." *Thou shalt do unto others as you would have them do unto you.*[3]

Time would change my emphasis on the above three related beliefs, and add others of equal importance. I still hold to the first belief in 1992 with the same fervor that I did in 1945. I have, however, become wary of government and less sure of belief No. 2. My trust in a benevolent government has been shaken by the all-to-common practice of the rich and powerful using government to become even richer and more powerful. Still I see no alternative to government assistance for the poor. Finally, I have become much more tolerant of views held by experts that differ from mine. I have no time for expert opinion which I consider dishonest or self-serving, but I recognize that there is often more than one way, my way, to achieve a specific goal, and that truth and knowledge are relative things.

The latter development of my belief and value system results from four major activities in my adult life, which are also responsible for my deepened, as well as growing, understanding of the functioning of the American farm economy. Those activities are: (1) active participation in the never-ending farm policy debate, (2) actual participation in policy formulation in the 1960s, (3) an active involvement in overseas development work, and (4) a deep commitment to teaching, research, and writing. I was a charter member from the University of Minnesota of the land grant college regional and interregional research committees on farm policy in the 1950s. I produced a steady stream of research publications in this period, including my favorite writing effort *Farm Prices: Myth and Reality.* I acted as the unofficial advisor on agriculture to Orville L. Freeman, governor of Minnesota, and served as chairman of his study commission on agriculture 1957–1958. I wrote position papers and legislative proposals for Senator Hubert H. Humphrey. I debated the supporters of the farm policies of Ezra Taft Benson across the land.

I served on the personal staff of Senator John F. Kennedy during the 1960 presidential campaign as his agricultural advisor. I served as director of agricultural economics (now called assistant secretary for economics) in the U.S. Department of Agriculture during part of the Kennedy-Johnson administrations and as the chief program planner of the department with the administrative responsibility for two agencies: the Economic Research Service and the Statistical Reporting Service. In 1965 I became dean of international programs at the University of Minnesota and for the next five years was deeply involved in the initiation, administration, and work of overseas development projects. In the 1970s I turned almost exclusively to teaching and research in the areas of farm policy and agricultural development; in 1978 I turned out my last volume prior to this one, *The Development of American Agriculture: A Historical Analysis.* It has been a rich experience with many lessons, which I hope are reflected in this volume.

In the years since 1965, I have developed another belief which I consider of paramount importance. It is that man through the rapid exploitation of natural resources, pollution, and unbridled population growth is destroying the earth on which he lives. Related to this belief is that man is not God's chosen creature with the right to wantonly destroy other forms of life for his pleasure. Thus, I have become an ardent environmentalist in the belief that we will need to take extraordinary measures in the years ahead to protect the physical environment and thus maintain an environment in which man and other forms of higher life may survive.

Finally, my exuberant idealism of the 1940s has given way in the 1980s and 1990s to a profound skepticism about the future.[4] Everywhere I look in America, I see the forces of enlightenment, knowledge and reason, the Golden Rule as a guide for human behavior, beauty in nature and the arts, and fair treatment under the law for all countered and checked by the forces of evil, human greed, mediocrity in education, lying and dishonest acts by political leaders, massive pollution of the environment, and cultural vulgarity. My vision of the future is thus no longer one of a good society striving for perfection; it is one of a constant struggle by American society to see that the forces of enlightenment are not defeated.

People who read this book on farm policy—what is wrong about it and what needs to be done about it—can now read it against the backdrop of Cochrane's own view of his belief and value system.

C. Ford Runge, (1953–): I was born in Wisconsin, and grew up in the southern part of the state, west of Madison. My father and mother were teachers and small-town Wisconsin Progressives and New Deal Democrats, active in state politics and early opponents of Senator Joseph McCarthy. Their families were in the farming, fertilizer, and lumber businesses of the state, my father's family settling frontier Wisconsin in the 1840s. My mother died after a struggle with multiple sclerosis when I was eleven, and my father remarried several years later into a prominent Wisconsin family. My stepmother, Eleanor Vilas Runge, raised me, my two sisters, and her own two children.

I grew up under the influence of the great state university of Wisconsin, where my parents were educated and where my father played various roles. The traditions of state service, sometimes called the Wisconsin Idea, were a part of the social culture and my own upbringing. Wisconsin and its university are also great agricultural centers. Beginning early in high school, I earned extra money at the University of Wisconsin experimental farms.

In 1977, I returned to Wisconsin for my Ph.D. in agricultural economics at the University of Wisconsin after having received my M.A. in economics as a Rhodes Scholar at Oxford University, and my B.A. at North Carolina–Chapel Hill. While in college, I was politically active, working to support the formation of student consumer groups, and serving as president of my student body. After college, I spent a year at Duke University at the Institute for Public Policy Sciences, where I met my wife, Susan Mackenzie. I then left for Oxford. It was in England that I first realized the opportunities that might exist in international affairs, and I returned to Wisconsin dedicated to a life in agricultural research and development, focusing on its international impacts. Throughout these years in education, I also took time out to work in government. During 1976, I served on the staff of the House Committee on Agriculture, working for then Chairman Thomas S. Foley, Democrat from Washington, the current Speaker of the House. During college, I was an intern in the office of then Senator Gaylord Nelson, a Wisconsin Democrat. It was Nelson who first impressed me with the power of the environmental issue in American politics, which he appreciated long before others understood its significance. After receiving my Ph.D. under Professor Daniel W. Bromley, to whom I owe a great intellectual debt, my first job was in Political Science and Environmental Policy at the University of North Carolina–Chapel Hill. I also held a position in Forestry at Duke University. There I taught courses in American government, democratic theory, public policy analysis, and environmental policy. In 1982, I left Chapel Hill to spend a year in Washington to work in the U.S. Agency for International Development (AID) on food aid and trade issues as a fellow of the American Association for the Advancement of Science.

In 1983, I was offered a position at the University of Minnesota, working to build the North American Granary Project, an international research effort created by G. Edward Schuh, Vernon Ruttan, and other Minnesota faculty. I came to Minnesota eagerly, excited to have the chance to interact with such well-known academics, and to return to my political roots. Shortly after joining the Minnesota faculty, I was appointed chairman of the governor's Farm Crisis Commission by Governor Rudy Perpich, structuring recommendations on farm credit and land markets in Minnesota during the Minnesota farm depression of the 1980s. At the time of this appointment, thousands of farmers were massing on the Capitol steps, demanding debt relief. I am proud of having helped structure the first state program of financial relief to farmers to emerge from the crisis in land values. While I did not experience the Great Depression, I learned something of the politics of that era in the farm depression of the 1980s. During the same period, I also helped to design a state environmental land retirement scheme, the Reinvest in Minnesota (RIM) program.

In 1986 I was awarded an International Affairs Fellowship by the Council on Foreign Relations, and in 1987 was selected as a Bush Foundation Leadership Fellow and Ford Foundation Economist. I used these awards to spend a year working in the ongoing trade negotiations over agriculture. During 1988, I served as a special assistant to Michael Samuels, the U.S. ambassador to the General Agreement on Trade and Tariffs (GATT) in Geneva, Switzerland. Working under our overall trade representative and subsequent Agriculture Secretary Clayton Yeutter, I observed at first hand the problems of negotiating new international trade rules for agriculture.

This experience confirmed a growing belief that agricultural policy was in serious need of reform, not just in the United States, but around the world. Upon returning to Minnesota in 1988, I was asked to serve as first director of the Center for International Food and Agricultural Policy. The center is structured around improving agricultural export competitiveness, while giving equal weight to maintaining the quality of soil and water resources on which midwestern competitiveness ultimately depends. I served in this role from 1988 to 1991, and remain in the Department of Agricultural and Applied Economics. I also hold appointments in the Hubert H. Humphrey Institute of Public Affairs and in the Department of Forest Resources.

I have had a series of remarkable opportunities to be involved in the policy process. Although an academic, my beliefs and values arise largely from a practical background and set of experiences: I am convinced of the necessity of government intervention to improve social and economic life in rural areas, yet I remain skeptical about the capacity of government to solve all economic problems. In agricultural policy, I am a committed internationalist, and believe strongly in maintaining U.S. trade competitiveness in an international market economy. I am convinced that agricultural policy is no longer the province solely of commodity price support programs, and must be broadened to include rural development and environmental quality objectives. The opportunity to bring these values to bear on current issues of policy, in collaboration with my distinguished colleague, Willard Cochrane, is a great challenge.

Compromise: The Essence of Policy

Although the belief and value systems of the two authors are similar in many respects, their backgrounds are very different. They came of age in vastly different socio-economic time periods; their family backgrounds are very different; and their professional training occurred in different stages in the development of their discipline. Thus, Cochrane is inclined to emphasize his belief in the inherent instability of the agricultural sector, while Runge is less convinced that this instability can be overcome. While both authors place a high value on the protection of the environment, Runge places greatest emphasis on the utilitarian aspects of the environment, and Cochrane more emphasis on the ethical and survival aspects of environmental protection. With respect to market phenomena, Runge has a greater belief in the beneficial consequences of a free market than does Cochrane.

For these and other differences, some large and some small, the two authors found when they sat down to try to formulate a desirable policy, that each had to compromise some of his beliefs and values to find a common policy ground. Two men who hold similar views regarding the limitations and deficiencies of current farm policy, found that in articulating a positive policy each had to compromise certain of the beliefs and values that he held with respect to the broad area of food and agriculture.

Further, in trying to formulate a policy that was both desirable *and acceptable to the body politic* based on their interpretations of the belief and value systems of that body politic, they found that more compromising became necessary to reconcile their different interpretations. In other words, even where the belief and value systems of two people are similar in many respects, differences in emphasis and priorities force compromises if a common policy ground is to be found.

The problem of building a desirable and acceptable farm policy at the national level obviously becomes an exceedingly complex and difficult task. At this level we have people on the far right with their belief and value systems, people on the far left with their belief and value systems, and all kinds of people in between with belief and value systems that may emphasize religious goals, or environmental protection, or national security or health and housing, or the arts, or some other subject areas. Finding such common ground, is, of course, what politics is all about. In a pluralistic democracy such as ours, it is achieved through endless compromise among the competing policy goals advanced by the varied groups noted above. The agents for effecting these compromises are our political and opinion leaders. And the process goes on endlessly in public debates, convention deliberations, over business lunches, in congressional hearings, debates, and votes, and through the interaction of the Congress and the president.

The farm policy presented in Chapter 6 with its various program features represents the Cochrane-Runge version (itself a compromise) of what could be the policy product of the process described above. It is viewed by the authors as desirable in terms of its possible consequences and as acceptable to the body politic.

But it must be immediately recognized that the farm policy statement presented in Chapter 6 is not likely to be enacted into law as it now stands. If it is taken seriously, as we hope it will be, it will be pushed in one direction and pulled in another by interest groups in the farm-food sector, each with its own policy goals based in turn upon the compromised belief and value systems of its members. And if it should be introduced into the legislative process, it will be further modified and reformulated by interested members of the two major political parties. Thus, the farm policy ideas of Cochrane and Runge as presented in Chapter 6, even if they are taken seriously, are certain to emerge from the legislative process in a far different form from which they entered it. The authors fully recognize this probable result.

If this is the case, what is the purpose of this exercise in the first place? First, we believe our analysis can assist in bringing together the political will to start the process of a major farm policy reform. Second, if the Cochrane-Runge interpretation of the policy goals of American society is deemed to be broadly valid, it can point the way, or give direction to, the reform process.

In thinking about policy formation, it is important to recognize that there is no perfect or unique solution as in the case of a multiplication problem or the solving of an algebraic equation. The process is totally different. In a pluralistic, democratic society, we seek through compromise a policy solution that is acceptable to groups with widely differing beliefs and value systems. Thus, the policy agreed upon for execution is not likely to please the members of any of the different interest groups. But through compromise a policy solution is reached that is tolerably acceptable to all concerned. This is the way the Cochrane-Runge policy statement should be viewed.

Notes

1. Based on estimates of cash receipts from farming.
2. Robert C. Lamphier III, president of the American Faculty of Agricultural

Engineers, organized a roundtable to discuss the concept of agriculture's contract with society at the annual meeting of that Society on December 18 and 19, 1990 in Chicago, Illinois. Mr. Lamphier developed this concept in some detail in a lecture entitled "Agriculture's Contract With Society" to the College of Engineering, University of California, Davis, January 30, 1990.

3. See the discussion in Cochrane (1958) pp. 129–30.

4. For an example of my youthful exuberance see my Presidential Address to the American Farm Economic Association in 1959 (Cochrane 1959).

References

Cochrane, Willard W. 1959, December. "Farm Technology, Foreign Surplus Disposal and Domestic Supply Control." *Journal of Farm Economics*. Vol. XLI, Number 5: 885–89.

Cochrane, Willard W. 1958. *Farm Prices: Myth and Reality*. Minneapolis: University of Minnesota Press.

Paarlberg, Robert L. 1990, December 18. "The Social Contract between Society and Agriculture: The Changing Rules by which the Contract is Determined." Remarks to the Annual Meetings of the American Society of Agricultural Engineers. Chicago, Ill.

Kalbacher, Judith Z. and Nora L. Brooks. 1990, First Quarter. "Centerfold: Farmers are Part of American Mainstream." *Choices*.

Myrdal, Gunnar. 1962. *An American dilemma: The Negro Problem and Modern Democracy*. New York: Harper and Row.

U.S. Department of Agriculture/ERS. 1991. *Economic Indicators of the Farm Sector, National Financial Summary, 1989*. ECIFS 9-2, Washington, D.C.: USDA/ERS.

2 Imagery, Reality, and Policy Principles

At the end of the 1980s, the Federal Reserve Bank of Kansas City reported that over half (56 percent) of government farm program payments went to farmers with net profits in excess of $100,000 (Duncan 1989). Even more striking, a report issued by the Economic Research Service of the U.S. Department of Agriculture stated that in 1988, some 18 percent of the farms of the nation (the larger farms producing program crops) received approximately 90 percent of direct government payments; another 18 percent of the farms (smaller farms producing program crops) received only 10 percent of direct government payments; and some 64 percent of the farms of the nation received no government payments at all (USDA 1990). This highly skewed system of commodity and income price support is one of the least understood mechanisms of public policy in the U.S. government. It has existed for years, continuing to reward those farmers (and nonfarm landowners) the most who bought or inherited large tracts of farmland, and who agree to produce those crops for which the government pays large subsidies through the commodity price and income support programs.

Sadly, the American public is largely unaware of how different farming is from the imagery of the past. A great gap exists between these images and the reality of farm activity today. In this chapter, we discuss five images that mask the reality of how the commodity programs really operate.

Imagery

The *New Yorker* magazine several years ago depicted an East Coast perspective on the continental United States. The great middle of the country was essentially a blank. It began somewhere after the Hudson River, with Iowa vaguely centered between the foreground of Manhattan and the distant point of Los Angeles. The myopia depicted was at once accurate and self-congratulatory. A similar cartoon soon appeared on the

West Coast, showing the same view, but with Los Angeles in the foreground.

The concentration of population, media influence, and popular culture on the East and West Coasts creates a sort of informational dumbbell, in which what goes on in between appears in narrower and less accurate terms in many journalistic and media accounts. Scholarly studies have confirmed the existence of this bias. John Borchert, the distinguished geographer, reports that the upper Midwest "is a blank on the mental maps of most Americans" (Borchert 1987). The major metropolitan area of Minneapolis-St. Paul becomes "a vague, inexplicable anomaly amid the wastelands, glaciers, and boondocks." This lack of awareness about America between the coasts has a stifling effect on treatments of farming and farm policy, giving rise to a variety of false images about how it really operates.

The first image is that there exists an undifferentiated land mass of red barns and tall corn or golden wheat growing in flat, featureless landscapes collectively described as "farm states." While some areas conform to type (making them favorite visuals for the occasional nightly news story on farm policy), the reality is strikingly different. Obviously, the great middle is a highly diverse landscape. In addition to the flat, fertile soils of Iowa and Illinois, which are the prototypical agricultural landscapes, there is also great diversity, from the rolling hills and woodlands of southwest Wisconsin or the Ohio Valley to the wet, humid semi-tropics of the Mississippi delta; from the arid High Plains of Kansas and Nebraska to the uncropped grazing lands of the mountainous West. In this vast land area a wide range of crops and livestock are grown and raised, although it is less diverse, as we shall see, than in the past.

Each state's agriculture is sufficiently different that very broad generalizations are needed to sustain any picture of a "typical" farm state. Perhaps more importantly, the economies of the great middle of America, while heavily dependent on agriculture, are less so today than ever before. The Federal Reserve Bank of Kansas City reported in 1987, for example, that fewer than 12 percent of rural families received the majority of their income from farming (Drabenstott, Henry, and Gibson 1987). In the upper Midwest, a pattern of regional service centers has emerged, focused on medium-sized cities such as Rochester, Minnesota; Iowa City, Iowa; or Billings, Montana. Although farming itself serves as a diminishing source of employment, agricultural processing, finance and services are substantial employers, including international companies headquartered in "farm states" like Hormel, International Multifoods, Pillsbury, and General Mills.

The first image, then, is that commodity programs are the product of general farm state interests, with benefits that are widely distributed to the residents of this undifferentiated land mass. In reality, the interests (and politics) of farm programs break down along lines of specific commodities and regions, each with its own features and peculiarities. Farmers are a distinct minority in every "farm state," and in every congressional district in these states. The most "agricultural" congressional district in the country, Minnesota's second, has only 25 percent of its population engaged in full-time farming. Reliance on agriculture has increasingly come to mean *part-time* reliance, with other employment in processing or service sectors. It is a particular irony of the midwestern "farm state" illusion that California is the biggest farm state of all, with net farm income of $6.0 billion in 1989, compared with $2.4 billion for Iowa, $2.1 billion for Nebraska, and $1.1 billion for Kansas (USDA/ERS 1991a).

To understand agricultural policy, therefore, it is not enough to understand "typical" farm state interests. The student of policy must grasp an intricate web of specific commodity and geographic interests, and a complex historical evolution of farm programs. Faced with this complexity, it is easy to see why the urbane President Kennedy is reported to have said to his newly designated secretary of agriculture, Orville Freeman, "I don't want to hear about agriculture from anyone but you ... Come to think of it, I don't want to hear very much about it from you either."

A second image characteristic of many treatments is what might be called the picture of a "Little House on the Prairie." This soft-focus view of rural life, while conceivably part of a romantic past, is not of the present. Laura Ingalls Wilder's own life history, on which the recent television series was based, suggests that her rootless frontier experiences in Wisconsin, Minnesota, and the territories was anything but bucolic. The image of a "family farm" associated with the little house is reinforced by a democratic conception of a majority of farmers providing a stable basis for an agrarian republic. This Jeffersonian idealism, despite its powerful hold on the political traditions of our nation, began a long decline in its actual relevance to American political life as early as Jefferson's own time, when the Hamiltonian conception of a manufacturing-based economy began to take hold.

Today, the majority of families who farm are incorporated as businesses and file farm income form F-1040 with the IRS. A large share of the profits in this business, including government commodity payments, go to a small percentage of those categorized as "farmers." As we shall see, the commodity programs tend to aggravate this skewed distribution of benefits. Those farmers who do live on relatively smaller farms, because of the way these government programs are structured, receive the least in payments. Earl Butz, President Nixon's secretary of agriculture, was famous for his proclamation that to survive, farmers had to "get big or get out." Yet it is the commodity programs, as well as market forces, that have rewarded the bigger land owners. Their reward is not just for efficiency, but because they own more acres. This contributes, as we shall document, to the cannibalization of the small by the big. This reality is a far cry from the Jeffersonian ideal, or the symbolism of Laura Ingalls Wilder.

The third image, related to the first two, is that farmers in general are "stewards of the land," and that agriculture is an environmentally benign and naturally healthy activity. In reality, agriculture is increasingly dependent on chemical and mechanical inputs that, when left uncontrolled, have contributed in major ways to environmental pollution of lakes, streams, and groundwater. As more and more farmers have left the land, the fewer, bigger farmers that remain increasingly rely on larger and larger machinery to till their soil and chemicals to maintain its fertility and protect it from weeds and pests. Commodity programs have rewarded the specialized cultivation of crops that are particularly prone to erosion, and encouraged heavy use of fertilizer and chemicals to keep yields high so that larger government payments can be garnered. Heavy equipment, long hours, and steady exposure to hazardous materials also make modern agriculture one of the riskiest businesses in America, with accidents and occupational mortality and morbidity rates among the highest of any major occupational category. Some of the most dangerous features of modern agriculture, we shall argue, are aggravated and encouraged by commodity programs that reward behavior which is inconsistent not only with the health and safety of farmers, but with the health of the larger consuming population that eats what these farmers produce.

The fourth image is that American agriculture remains a domestic industry, for which domestic policies, such as the five-year farm bill, are most important. In reality, American agriculture in the postwar period has emerged as the quintessential export industry, highly dependent on foreign markets and international market forces over which domestic commodity and economic policies have comparatively little influence. Far from being isolated between two coasts, the great middle of America depends upon, and looks to, global markets for its survival and livelihood. Part of what New Yorkers and Los Angeleno's miss when they look west or east is that vast quantities of American agricultural exports are moving south to New Orleans on Mississippi barges, or north through the Port of Duluth and Great Lakes, to destinations all over the world. Nearly half of many fields of corn, wheat, and soybeans in the Midwest are destined for these markets. Farm incomes and assets of Iowa and Nebraska farmers depend, daily, on the quoted prices in Rotterdam. The modern farmer is thus increasingly a global trader, with an increasingly sophisticated grasp of international commerce, logistics, and transport. A major trading firm located in Minneapolis and serving this market is estimated to be the largest privately held company in the world.

The fifth and final image is that the number of farmers leaving the land is so great, and the remaining survivors so beleaguered by debt, crop failure, and hardship that farmers amount to an endangered species. In this view, no expense is too great to preserve and protect them from the hostile march of corporate takeovers. They must be preserved by farm programs so that the other images cited above can also be maintained. The reality is that farm programs have actually hurried the exodus of farmers from the land, by encouraging large farmers to buy up their smaller neighbors. In records kept of farmland purchases in Minnesota going back to 1910, the distinguished economist Philip M. Raup has observed a consistent and steady pattern of farm enlargement, not of corporate takeovers from outside, but of neighbors buying out neighbors. During the period 1981-88, 89 percent of all farmland purchases in Minnesota were made by buyers living within 50 miles and 74 percent within 10 miles of the land they purchased. In the same period, 75 percent of all purchases were to expand existing farms, and only 12 percent were bought by investors (Schwab and Raup 1989).

It is true that millions of farmers have left the land, and that those remaining constitute only about 1.5 percent of the American electorate. But those that remain are hardly poor. And farm programs, as currently structured, do almost nothing to help those who are the poorest and most disadvantaged.

Related to this endangered species image of American farmers, is the fear on the part of many urban consumers that their food supply may in some way be impaired. The idea is often expressed: "If farmers keep going out-of-business who will produce our food?" The answer is that the remaining highly productive, efficient big farmers will produce it. Total farm output in the United States has increased in almost every year since 1947—with total farm output just about doubling since 1947 despite a decline in the number of farms from 5.9 million to 2.2 million over the same period (USDA/ERS 1989; USDA/CRB 1962).

Policy Realities

These five images and their numerous variations tend to mask the important agricultural policy issues—the policy realities—which confront the nation. Let us set forth certain of those realities.

First, how can the diverse needs of many different types of farmers in different farming areas be adequately met by national farm programs? How can sufficient flexibility be built into the programs to meet the diverse needs of individual farmers and still achieve the overall price, income and production goals of the programs? This is a continuing problem with which the Congress and succeeding administrations have struggled every four or five years, and usually each year in between. The result, as of the early 1990s, is a set of commodity programs so complex in content and involving so many operating options that participating farmers usually require technical assistance in the form of legal, tax, and financial advice before signing on with the program. Trying to construct national commodity programs to meet the diverse needs of modern commercial farmers has become an almost impossible task.

Second, how can the benefits of the farm programs be distributed more equitably, so that those who are relatively poor receive proportionately more support than those who are rich? Three important obstacles stand in the way of a satisfactory resolution of this problem.

1. The large, aggressive, rich farmers are well organized and well represented in Washington, hence are able to influence legislation on their behalf, while the small farmers with low incomes are poorly organized and poorly represented in Washington.

2. Commodity programs with the goal of raising farm prices by controlling production must include the large farmers who account for the bulk of the production; thus financial incentives must be built into such programs to induce the large farmers to participate in the programs.

3. Related to (2) above, commodity programs since the 1930s have provided income support to farmers based on the number of units produced by the program participant; this may have been a logical and equitable way of distributing program benefits in the 1930s when the size distribution of farms was not nearly as skewed as it is now; but the tradition which began in the 1930s, and which clearly works to the advantage of the large farmers, is very difficult to break.

Third, how can the objectives of environmental quality and human health be made more consistent with the commodity programs, so that some of the negative environmental and health impacts of modern agriculture are reversed? This policy issue does not lend itself to easy resolution. The commercial farmer is a profit seeker. For 50 years the aggressive commercial farmer has been able to get his costs down and improve his profit position by adopting new and improved technologies—bigger and more efficient machinery, new and improved crop varieties, more intensive use of chemical fertilizers and more intensive applications of chemical pesticides. The commodity programs have reduced the price and income risks to aggressive, innovative farmers for investing in these new cost-reducing technologies. This has increased their incomes as well as their appetite for increasing the size of their operations, which further increases their incomes. In this dynamic scheme of things driven by the private profit motive, little thought has been given to the protection of the rural environment, except perhaps through the back door of the work of the Soil Conservation Service. And the health of the consumer of agricultural products has been given a low priority. With recent interest in the protection of the environment and the high priority assigned to a healthful diet by urban consumers the question now arises: how can these new priorities be made an integral part of American farm policy?

Fourth, how can domestic commodity programs be made consistent with the global marketplace, so that American farmers can compete successfully and the farm sector can prosper? American agriculture was richly endowed with soils, water and climate, and it has been abundantly supported by a public research and extension system and by private transportation, marketing and input supply systems. Thus, it should have a comparative advantage in the production of many, if not most, agricultural products. However, since the end of World War II, the goal of the commodity programs through the operation of price support and production control programs, has been to hold domestic farm prices (or domestic farm incomes through the employment of deficiency payments), above world market prices. This has placed a great handicap on the farm sector economy in the way of developing and supplying foreign markets. Now that almost half of American farm production must find market outlets outside the domestic economy, the goals and operations of government farm programs must be made consistent with the imperative to maintain and develop export markets. However, this new export imperative runs head on into the policy ideas of many farmers and farm leaders who want it both ways—a protected domestic market and a subsidized export market.

Fifth, has the dramatic decline in the total number of farms in the United States since the end of World War II seriously endangered either American society or the economy? If so, what should be done about it? This issue is tied closely to the save-the-family-farm issue. It is both a complex and an emotional one. But it will help our thinking to get a series of facts straight. (1) A relatively few large to very large farms and their family proprietors—some 300,000—have prospered, expanded and have shown no signs of going-out-of-business over the past two decades;[1] these are the farms that produce the bulk of American farm products and have been the principal beneficiaries of the government commodity programs. (2) There is a large and growing number of part-time farm families who regularly earn more than half their total net income from off the farm—some 1.5 million—and who undoubtedly would like to see their family incomes increase. But this increase is unlikely to occur through sweetening the traditional government commodity programs; their farm operations, on the average, are too small and too diverse to benefit importantly from the traditional commodity programs. Their hope lies with more productive, hence more remunerative, off-farm job opportunities. (3) There are a sizeable number of small family farms, with low net farm incomes and even lower off-farm incomes in most years—some 300,000—which could be helped by commodity programs targeted to their situations. But their greatest need is for management and credit assistance which would enable them to enlarge their operations and increase their gross incomes, and thereby their net farm incomes. Many, if not most farms in this class, are too small to be economically viable in the modern commercial world. In sum, many small family farmers and part-time farmers live close to the poverty line in the United States. However, simply redirecting the commodity programs will not, in most cases, solve their income problems because their farm resource base is too small. What they need is more productive job opportunities either on or off the farm.

These are the pressing policy issues that cry out for resolution in the 1990s.

Political Realities

The images described earlier in the chapter are those of the urban citizen, voter, media, and representative in government. The farm commodity organizations—their spokesmen and their representatives in government—know exactly what the hard facts of agriculture are: farm numbers, farm input requirements, supplies and costs, the size distribution of farms. They know within that size distribution who are the efficient, large producers, who are in financial difficulty, and who are small or part-time farmers. They also know exactly what they want from government, commodity by commodity, in the way of credit assistance, income protection, export assistance, research assistance, and tax exemptions. And they have been able to get most of what they have wanted in the post–World War II years. There may be disagreement among these commodity groups from time to time over program priorities and specific program features, but there is no confusion about what each group is seeking from the government in the way of protection or assistance.

The confusion is on the urban side. The false and misleading images described above create and magnify this confusion. Some urban voters, leaders and representatives in government want to "save the family farm" as a part of the Jeffersonian dream of a good society. Some want to help young people to get started in farming to insure an adequate food supply. Some want to support farm prices and incomes as a means of protecting the small family farmer. Some believe that farmers are good stewards of the land; others believe farmers are destroying our land, polluting our water and producing an adulterated food supply. Some want to enhance farm exports, while others believe farmers need more protection from foreign suppliers. And most have no appreciation at all of the resource concentration that has taken place in farming since the end of World War II; the fact that some 300,000 farms, each grossing over $100,000 per year, now produce some 75 percent of the total farm product (USDA/ERS 1991b).

The typical urbanite, as he or she worries about the plight of the family farmer, is largely oblivious to the fact that poultry is now produced in large factories in Georgia and Arkansas, not on family farms across the nation, that cotton is now largely produced in huge operations in the San Joaquin Valley of California and in west Texas, not on family farms or plantations in the Deep South, that large cash grain farms in Illinois and Iowa produce corn and soybeans principally for export to livestock producing centers elsewhere in the nation and overseas, and that wheat farms on the Western Plains are often several thousand acres in size on which nary a horse or a cow is to be found.

In this state of confusion, or misinformation, regarding the state of the farm economy, the typical urban representative in Congress has little or no idea what should be either the goals of farm legislation or the program features of that legislation. In this state of confusion and/or ignorance, one of two things is likely to happen: (1) urban leaders and congressional representatives lose their effectiveness as they bicker over legislative objectives in this area of farm policy, or (2) they throw up their hands in despair and say "Let the farm experts representing farming areas, both in and out of Congress, write the farm legislation, so long as that legislation does not raise food prices."

Urbanites and their representatives in Congress have the votes to write the farm legislation, if they knew what they wanted. But they don't. They are so deeply mired in a set of false and misleading images about farmers, farming and rural America, that they cannot take effective legislative action.

Policy Decision Principles

Are there principles to guide the electorate and its elected representatives in dealing with complex, stubborn farm policy issues? We believe there are, and that in articulating a set of policy reforms, these principles should be made explicit.[2] These principles are a reflection of the belief and value system of American society.[3] They are not engraved on the walls of the House and Senate agriculture committee rooms, or carved in stone at the entrance to the U.S. Department of Agriculture's administration building. They are subjective things, which must be revealed by some person or group of persons with experience in the agricultural policy area. The specific formulation of those principles will, of course, be influenced by the belief and value system of that person or persons. But, because they are subjective, it does not follow that they are devoid of meaning or power as guides to policy formulation. They have meaning and power (i.e., are real) because they are a reflection of the belief and value system of society. They define its "moral compass."

One important way in which these principles may be revealed is through the speeches, stands and votes of elected politicians; over time an elected politician through his or her stands on issues must reflect the basic beliefs and values of his or her constituents. Other indicators of these principles include: the results of opinion polls, the platforms of political parties and interest groups (e.g., farm groups, labor unions, trade associations, and environmental groups), writings in journals of opinion and editorials and columns in newspapers and trade and news magazines.

We believe four policy decision principles are critical to the arguments in this book. First and most determining is the *Majority Rule* principle. Unless a policy has the backing of the majority of members of the political universe involved, it has little chance of success. Of course, the larger the majority support for a policy, the more likelihood that it will be a successful policy. This principle flows directly from the democratic ethic which invests in each man the power—the right—to participate in shaping the rules which each must observe. This is obviously not a new or unusual guiding principle for making policy decisions. It is the rule for political decision making in all Western, pluralistic democracies.

A key point in this concept of *Majority Rule* is the definition of the political universe. This becomes especially important with respect to national policies in the food, farm and rural sector. Since the incidence of many federal farm policies falls upon farmers and their closely related industrial, commercial and financial allies, members of that economic grouping commonly argue that they, and they alone, should determine what should be the content of federal food, farm and rural policies. In the words of Robert Paarlberg farmers feel, or at least their spokesmen feel, that they are a party to a social contract in which they are granted "sovereignty" over policy decisions in their sector of the economy. But as was made clear in Chapter 1, events have long since rendered this concept of sovereignty for farmers invalid.

In the national economy of the 1990s it is inconceivable that the political universe for formulating and executing policies for the food, farm and rural sectors be limited to the farming community. This is true for a number of reasons. First, such policies often involve transfer payments from the nonfarm sector to the farm sector, in which most of the revenues are raised in the nonfarm sector. Second, the products of the farm sector are largely consumed in the nonfarm sector; and the prices of, the quality of, and the availability of those products are of crucial importance to nonfarm consumers. Third, to the extent that the farm sector is a major exporter of products, which is the case in the United States, those farm-produced exports can play an important role in determining the prosperity of the nation.

Thus, it is of critical importance that the universe of political decision making for policies concerned with the food, farm, and rural sector be recognized to be the full national society. Until this principle of policy making is clearly recognized, policies developed for this sector will be of the special interest type. They will not fully recognize the legitimate interests of the national society in the economic and social developments of the food, farm, and rural sector.

The second guiding principle may be described as *"Protection for the Minority."* Like the first principle, Protection for the Minority has a long history in Western pluralistic democracies; a large body of law has been built, both in legislatures and in the judiciary, to protect the personal and property rights of minorities from the rule of the majority. This rule states that policies formulated and executed by the majority shall not do irreparable harm to a minority—shall not adversely affect the personal and property rights of the minority in an undue fashion. This principle flows naturally from the democratic ethic, but is reinforced by the right of citizens to accumulate capital and run their businesses as they choose.

Undue is the key word in this concept. Almost every policy put in place by the majority to achieve some desired purpose will have some adverse effects for some members of society. But this principle states that the human rights of members of the minority should not be abrogated or the asset position of members of a minority be destroyed by a policy put in place by the majority. In such cases, the position of members of a minority would be adversely affected in an undue fashion. The purpose of this second guiding principle is to insure minority members of society fair treatment in policy formulation and execution where policy decisions are made by majority rule.

The third guiding principle states that it is *the Duty of Government to Assist the Poor and the Downtrodden to Become Productive Members of Society.* Thus, policies should be put in place which provide opportunities for the poor and the downtrodden to learn skills, find jobs and earn decent incomes. The historical tradition for this principle in the United States is much shorter than for the previous two principles. This tradition emerges with the increased weight—value—given to the democratic ethic in the twentieth century. Consequently, since the 1930s, this principle has gained reasonably wide acceptance in American society for two basic reasons. First, it is consistent with the Christian creed "to do unto others as you would have them do unto you." Second, it is increasingly recognized that the poor and the downtrodden represent a drag on both society and the economy, and that society would be healthier and the economy stronger if such members of society were working regularly in productive jobs. Thus, it is a form of social self-interest to formulate and execute policies that assist the poor and the downtrodden to learn skills, find productive jobs and earn decent incomes.

The fourth guiding principle might be called *Governmental Responsibility for the Economic Health of the Nation*. This principle states that policies should be undertaken by the federal government which make a contribution to the smooth and effective operation of the national economy. Certainly, the federal government should not undertake policies which hinder the growth and operation of the national economy. This guiding principle, like the third one, is a product of the twentieth century. It has emerged and become a force on the national scene as the belief in unfettered private proprietorships as the perfect form of economic organization has weakened. While there is much controversy over how much the federal government should intervene in the operation of the economy, it is today widely held that the federal government is ultimately responsible for its overall operation. As Richard Nixon reportedly remarked: "We are all Keynesians now."

How do these principles relate substantively to food, farm and rural policy?

THE MAJORITY RULE PRINCIPLE

The majority rule principle plays both procedural and substantive roles in public policy discussion. Procedurally, for any policy to have validity it must have the majority support of the body politic. Without majority support in a pluralistic, democratic society a policy is not going anywhere.

Substantively, what food, farm and rural policy areas can we identify as having broad political support, majority support? First and foremost, Americans support policies which contribute to the production of an abundant supply of food. Above all else, Americans want an agricultural industry that provides them with a healthful, abundant supply of food at moderate prices. And they have supported policies overwhelmingly in peacetime and wartime over the past 100 years that produce that result. This national goal, and the policies that make its achievement possible, stand on a plane above all others for the food, farm and rural sectors.

Majority support by society for the production of an abundant supply of food raises once again the validity of the "social contract" argument. To the extent that the argument is valid, and the authors believe that it has some validity, then society must provide some form of price and income protection to farmers. The question is: which farmers and under what conditions?

Enjoying somewhat less support than the policy goal discussed above, but still having broad political support, is the Jeffersonian dream of an agriculture comprised of many relatively small family farmers. In this dream American society will be a good society so long as agriculture is made up of many prosperous owner-operated farms. We have argued that this imagery masks the reality—over the past 40 years productive farm resources have concentrated into the hands of relatively few large farmers. Still, the American people are inclined to support policies that will keep as many farmers on the land as modern technology and economics will permit. This is a policy goal with fading support in 1992, but we believe still a goal with majority support.

Support for protection of the soil, water and environment, has moved in a direction opposite that of the family farm goal. In the past 20 years support for protecting the rural environment from pollution, protecting soil and water resources for future generations, and protecting open spaces from mindless development has skyrocketed. Thus, without question, this policy goal enjoys majority support of the body politic as of the 1990s. If support for this policy goal continues to grow at the pace of the previous 20 years, it could be a dominant policy goal by the year 2000.

Broad support for the above policy goals, and the programs to achieve them, will serve to guide and direct the actions taken by the Congress in the 1990s in the enactment of specific laws dealing with the food, farm and rural sector. The president and the Congress can no more ignore broad majority support for these policy goals than can the authors of this volume.

PROTECTION FOR THE MINORITY

Since the policies that we have been discussing are national in scope with a universe of the national electorate, the minority in this case is the rural sector and the people who comprise it. What protection from majority rule then is deemed critically important by farmers and other rural residents?

Two areas of minority protection are identifiable, although the degree of majority support for these areas of protection may be questionable. First, the national majority shall make no changes in policies dealing with farming and related industries which either destroys or seriously impairs the monetary value of assets in those industries. The point at issue here is—how much erosion of asset values in farming and related industries through a shift in farm policies (e.g., changes in the commodity programs) will the body politic support? Certainly, the majority would not want to see the asset values of farmers destroyed by a change in farm commodity programs. But the majority would probably not be concerned about some diminution of asset values in farming as the result of a restructuring of farm policies. The question is: how much? The answer to this question will occupy the attention of farm policy experts, leaders and legislators for much of the coming decade.

Second, the national majority shall make no changes in farm policy which further infringes on the freedom of individuals to farm. Farmers prize their freedom of decision making in their farming business very highly. In general, the body politic is supportive of farmers in this personal right, except when farming practices damage the environment or threaten the public health. Thus, in the past the Congress in enacting farm policy legislation has been highly solicitous of farmers and their rights of decision making in their farming enterprise. The only basis for believing that this protection will be compromised in the future arises from environmental, health and safety concerns. Freedom to farm is highly prized by the typical farm operator, and generally supported by the national majority.

THE DUTY OF GOVERNMENT TO ASSIST THE POOR AND THE DOWNTRODDEN TO BECOME PRODUCTIVE MEMBERS OF SOCIETY

This principle has been held with varying degrees of intensity and broadness of support over time by the American electorate. As a guiding principle to policy formulation and execution, it had strong support in the 1930s and 1960s. In the 1980s it was a weak reed for policy guidance. Nonetheless, it has never been lost as a guiding principle, because a strong and vocal group of opinion leaders in the United States continually reminds the American people of their duty to help the poor and the downtrodden.

One way this principle has manifested itself in the food, farm and rural sector is through various food and nutrition assistance programs. Certainly, the abundance of food supplies has worked in favor of this benevolence. Still the various food and nutrition assistance programs for helping the poor and the needy have become institutionalized so that they continue, at least domestically, in periods of short supply as well as in periods of surplus.

In contrast, efforts to assist the poor and the downtrodden in rural areas to learn new skills, locate new jobs and to earn decent incomes have been very intermittent. At times Americans have been generous in such support and at others times niggardly in the extreme. How much policy guidance this principle will provide in the 1990's remains to be seen. But the authors believe its power is on the upswing.

GOVERNMENTAL RESPONSIBILITY FOR THE ECONOMIC HEALTH OF THE NATION

There is widespread agreement that the federal government has the ultimate responsibility for the economic health of the nation. The problem is that support breaks down and fragments with regard to specific economic policies and programs. This becomes evident when we consider the role of this fourth principle in formulating and executing policies in the food, farm and rural sector. The body politic has long been supportive of the use of public funds to underwrite research, development and extension education for the rural economy. But when we move into the farm policy area of the commodity programs—programs concerned with price support, production control, deficiency payments, and government stock accumulation—support fragments. Government economic intervention of this sort to assist farmers runs head-on into the widely held belief that free markets constitute the best form of economic organization. Controversy has thus raged for 50 years or more over the content of specific programs to create a productive, healthy, prosperous agriculture. Some farmers and their spokesmen want more governmental intervention via the commodity programs; other farmers and their spokesmen want less government intervention and a move toward the free market. In this struggle between contending farm groups, the dominant group on the American political scene—the urban electorate—has not, to this date, resolved this essentially national policy issue. The major objective of this book is to help to form this resolve, by linking food, farm and rural policy to economic and social programs of vital concern to urban voters.

Since the beginning of the Republic, the body politic has also sought to stimulate and strengthen the national economy by foreign trade policy. In the first hundred years of the Republic trade policy first involved industrial protection, then prior to the Civil War there was a movement toward freer trade, but after the Civil War trade barriers went up again. Since 1933, public opinion in the nation has moved steadily in the direction of more open trade, with corresponding actions to lower trade barriers. As of the 1990s, majority opinion would appear to favor an open trade policy, although when it comes to certain specific products such as shoes or sugar minority views may dominate the political process.

In the food, farm and rural sector views with regard to trade policy are decidedly mixed, much as in the case of commodity programs. Farmers producing wheat and feed grains mainly favor policies that reduce trade barriers at home and abroad. However, producers of dairy products, sugar, and other products protected at the border actively support protectionist policies. As of 1992 there is a widely held belief that a more open trade policy is good for the nation—it brings lasting benefits to the national economy. But the pursuit of such a policy with respect to specific commodities—particularly in the agricultural sector—encounters strong political obstacles. Tinkering with trade policy is thus a commonly accepted way of influencing the operation of the economy in the United States, but the pursuit of such a policy with respect to specific commodities—particularly in the agricultural sector—encounters political obstacles.

Stability is another much sought after goal in the food, farm and rural sector. Consumers want stable food prices. Producers want stable incomes. But these goals are not easily achieved. Agriculture is a feast or famine industry in which small shifts in world demand, or supplies, can send farm prices, hence food prices, skyrocketing or plummeting. So here again we have the strongly held, and widely shared, view in American society that the federal government should undertake policies that contribute to stability in the food and agricultural sector, and avoid destabilizing policies for that sector.

But here the consensus ends. Some believe that stability can best be achieved through reliance on the free market, in which producers and marketers protect themselves against sharp and unpredictable price movements by hedging in the futures market. Others, typically the commodity associations, which have supported the existing commodity programs for decades, continue to give them their strong support as a proven way of providing income stability to commercial farmers. Then there are others, hardly a group, comprised of consumer advocates, budget reformers, disenchanted agricultural economists, and some farmers who recognize that instability is a real problem but lack faith in the free market. They also believe that the commodity programs have become special devices for transferring large sums of money from all of society to a few hundred thousand very large commercial farmers. This amorphous group does not have an internally consistent, generally accepted farm policy proposal to deal with the instability problem. The elements of such a proposal are the subject of the chapters to follow. In this political vacuum, the existing farm commodity associations continue to win acceptance of their commodity programs in the complex, vote-trading milieu of the Congress.

QUESTIONS OF PRIORITY AND CONSISTENCY

The greater the majority support for a policy in a pluralistic democratic society, the higher the priority of that policy. But where majority support for a policy does not exist, or is unclear, is there any basis for assigning priorities to policies falling under guiding principles two, three and four? We think not. The authors find no logical basis for assigning a higher priority to a policy falling under one of the principles enumerated above than to policies falling under the other two. For this reason, we have political parties in pluralistic democracies, and sub-groups within parties. Parties, or sub-groups of parties, assign priorities to policies and then provide support for such policies in accordance with their own values and beliefs. The authors, of course, have their own beliefs and values which will become obvious when they set forth certain policy proposals. But they cannot, when seeking to analyze and understand the way in which policy decision principles operate, say either that their belief and value systems are superior, or that the belief and value system of some particular group is superior.

There is also the problem of internal consistency among policies falling under the four guiding principles. For example, it is entirely conceivable that a policy put in place to contribute to the effective operation of the national economy would do irreparable harm to some minority, and thus violate the second guiding principle. This could happen, for example, if when an import restriction was eliminated, the protected industry was destroyed economically and all the jobs in the industry were lost. In this hypothetical example, pursuit of one desired policy jeopardizes the realization of another desired policy.

Case after case could be presented illustrating this tendency for policies based on different principles to come into conflict. In fact, policy conflicts are the norm in a pluralistic democracy like the United States. Policy conflicts and compromise are the essence of the policy formulation and execution process in a pluralistic democracy like the United States. Is this bad? The answer is definitely no. How else are groups with widely differing belief and value systems to live together peaceably in a pluralistic society?

LESSONS FOR THE POLICYMAKER

From this discussion of "Policy Decision Principles" what have we learned to aid, or guide, the policy decisionmaker? The short, cynical answer might be—"not much." In the last few sections we have learned that different groups in a pluralistic society assign different priorities to particular policies based upon the different belief and value systems and that a policy pushed by one group on the basis of a commonly held belief and value system often comes into conflict with policies pushed by other groups. In this uncertain, heterogeneous socio-political context, the policy decisionmaker (whether the president, the secretary of agriculture, congressman, or a private organizational leader) must thrash around, interact with many different interest groups, trade votes, accept positions distasteful to him or her and through this process come up with a policy solution, a workable solution, that is acceptable to the various different and contending groups.

But the policymaker does not operate in a socio-political vacuum. The four guiding principles outlined earlier define the parameters of the socio-political system in which he or she must operate. They are like the points of a moral compass. On this compass, majority rule is due north. The policymaker knows that to get his or her policy accepted and/or enacted into law it must have the majority support of the electorate; and the larger that majority, the greater the likelihood that the policy will prove to be effective in practice.

Second, the experienced and successful policymaker is well aware of the long tradition of minority rights in the American political system. He or she knows that it is bad policy to push for the acceptance of a policy that does irreparable harm to a minority group. The third guiding principle, "The Duty of Government to Assist the Poor and the Downtrodden" is an uncertain guide. At times this principle has been a powerful guiding force in the policy formulation process; at other times it has been weak. In the 1800s this principle manifested itself in policies of unlimited immigration and the distribution of free land. In the 1900s it has taken the form of the many and varied social programs of the New Deal, and again the social programs in the Kennedy-Johnson administrations. In other periods it has provided policy guidance, but weak guidance. Thus, the policymaker and the policy analyst must know and understand the social trends of a given time period, before they are able to make an accurate judgement of the force, or power, of this guiding principle in the period in question.

The fourth guiding principle, "Governmental Responsibility for the Economic Health of the Nation" has in the twentieth century become a powerful force in formulating and executing policies that relate to the national economy or segments of it. Americans hold the federal government ultimately responsible for the smooth and effective operation of the economy. Any political representative of the people who ignores this responsibility of the federal government in his or her actions or votes is likely to find himself or herself in political difficulty.

In sum, we have identified four guiding principles, which serve like the points of a compass to orient us in the space in which farm policy decisions must be made. These policy principles will guide the authors in their evaluation of existing policies and programs in Chapters 3, 4, and 5 and their development of proposals for policy and program reform in Chapter 6.

Notes

1. It is true that certain of these farmers over-expanded, took on too much high priced debt, and had tough financial sledding in the early 1980s; but the group as a whole weathered the stressful period of the early 1980s without any substantial loss in numbers.

2. As noted in Chapter 1, we follow in the tradition of Gunnar Myrdal (1962 and 1954), who argued that all policy analysis is normative, and that the values driving it should be made explicitly a part of the analysis.

3. We define beliefs and values as John Brewster defined and developed them in his essay "The Cultural Crisis of Our Time." (Madden and Brewster 1970).

> Beliefs are *concepts* of ways of living and making a living which people feel obliged to follow so as to be the type of person they most prize. . . . Values are the relative weights (degrees of desirability or importance) which people assign to their various beliefs . . . Beliefs and values are as interdependent as the sides of a coin. Neither exists without the other. . . . There are no beliefs without concepts of practices which are *valued* in some degree as valid evidence of prized personal and social qualities. Conversely, without concepts of given ways of life there are no values, as there is nothing to value.

References

Borchert, John R. 1987. *America's Northern Heartland*. Minneapolis: University of Minnesota Press.

Drabenstott, Mark, Mark Henry, and Lynn Gibson. 1987. "The Rural Economic Policy Choice." Federal Reserve Bank of Kansas City, *Economic Review*. 72:1.

Duncan, Marvin R. 1989. "U.S. Agriculture: Hard Realities and New Opportunities." Federal Reserve Bank of Kansas City, *Economic Review*. 74:2.

Madden, Patrick J. and David E. Brewster, eds. 1970. *A Philosopher Among Economists: Selected Works of John M. Brewster*. Philadelphia, Penn.: J. T. Murphy Co., Inc.

Myrdal, Gunnar. 1962. *An American Dilemma: The Negro Problem and Modern Democracy*. New York: Harper and Row.

Myrdal, Gunnar. 1954. *The Political Element in the Development of Economic Theory*. Cambridge: Harvard University Press.

Schwab, Andrew and Philip M. Raup. 1989. *The Minnesota Rural Real Estate Market in 1988*. St. Paul: University of Minnesota Economic Report ER 89-3.

U.S. Department of Agriculture. 1990, April and errata May 1990. "Payments Go to Largest Farms." *Agricultural Outlook*.

U.S. Department of Agriculture/CRB. 1962. *Number of Farms and Land in Farms*,

1910–1959. Washington, D.C.: USDA/CRB.

U.S. Department of Agriculture/ERS. 1991a. *Economic Indicators of the Farm Sector, State Financial Summary, 1989*. ECIFS 9-3. Washington, D.C.: USDA/ERS.

———. 1991b. *Economic Indicators of the Farm Sector, National Financial Summary, 1989*. ECIFS 9-2. Washington, D.C.: USDA/ERS.

———. 1989. *Economic Indicators of the Farm Sector, Production and Efficiency Statistics, 1988*. ECIFS 8-5. Washington, D.C.: USDA/ERS.

3 A Concise History of the Commodity Programs

The purpose of this chapter is to provide a concise but necessarily detailed history of how the commodity programs came to be. While commodity price and income supports covering the main field crops are the centerpiece of farm programs, there are also a variety of other programs that will be described in Chapter 5.

The origin of commodity price supports may be traced to attempts during the farm depression of the 1920s to establish "parity" prices for farmers based on a 1910–1914 index, when farm prices were especially attractive.[1] The first serious attempt to achieve parity prices for farmers involved the division of the market for a commodity like wheat into a domestic market and a foreign market. Supplies in the domestic market would be limited to an amount that would drive up domestic farm prices to the parity level; the remainder, or the surplus, would be dumped on the foreign market for whatever it would bring. The program mechanics of this dumping scheme were worked out in the USDA under the direction of the then Secretary of Agriculture Henry C. Wallace. The plan was introduced into the Congress in 1924, and in each succeeding year through 1928 by Representative Haugen of Iowa and Senator McNary of Oregon, becoming known as the McNary-Haugen plan. It passed both houses of Congress in 1927 and 1928, but was vetoed by President Coolidge on both occasions. The plan nonetheless laid the groundwork for subsequent efforts to raise farm prices through government intervention.

Between the stock market crash of 1929 and 1932, farm prices continued to decline, falling over 50 percent in three years. In the face of this near total collapse, President Hoover attempted to stem the tide with a Federal Farm Board, which made loans to stabilization corporations and acquired surpluses in an effort to hold them off the market. However, the board was not sufficiently capitalized to acquire and hold off the market those amounts of the staple crops—wheat, cotton, and corn—necessary to keep their prices from falling in world markets. And whenever the stabilization corporations released stocks from one crop to make room for commodities from next year's crop, prices in the domestic and world markets declined still further. The Farm Board and its stabilization corporations simply did not have the financial capacity to stem the decline in the world prices of the great staple commodities.

In April of 1929, President Hoover recommended to Congress a limited upward revision of tariffs as a means of protecting domestic agricultural markets. In response to the presidential recommendation, Congress passed the Smoot-Hawley Tariff Act of 1930, raising tariff duties to an all-time high. Today it is difficult to understand why Congress would take such an action, since it was well known at the time that one of the principal causes of the agricultural depression of the 1920s was the loss of export markets following World War I. But Congress passed the legislation, President Hoover signed the act, and farmers and farm leaders acquiesced to it. This action by the United States set off a wave of protectionism around the world, served to shut off foreign trade of all kinds and the export of American farm products, in particular.

After these abject policy failures, agricultural economists devised an alternative, the Domestic Allotment Plan, in which each farmer would receive an allotment, or "right to produce," based on his production history. The sum total of such rights was to coincide with domestic consumption levels. Processors purchasing this production for domestic use would have to account for all of it as a sum of pre-existing allotments, and the farmer would be paid the domestic price for the commodity, as determined in Washington. The allotment would thus provide a subsidy only on domestic production; the remaining surplus would presumably enter export markets at world prices. This second form of "two-price" scheme, while never enacted, raised a variety of ideas which resurfaced in the famous Agricultural Adjustment Acts of the 1930s, providing additional foundations for modern commodity programs.

The Agricultural Adjustment Act (AAA), adopted May 12, 1933, was established as part of a tripartite New Deal agricultural policy. Title I, the AAA, dealt with price and income supports. Title II provided for debt relief and farm credit, while Title III authorized the president to manipulate the exchange value of the currency. Title I, the AAA, did not take the form of either the McNary-Haugen Plan or the Domestic Allotment Plan, although it contained elements of both. The AAA contained a wide range of ideas and economic tools, including provisions to control production through acreage reduction on individual farms, the authority to purchase and store commodities, and the authority to regulate the marketing of specialty crops through the employment of marketing agreements and orders. To implement these authorities such tools as "base acres" on individual farms,[2] the parity concept and "nonrecourse loans"[3] were forged.

But the centerpiece of the AAA was the reduction of production through the control of crop acreages on individual farms. For complying with the approved reduction in crop acreage, farmers received a benefit payment. The money to make these benefit payments was to be raised through excise or processing taxes on the commodities involved.

This essential feature—acreage control in return for government payments—has remained at the heart of all subsequent policies despite continued evidence of problems. As early as the 1930s, appraisals of the operation of the AAA in the period 1933–36 reached two general conclusions. First, the production control features of the AAA were largely unsuccessful. Farmers in the 1930s found ways to circumvent the acreage control programs by "renting" their poorest acres to the government and by raising noncontrolled crops on the controlled acreage so that the total production of each farm was reduced very little, if at all. This phenomenon has come to be known as "slippage." (The great droughts of 1934 and 1936 did, however, reduce total agricultural production.) On the positive side, however, the benefit payments to farmers succeeded in bolstering the farm economy, helping farmers to purchase food, feed and supplies, and to pay their taxes when they had no other money income at all. Thus, all but a handful of farmers supported the AAA in the period 1933–35, as did their farm organizations.

The Supreme Court found the AAA unconstitutional in early 1936 on the grounds that use of processing taxes on the commodities involved to finance the control of their production was illegal. The Congress hurriedly passed emergency legislation in 1936—the Soil Conservation and Domestic Allotment Act of 1936—which dropped the processing tax feature and shifted the emphasis of the overall program from price enhancement to income protection and resource conservation. However, it retained the *quid pro quo* of acreage retirement for payment. Under the 1936 legislation the government paid farmers to take acres out of production in "soil depleting" row crops and plant those acres to "soil conserving" legumes and grasses. The government also continued to purchase surplus supplies on the market to support prices, to distribute surplus food stocks to the urban needy, and to operate the marketing agreements for the specialty crops and milk.

New, permanent farm legislation was enacted in 1938. The Agricultural Adjustment Act of 1938 reaffirmed the soil conserving emphasis and activities of the 1936 legislation, and provided for the first time comprehensive programs of price support and production control based on the constitutional authority given to Congress to regulate interstate and foreign commerce. The new features of the 1938 legislation included: mandatory nonrecourse loans for cooperating producers of corn, wheat, and cotton if marketing quotas had not been rejected; marketing quotas for corn, wheat, cotton, rice, and tobacco when supplies had reached certain defined levels; rules governing referenda to determine whether marketing quotas should be put into effect; parity payments to producers to raise their incomes when and if funds had been appropriated; and a crop insurance plan for wheat. All of these features were to be orchestrated into the operational concept of an "Ever-Normal Granary" plan as espoused by Agriculture Secretary Wallace, aimed at protecting the interests of both producers and consumers (Wallace 1967).

World War II did for the U.S. economy what the New Deal could not do; it brought full employment and pulled surplus labor on farms out of agriculture and into war industries. In this context, farm prices and incomes began to rise substantially. The discontent with the farm programs of the New Deal, which became an important political fact in the period 1938–40, was forgotten as farmers revelled in their newfound prosperity.

Yet almost everyone concerned with the well-being of farmers—farmers themselves, farm leaders, politicians and agricultural economists—worried about the prospect of a farm depression immediately following the end of the war. These fears had two consequences. First, administrators of the war food programs were determined to come out of the war with little or no reserve stocks; they pursued a "bare shelf" food stocking policy. This put the United States in a weak position to feed the hungry and destitute peoples of Europe and Asia at the war's end. Second, the Congress passed legislation in 1942 which guaranteed that twenty commodities would be supported at 90 percent of parity for at least two years following the end of hostilities. As the war came to an end in 1945, with victories in Europe and the Pacific, policy decisions taken during the war years were creating new problems for the postwar period.

Farm prices did not collapse at the end of World War II, as so many people expected.[4] Because of the destruction of the agricultural plants of Europe and Asia during World War II, and the strong demand for food stocks and supplies by the victorious and occupying powers to feed the hungry people of those areas, food stocks remained short and supplies inadequate. This was aggravated by the "bare shelf" policy pursued by the United States in the last years of the war. As a result, farm and retail food prices soared between 1945 and 1948. Farm prices dipped modestly in 1949 and moved upward again in 1950 and 1951 in response to the Korean police action.

When wartime price support legislation expired at the end of 1948, the debate over subsequent policy provided a prototype for much of the debate over commodity programs down to the present day. Two camps were clearly identifiable. The principal policy goal of the first camp was to lower the level of price support on farm commodities and thereby reduce the extent of government intervention in the farm economy. In this camp were to be found most, but not all, Republican party leaders, businessmen from the agribusiness complex, and most economists. The overriding policy goal of the second camp was to maintain a high level of farm price support as a means of protecting and supporting farm incomes. This camp would accept whatever programs of government intervention were required to implement the price support objective. Here were to be found Democratic party leaders from the South and the Plains; most, but by no means all, farm organization leaders (the president of the Farm Bureau was no longer supportive of high price supports) and some government economists and union leaders. The farm policy battle over the level of price support in the immediate postwar period became for the first time a clear battle between the political parties.

The struggle which ensued in the Congress produced a curious compromise. It was an agricultural act with two distinct parts. Title I of the Agricultural Act of 1948 continued price supports for the 1949 marketing year at 90 percent of parity. Title II instituted a concept of flexible price supports in which the level of support for the basic commodities in 1950 and thereafter would be set at 75 percent of parity for a "normal" supply, with price support adjustment downward as the supply exceeded the defined normal, and upward as the supply fell below normal. This attempt to make agricultural policy function like a hemostat, with rising price supports in times of scarcity and falling supports in times of surplus, was known in later debates as "market-oriented" commodity policy. The concept was to allow prices to set the terms of trade, rather than making them inflexible, and coupling them to production controls. Most agricultural economists were ecstatic with the market orientation of Title II of the compromise, which provided the first substantial self-correcting price support mechanism. But their high hopes for the future were dashed in late 1949 when the Congress extended the level of price support for the basic commodities at 90 percent of parity through 1950. The inability to overcome political impulses to force up the level of price support even when markets were strong became a regular feature of subsequent commodity policy failure. In the Defense Production Acts of 1950, 1951 and 1952, the Congress extended the level of price support for the basic commodities at 90 percent of parity for each year up through 1953. And in 1952 the Congress once again passed legislation making price support at 90 percent of parity mandatory for the basic commodities—this time for the year 1954—if producers of those commodities had not disapproved marketing quotas. Clearly the high-price-support camp won the policy battles in the post–World War II years, while advocates of flexibility and market oriented-policies lost.

But while these battles were occurring, another set of farm policy ideas was taking shape. Agriculture Secretary Charles Brannan had played a leading role in the 1948 presidential election by helping Harry Truman carry the farm vote. As a close political confidant of the president, Brannan was encouraged to develop new farm policy ideas. Early in 1949, Brannan held a series of seminars in the U.S. Department of Agriculture with trusted political aides and leading policy analysts. From these seminars emerged the Brannan Plan. This was a classic case of policy development by political and economic technicians.

The Brannan plan contained four new policy ideas. They were:

1.   An income standard to replace the old 1910–14 parity price standard.
2.   Production, or income, payments to support gross returns to producers of perishable products.
3.   A new list of farm commodities (including important animal products) to replace the old, so-called basic commodity list.
4.   No price or income support on production above a certain limit—with that limit to be determined by the size of the typical family farm.

The plan was presented to Congress by Secretary Brannan with the support and backing of President Truman in April of 1949. It was the administration's alternative to the Agricultural Act of 1948. While enthusiastically received by economists, its reception was cool on Capitol Hill. Congress had not been consulted in the policy development stage—a crucial tactical error. But the politicians had more serious objections to the plan. First, the large commercial farmers, who were well-represented in Washington even in 1950, were strongly opposed to Points 2 and 4 in the above list. They did not want to see the extent of their income subsidy exposed to public view (which could occur if it were paid directly instead of disguised as a "price support"), nor did they want any limit put on the amount of price and income support that any farmer could receive.

Second, Secretary Brannan's proposed income support standard was so high that it drove away many of his logical allies. Congressmen who were friendly to the basic ideas of the plan were appalled by estimates of its costs—which ranged from three to eight billion dollars per year. Finally, the Republican party was badly frightened by the political appeal of the Brannan Plan; thus, Republicans closed ranks and fought it vigorously and successfully. Legislation which contained some, but not all, of the important features of the Brannan Plan was defeated in both the House and the Senate in the summer of 1949. An upward surge in farm prices in 1950 drained away support, and by the fall of 1950 the Brannan Plan, as a coherent package, was dead.

Dwight D. Eisenhower was elected president in 1952, and appointed Ezra Taft Benson secretary of agriculture. Benson believed that government intervention in the economy was wrong on both moral and economic grounds, and was determined, with the support of the American Farm Bureau, to move to a system of flexible and market-oriented price supports as soon as possible. Also, farm prices began to sag in 1952, and by 1953, were sagging badly. Concurrent with this decline in farm prices, productivity in agriculture due to technological advance was increasing rapidly. The result was a large increase in the aggregate supply of farm products. In this context, Benson tried to persuade Congress to adopt a system of flexible price supports. With the support of the American Farm Bureau and the Republicans in Congress, Benson won a limited victory in August, 1954, with the passage of the Agricultural Act of 1954. The Act authorized the use of flexible price supports for the basic commodities ranging from 82.5 percent of parity to 90 percent in 1955, and from 75 percent of parity to 90 percent in 1956 and thereafter. The act also provided for the use of payments as a means of directly supporting incomes of wool producers; thus, one important idea from the Brannan Plan had become operational.

The modest lowering of the price supports for wheat, feed grains and cotton in 1955–56, in conjunction with the administration's aversion to strict production controls, did not, however, stem the tide of agricultural output. Total farm output took a large upward jump in 1956 and then continued on a trend upward throughout the 1950s. The result was a large increase in the stocks of wheat, feed grains and cotton in government hands and a further decline in net farm incomes.

To deal with the growing surplus problem, the administration, with some support from farm leaders, developed the "soil bank" concept. The soil bank idea, which was enacted into law in the Agricultural Act of 1956, had two main parts. One was the Acreage Reduction Program (ARP) which operated in 1956, 1957 and 1958. Under this program, some 21 million acres were "banked" in 1957 on which no crop could be harvested and which could not be pastured. The second part of the soil bank, the Conservation Reserve Program (CRP), was designed to assist farmers to reduce the production of crops through shifting below-average cropland into long-range conservation uses. The first acres went into this program in 1956 and the last acres came out in 1972; a maximum of 28.6 million acres were under this program in 1960. (A new version of the CRP would return to the policy arsenal in the 1985 Farm Bill.)

For several reasons, this Acreage Reduction Program was brought to an end in 1958, and the Conservation Reserve was not pushed after 1959.

These reasons included: (1) the high cost of removing crop acres from production under these programs; (2) dissatisfaction in rural areas and rural towns with the provision that permitted whole farms to be taken out of production under the soil bank; and (3) the lack of success in reducing total farm output. In 1959 and 1960 Secretary Benson once again tried to stem the tide of rising farm output by lowering loan levels to the minimums permitted under the law. But once again this strategy failed. Total farm output increased significantly in 1959 and 1960.

One more policy idea that was developed in this period needs to be considered. It was the idea of disposing of surplus agricultural products abroad, primarily in the less developed world, through sales for nonconvertible foreign currency and other "soft" or concessional terms. This idea was enacted into law in the Agricultural Trade Development and Assistance Act of 1954; this act became better known as P.L. 480 or "Food for Peace." Exports under various governmental export programs in 1952, prior to the enactment of P.L. 480, stood at a value of 449 million dollars; by 1957, following the passage of P.L. 480, those exports had risen to a value of $1.9 billion, and they averaged well over a billion dollars per year thereafter. P.L. 480 became a powerful mechanism for expanding the total demand for American farm products, and helped drain away farm surpluses, saving American farmers and their programs from complete disaster in the late 1950s. The impact of such food aid on receiving nations, while not an issue then, became increasingly controversial in time, as evidence accumulated that dumping of surplus stocks lowered prices and aggravated the problems of poor farmers. In the 1950s these problems in far away nations did not intrude greatly on agricultural policy in the United States.

The 1960s brought a new administration to Washington, convinced that farm prices could be increased, and government costs could be reduced through a combination of demand expansion and mandatory production controls. President Kennedy's USDA secretary, Orville L. Freeman, established a three-part policy designed to stimulate demand and reduce surpluses:

1. Meeting the food needs of those living in poverty at home.
2. Providing food aid to poor nations.
3. Expanding commercial exports wherever possible.

To this end the administration initiated the Food Stamp Plan and pushed a variety of domestic food programs; it supported and expanded the coverage of P.L. 480 programs initiated in the Eisenhower administration; and it sought to expand commercial trade through the Kennedy round of trade negotiations, part of the General Agreement on Tariffs and Trade

(GATT). In response to rapid technological change and mounting surpluses, foreign market creation entered the tools of agricultural policy, and the steady growth of dependence by American farmers on international trade began in earnest.

But Freeman and his lieutenants recognized that these demand-expansion activities could not entirely solve the surplus problem that confronted farmers and the government in 1961, and had dogged the entire postwar experience in agricultural policy. They thus proposed a system of mandatory supply management devices—ranging from strict acreage controls to marketing orders—to adjust supplies to demand at prices administratively determined by the Congress to be fair to farmers and consumers alike. They started down that path by introducing legislation in the spring of 1961 that would have established procedures for placing mandatory controls in operation for a commodity without specific congressional approval. Congress would not accede to such procedural arrangements and the legislation died in committee.

In the meantime, the farm income problem and the surplus problem worsened. Thus, the administration embarked upon a series of emergency production control programs of which the emergency feed grain program of 1961 became the prototype. This program held the level of price support at approximately the 1960 level, and paid farmers on a voluntary basis to take from 20 up to 50 percent of their feed grain base acreage out of production. The land "rented" to the government had to be held in a nonproductive soil-conserving use. This phase of the program was strictly enforced, and as a result some modest reductions in output were achieved.

Other crop control programs for the period 1961–63 were similar to the feed grain program described above, with one exception, wheat. The Food and Agriculture Act of 1962 gave wheat farmers a choice of two alternatives for their 1964 crop to be decided in referendum in 1963. The first alternative, and in fact the administration program, involved a mandatory control program with no payments for land removed from production, stiff penalties for overplanting individual acreage allotments, and price support at $2.00 per bushel for the farmer's share of the national market. The second alternative involved no penalties for overplanting individual allotments and price support for complying farmers at the low level of 50 percent of parity, or roughly $1.22 per bushel. The second choice was very close to a free market alternative.

Wheat farmers voted down the first alternative in referendum on May 21, 1963. This vote ended all efforts by the Kennedy-Johnson administration to deal with the farm price and income problem through the use of mandatory production controls. But wheat farmers were not forced to accept the second alternative either. Seeing little economic advantage in the first alternative, they voted it down, betting that the administration and the Congress would come up with something even better than the second alternative. They won. Congress immediately passed the Agricultural Act of 1964, which gave farmers participating in the acreage control program price support at $2.00 per bushel on their domestic share of the market, plus a voluntary acreage control program in which farmers were paid to retire their wheat base acres from production. This "paid diversion" added yet another twist to the basic *quid pro quo* of dollars for reduced production.

But the 1964 programs for both wheat and cotton had another new direction arising from the increasing role of export markets as a vent for surplus. Commercial exports of all the grains were expanding, and the high domestic price of cotton was dampening exports and encouraging the use of synthetic cloth. Thus the administration largely turned away from production control as a *modus operandi* for dealing with the joint problem of farm surpluses and low farm incomes, and thereafter focused on expanding exports. To make cotton and wheat more competitive in international markets, the administration concocted programs which lowered the domestic price support of these commodities down to the export (or world market) price while guaranteeing producers of those commodities that they would be paid the 1963 support value for their domestic share—$2.00 per bushel for wheat and 30 cents per pound for cotton. Once again, a form of "two-price" plan prevailed. The stage was set for the basic compromise of 1965.

It had become clear over a period of nearly two decades that farm price supports at higher than world-market-equilibrium levels were not consistent with an agricultural industry that is on an export basis, as in the United States. Further, program experience made it clear that although mandatory production controls were anathema to American farmers, buying cropping rights through voluntary controls with payments, if vigorously administered, could be reasonably successful. With these conclusions in mind, the administration, with the support of a somewhat reluctant Congress, effected a basic policy compromise in the Food and Agricultural Act of 1965.

Levels of farm price support, commodity by commodity, were lowered to world equilibrium levels. Farm incomes would be supported, when they were to be supported, through the use of income deficiency and/or land retirement payments. But payments would be made to farmers only if they participated in the authorized production control program for that crop year. Finally, storage and surplus disposal programs were continued to deal with any remaining surpluses and with future food shortages at home or abroad. This compromise was accepted and maintained for five years and with only modest changes throughout the 1970s. The compromise had one great drawback which succeeding administrations of both political parties have only slowly recognized; namely, voluntary production control programs coupled with deficiency payments come with very high price tags for the federal government.

This export-oriented strategy (or luck, depending upon whether one was in the administration or out) was not unanimously regarded as a great social good. Export-oriented agriculture in general received especially bad publicity as a result of the infamous Soviet grain deal, valued at 750 million dollars, in the summer of 1972. Described by Secretary Butz as the largest grain deal in history, it was widely criticized in the urban press. Another potent critic was Senator Henry Jackson, who was suspicious of both the Soviets and grain companies. As reserve grain stocks were pulled down in 1972–73, fear and panic set in around the world and a wild scramble by governments and private firms for the remaining stocks occurred. This drove grain prices sky high in 1973–74. Widely described as "the great grain robbery," the winners were the Russians and export companies, while the losers were American consumers.

New farm legislation was passed in the midst of this record-breaking boom in farm prices. Yet the provisions of the new act did not suggest that anything unusual was occurring in the world agricultural economy. The Agricultural and Consumer Protection Act of 1973 was a direct extension of the acts of 1965 and 1970. The voluntary features of the commodity control programs were maintained as was the basic principle of setting levels of price support at or near world equilibrium levels. The act also provided for production control for individual commodities if the situation required it. And the payment limitation per farm established in the Act of 1970 at $55,000 per commodity per producer was lowered to $20,000 per person. Like all such attempts at payment limits, it was widely and relatively easily circumvented by farmers working with their relatives and accountants to redefine and subdivide their farms.

There was one important new concept in the 1973 Act: the concept of a "target price"—a "what-ought-to-be price"—for measuring the size of the income support, or "deficiency payments" to farmers. This target price made the concept of deficiency payments (which will be described operationally below) a subsequent feature of farm income support programs. The Food Stamp Plan was also extended, and participation in the program was liberalized and expanded in a separate Food Stamp Act. By 1973–74 the Food Stamp Plan was approaching in dollar magnitude the total expenditure for the commodity programs. It was no longer a stepchild of the U.S. Department of Agriculture (see Chapter 5).

The Farm Act of 1973 did not get government out of agriculture, as Secretary Butz was fond of saying. It included all the program provisions of the acts of 1965 and 1970 and some new and expanded ones. But it is true that the commodity programs under the act of 1973 became nonoperational in the period 1974–76. This occurred as world market forces drove world market prices for the export crops far above the domestic support and target price levels for those commodities. Consumers in the United States thus learned in the period 1973–76 that a strong export demand, in which the U.S. agricultural economy is fully integrated into the world market, can cause domestic farm and food prices to shoot skyward. They further learned that the Agriculture and Consumer Protection Act of 1973 contained little in the way of protection for consumers, since it made no provision for a reserve stock program to be used to stabilize farm and food prices.

Jimmy Carter was elected president in 1976, and appointed Bob Bergland, a farmer from northern Minnesota, to be his secretary of agriculture. Secretary Bergland had served in the House of Representatives for several terms, and was thus experienced in the political ways of Washington. That experience would be needed in the passage of the Food and Agricultural Act of 1977, since the Congress was anxious to raise both target prices and loan levels, and the administration was equally anxious to hold down government program costs. The result was a compromise that pleased no one, in which target and loan rates were raised modestly, but the administration was able to hold loan rates at something close to world market levels. Otherwise, the Act of 1977 largely carried farm policies and programs into the period ahead as they had emerged from the acts of 1965, 1970 and 1973. However, payment limitations for wheat, feed grains and cotton were raised from $20,000 per farmer to $40,000 per farmer in 1978, $45,000 per farmer in 1979, and $50,000 per farmer in 1980 and 1981. In addition, the Secretary implemented the old notion of a "farmer owned reserve," dating to the early days of agricultural interventionism.

On January 4, 1980, President Carter announced an embargo on grain shipments to the former Soviet Union over and above those amounts specified in the U.S.-Soviet grains agreement, which had been forged in response to the 1972 grain deal in order to make Soviet purchases more predictable, and grain companies more accountable.[5] This action was taken by the president in response to the Soviet invasion of Afghanistan on December 25, 1979, and was done with a minimum of discussion with USDA officials. In fact, those officials were not brought into the discussions concerning the proposed action until the evening of January 2, and then only to deal with the issue of how to minimize the adverse impact on farmers. The political fallout from this action, which was immensely unpopular with farmers, helped ensure Ronald Reagan's victory in 1980.

Perhaps the major contribution of the Carter administration to agricultural policy was a frank recognition of the growing concentration of large farmers, and the decline of the small and medium-sized farm.

Secretary Bergland had observed the great decline in the number of farms during his lifetime and the growing concentration of the productive resources in the hands of fewer and fewer and larger and larger farmers. The number of farms in the United States declined from 6.7 million in 1934 to 2.7 million in 1978. Some 64,000 farmers in 1978 with sales valued at $200,000 or more accounted for 39 percent of the total sales from farming. Secretary Bergland and his staff spent much of their last two years in office studying these developments. In his last days in office, Bergland issued the report, *A Time to Choose*, which analyzed these structural developments with a series of recommendations to target commodity program benefits more equitably (USDA 1981). But defeat at the polls in November, 1980, cut short the administration's hopes for corrective action.

The election of Ronald Reagan in November, 1980, with landslide support in farm districts in reaction to the Carter embargo, brought what many felt would be a hard-edged conservatism back to agricultural policy, exemplified by a reduction of government intervention in and spending on agriculture. Few could have predicted that after decrying Carter's excessive spending on commodity programs, which reached an annual high of $3 billion dollars, Reagan would go on to spend nearly $26 billion in 1986. Reagan's first task after election was the farm bill of 1981. Although John Block, an Illinois corn and hog producer, had been appointed secretary of agriculture, the real power in the early days of the Reagan administration was David Stockman, the new director of the Office of Management and Budget. Stockman faced a daunting challenge, since many of the compromises leading up to the 1981 Farm Bill had already been struck when Reagan entered the White House. As in the previous farm bill cycles, the timing of farm bill consideration, immediately after the presidential election, tended to perpetuate programs already in place, and to limit the power of the executive to steer a radically different course. In addition, record grain crops in 1981 and falling farm prices and incomes led to demands for a continuation and strengthening of income protection for farmers through high support prices.

The Agriculture and Food Act of 1981 was passed by the Congress and signed by the president in December, 1981. It contained 17 titles ranging from floral research to dairy price supports. It also contained all the major elements of the farm programs of the 1970s: target prices and deficiency payments, nonrecourse loans to support prices, acreage reduction programs, the continuance of the farmer-owned grain reserve, an extension of the P.L. 480 program and an extension of the Food Stamp Plan for one fiscal year (with a spending cap of $11.8 billion). It also called for a modest increase in target prices. In the face of stiff opposition from the Reagan administration, the Congress saved the entire price and income support mechanism for farmers, and even provided them with a modest increase in income support.

But the implementation of those price and income support measures rested with the new administration. Faced with a supply of wheat that was only slightly greater than what would be considered desirable, but a large and burdensome supply of corn, the Reagan administration implemented a weak acreage reduction program in 1982. A combination of good weather and weak controls in 1982 (a repeat of the 1950s) produced record breaking crops in 1982. Grain exports, given the mounting world recession, also declined in 1982. These developments caused Commodity Credit Corporation (CCC) inventories and loans outstanding to soar in 1982–83 to heights never before experienced. Many farmers and their leaders felt that surpluses were pushing the agricultural sector into a crisis.

It was the convergence of these events which forced the administration to reassess its approach to the 1983 commodity programs, and to propose the Payment-In-Kind (PIK) program. Under this approach, the Office of Management and Budget hoped to keep farm program payments "off-budget" by paying for massive land retirements with stocks already owned by the U.S. Department of Agriculture. At the same time, surplus stocks in government hands would be reduced.

In part, the emergency PIK program of 1983 was successful. It prevented large increases in the wheat carryover, and in conjunction with the drought of 1983, it reduced the carryover of corn by about 2.5 million bushels. However, the payment rates employed in the program to induce farmers into participation were excessive, and requirements that farmers be paid in physical product were highly inefficient. PIK payments were made in certificates redeemable to the USDA, creating a form of fiat currency, and a variety of arbitrage and laundering opportunities. These program errors contributed to the high cost of the Reagan farm program in the first term. But the basic problem with the 1981–84 Reagan policies was not these program errors; it was misjudgment regarding the potential excess productive capacity relative to total demand, as export demand failed to grow at the pre-1981 rate. Faced with this misjudgment, the administration had to embark on the PIK program in 1983 to bring aggregate supply back into balance with aggregate demand. It is estimated that total cash expenditures of the federal budget for this huge 1983 program of price support and production control, not including commodity payments under PIK, amounted to $18.5 billion in fiscal 1983. If PIK payments, valued at $10 to $11 billion, are added to the above budget total of $18.5 billion, the cost to the federal government of commodity price support and related activities comes to between $28 and $30 billion in fiscal 1983 alone. These unprecedented costs were run up by an administration that promised a new conservatism in agriculture.

Even as the emergency PIK program attempted to cut into surpluses, the forces of nature intervened unexpectedly—a major drought hit the corn belt in 1983, reinforcing the effects of PIK and driving down surplus stocks. However, even more powerful events were conspiring to drive agriculture into a true crisis. Falling export demand was coupled with rising real interest rates,[6] as the inflationary period of the 1970s was forced to an end. The Federal Reserve Bank under Chairman Paul Volcker concluded that the pain of deflation was to be endured in the name of slaying the inflation dragon. The result was an extraordinary turn-around in real interest rates. These rates, which had actually been negative in 1979, at the height of the Carter inflation, were allowed to rise by 1983 into double digits, and actually exceeded 20 percent for a time, as the Fed hit the money supply brakes.

The farm sector was caught in a pincer: falling export demand resulted in declining overall farm prices and incomes, while rising real interest rates made large investments in farmland and equipment, which had boomed in the 1970s, suddenly appear to have been grave mistakes in judgment. Farmland and asset values, which had appreciated by over 500 percent in many rural areas, suddenly began a downward spiral that would not end until the middle to late 1980s. As farmland fell in price, loans taken out in the boom days of the 1970s started going bad, and highly leveraged farmers (including Secretary Block) were seriously threatened with total losses.

As in the case of Block, this pincer caught many of the most sophisticated and highly capitalized farmers by surprise. In large part, this was because agriculture had ceased to be controllable through domestic farm legislation alone. While high target prices appeared to guarantee farm incomes, the reliance of the sector on export demand, and borrowed capital, made both exchange rates and interest rates of equal or greater importance than commodity price supports to farmers' fortunes. To close this vicious circle, real interest rates increasingly drove export demand itself: as real interest rates rose, international money managers and foreign exchange dealers responsible for billions of dollars of financial flows looked to the United States in the early 1980s as a source of very attractive and safe returns on Treasury bills and bonds. To acquire these securities they needed dollars, leading to rapidly increasing demands for the U.S. currency. Because the anti-inflationary Federal Reserve was loathe to print more dollars, the exchange rate climbed dramatically between 1981 and 1985, reaching its apex in February 1985. This appreciation of the currency choked off the demand for U.S. farm exports which were also priced in dollars.

Hence, the Federal Reserve's decision to tame inflation not only drove down the value of holding real assets, such as farmland; it also contributed significantly to reduced export demand for what this land could produce. The growing integration of global capital and commodity markets made farmers hostages to exchange rate and interest rate policy as never before.[7] Finally, the huge budget deficits that resulted from the failure of the Reagan administration to reduce spending proportionately with their "supply side" tax reductions made the government's need to borrow on international capital markets nearly insatiable, locking in a reliance on high returns to Treasury securities in order to finance continued government spending.

This situation developed rapidly into an agricultural depression in which many large and previously wealthy farmers appeared to face total ruin. This set the scene for the 1985 farm bill debate. Although the Reagan administration initially proposed major cuts in farm price support levels, attempting to make good on its earlier conservative promises and to reduce a yawning budget deficit, the farm debt situation made the bill politically impossible, and it was declared "dead on arrival." Never had so many "technical experts" entered the fray as in the 1985 bill, calling for major changes in policy. And yet, when the nearly 1,000 page bill was signed into law, it retained all of the old mechanisms of target prices, loan rates and acreage reduction. The essential compromise resulted from a desire, first, to protect farm incomes by holding target prices steady. In order to reduce the number of acres on which generous subsidies were paid, large Acreage Reduction Programs (ARPs), as high as 27.5 percent in wheat, were implemented. The second objective was to regain lost export markets. This was to be achieved by ratcheting loan rates downward using administrative authority vested in the secretary of agriculture (so-called "Findley amendment" authority). Billions of dollars were also targeted to "export enhancements," in which export companies were paid in-kind to lower their prices at the border to selected U.S. customers, particularly in traditional markets of the European Community (EC). Europe, the primary target of the Export Enhancement Program (EEP) subsidies, was increasingly the agricultural trade nemesis of the United States, because its own price supports and export subsidies had triggered huge surpluses and export dumping, reducing world market share for the United States.

In addition to these subsidies, "marketing loans" were approved for rice and cotton, in which the government paid down the difference between the support price and the export price using PIK certificates, creating another form of two-price system. Another major distinguishing feature of the 1985 bill was the re-creation of a Conservation Reserve Program (CRP), this time with the objective of removing 45 million acres from production. The new CRP, together with much stricter conservation requirements accompanying price supports, signalled the emergence of a potent new lobby in agricultural policy: the environmental interest groups.

Environmental interest groups were responsible for establishing the "sod- and swamp-buster programs" in the 1985 farm bill. The programs were established to discourage conversion of highly erodible land and wetlands. Under the sod-buster program, producers would lose all future eligibility for deficiency payments and other USDA program benefits if highly erodible grassland or woodland was used for crop production without appropriate conservation measures. The swamp-buster program similarly caused eligibility for USDA programs to cease if a producer converted wetland areas to cropland. A related environmental addition to farm policy in 1985 was "conservation compliance." It required producers with highly erodible cropland to implement an approved conservation plan by 1990. To maintain eligibility for federal program benefits the plan must be completed by 1995. Again, failure to comply would lead to loss of eligibility for program benefits.

Resulting from the push to reduce the negative effects of agriculture on the environment, and more market oriented, were also the "0-92" and "50-92" provisions of the 1985 farm bill. Both programs were optional. The "0-92" program allowed wheat and feed grain producers to change all or a portion of their permitted acreage[8] to conserving uses while continuing to receive deficiency payments for a maximum of 92 percent of their permitted acreage.

The export competitiveness sought by the 1985 farm bill appeared to have been achieved by the late 1980s, but whether through export subsidies alone remained a hotly contested issue, since a falling dollar and lower loan rates contributed significantly as well (Coughlin and Carraro 1988). As a result of increased export demand, farm prices and land values recovered in 1987, confirming the link from farm asset values to export demand (Runge and Halbach 1990). However, because target prices were held particularly high, especially in corn, the costs of the 1985 farm bill were enormous. Those costs, rising to as much as $26 billion in 1986 alone, contributed to a growing sense that something was seriously wrong with the way in which the United States conducted its agricultural policy. This view was pressed especially in international forums such as the General Agreement on Tariffs and Trade (GATT), where competing exporters such as Australia, Argentina, and Brazil decried the lowered world prices resulting from subsidized competition between the United States and EC.

In the United States, a conviction to use the GATT to help move toward changes in domestic policy led to a radical trade proposal to reform agricultural programs by doing away with the majority of them and substituting direct income supports in their place, "decoupling" payments from specific crops. Reagan's new secretary of agriculture, Richard Lyng, and U.S. Trade Representative Clayton Yeutter together introduced such a proposal in July 1987 to members of GATT in Geneva. While it was obvious that total elimination of agricultural price supports was unlikely to be achieved, the U.S. negotiating proposal reflected a growing international realization that agricultural policy merited reform.

In any event, dismay with agricultural spending professed by the administration in Geneva did not deter it from continuing to spend at home, helping lock in a substantial Republican victory in the 1988 presidential elections. Agricultural policy, together with many other issues in this highly media-oriented election, was given almost no treatment by the candidates. Democratic candidate Dukakis briefly flirted with a warmed-over proposal for supply control, then abandoned it. President George Bush entered office with a vague commitment to Reagan's policies, and a new agriculture secretary, Clayton Yeutter, who had served as the chief U.S. trade representative and architect of the U.S. GATT proposal.

As the 1990 farm bill drew near (the 1985 bill created a five-year cycle, in an attempt to allow new administrations greater influence over policy), there was increasing recognition that farm policy was an antiquated and extraordinarily expensive enterprise. But the basic question remained: what should be done? Or what could be done?

As the deadline for the 1990 bill approached, the concurrent budget talks put pressure on Congress to rethink the way farm programs were administered. With an estimated budget deficit of $161 billion in 1990 and the threat of across the board budget cuts under the so-called Gramm-Rudman law, Congress was forced to cut farm program spending as part of the larger deficit reduction plan. The Balanced Budget and Emergency Deficit Control Reaffirmation Act of 1987 (known popularly as Gramm-Rudman) mandated deficit targets of $64 billion in 1991 and zero by 1993. If a deficit reduction plan was not submitted in time, the law called for "sequestration," or equal cuts of all eligible programs, with agriculture prominent among the eligible candidates.

A by-product of this need for deficit reduction was the greatest of all political imperatives: re-election. How could costs be trimmed in a way that was least painful to politicians facing races every two or six years? The result was a compromise 1990 farm bill feature known as "flexibility." Flexibility was an extension of the "0-92" and "50-92" provisions of 1985 to include other acreage "bases."

The "flexibility" debate of 1990 occurred in essentially two phases. The first was a political exercise in the spring and early summer, in which the members of Congress indulged the wishes of a variety of commodity groups with promises of increased levels of support. During this phase, the administration issued its own version of a wish-list, a document detailing its proposals for a whole farm base, or Normal Crop Acreage (NCA) scheme, together with a variety of other more-than-incremental proposals. The NCA proposal would have merged all existing crop bases and established a single payment determined by cropping history. In effect, under the NCA scheme farmers could produce whatever program crops they chose on the NCA acres. Rather than "decoupling," which had gained a bad reputation with many farmers, the word chosen to characterize the NCA proposal was "flexible base."

The second phase of the farm bill process was driven by budget realities, during which most of the promises (though not all) were laid to rest both in Congress and at USDA. As the "budget summiteers" flailed away in attempts to conform to the Gramm-Rudman deficit reduction targets, it became evident that even major attempts to staunch the flow of red would not contain the hemorrhaging federal budget, especially as recession deepened and a military buildup began in the Middle East in response to Iraq's invasion of Kuwait. Agricultural spending was, however, a virtually unanimous candidate for cuts, and as the need to eliminate roughly $13.6 billion from agricultural commodity programs over five years emerged from the budget talks, it dictated that the agriculture committees and USDA save money while saving their seats.

The budget pressure dovetailed (though not perfectly) with the "flexibility" which had underpinned the administration's argument for NCA. Since total flexibility under NCA was neither necessary to achieve the budget targets nor desirable to many commodity groups and their supporters in Congress, a "triple-base" emerged as a natural compromise. The triple-base acreage concept continued the idea of splitting the historical crop acreage into permitted and idled acreage under the Acreage Reduction Program (ARP). Permitted acreage was then divided into two parts: a base for program crops which continue to receive payments, and a "flexible base," set at 15 percent of total for 1991 on which no payments are made. This flexible acreage could be planted to any program crop that was not a "fruit or vegetable." The political bargain was: "we will give the farmer flexibility, and he will surrender a portion of his deficiency payment guarantee."

In addition to the 15 percent "flexibility" farmers gained from the triple-base program, a little known 1985 provision was expanded in 1990 to give farmers full "flexibility" if they choose. The provision, called zero certification, allowed farmers to plant any nonprogram crop, other than a fruit or vegetable crop, on their crop base acreage while protecting that base. The 1985 provision only allowed conserving crops to be planted. The new provision allowed farmers to make planting decisions via market forces.

However, the nonprogram crops continued to compete with the artificially high returns of program crops.

Another force driving the 1990 bill was the environmental movement, which gained strength between 1985 and 1990. The CRP was extended and expanded, while a new Wetlands Reserve Program (WRP) was established. Arising from the neglect of water issues in farm policy, water quality was addressed with a new Water Quality Incentive Program (WQIP). A new Integrated Farm Management (IFM) program was established to allow farmers to combine overall productivity with profitability. In addition, the existing conservation compliance provision and sod- and swamp-buster programs were revised to administer more equitable penalties.

The impact of the GATT trade negotiations on the farm bill debate was more subtle than that of the budget or environment. Negotiations in the Uruguay Round were perceived as potentially affecting what the U.S. farm bill could do in terms of restricting trade and subsidizing agriculture. The United States had taken a strong liberal stand in the Uruguay Round and could not be perceived to be completely out of step in its domestic legislation. This did not, however, prevent the 1990 bill from adopting a variety of illiberal measures, continuing many more, and threatening to *raise* trade distorting subsidies if the Uruguay Round failed.

The 1990 bill included a provisional clause that if no agricultural agreement was reached by June 30, 1992, among the GATT contracting parties, the secretary of agriculture was permitted to spend an additional $1 billion on export subsidies. The secretary was also required to enact a marketing loan program on wheat and feed grains. In the case of a GATT agreement that is not enforced or not approved by Congress, the secretary can waive all program cost reduction measures, raise export subsidies and enact the marketing loan for wheat and feed grains.

What was to have been the final meeting of the Uruguay Round in Brussels occurred in early December 1990. Mr. Mats Hellstrom, Swedish minister of agriculture and chairman of the agriculture group, circulated a compromise proposal built around three areas: export subsidies, market access, and internal measures of support. Market access guarantees that other countries, particularly poor developing ones, would not be shut out of wealthy countries' markets. Internal supports were domestic policies such as price supports that artificially encouraged production, leading countries to dump these surpluses into world markets. To unload them, export subsidies made up the difference between internal and world prices. Market access and export subsidies were critical issues to most developing countries, for whom agricultural exports are the only way out of poverty and debt.

The EC immediately balked at the compromise. By paying farmers as much as four times world prices, the community accumulated chronic surpluses, which it then dumped into world markets at subsidy, lowering prices for everyone. Without the ability to pay such subsidies at the border, the EC would choke on its own surpluses, unless it cut internal supports, with political costs to pay. The compromise called for 30 percent adjustments over five years in market access and internal supports, based on policies in force in 1990. The EC had previously argued for 30 percent cuts—but based on 1986—when its own subsidies were at an all-time high. The compromise would also have required a commitment to specific percentage reductions in export subsidies, which was left open when the draft was circulated. The proposal was a major move for the United States, which had argued for 90 percent cuts in export subsidies, guarantees of market access and 75 percent cuts in domestic supports over several years.

The EC produced a list of reservations, complaints and demands that required major changes in the draft. They were joined in their objections by Korea and Japan. It was then that the negotiation broke down. The GATT Secretariat declared them "adjourned." In reality, the negotiations were in limbo, until and unless the EC came forward with a compromise on agriculture.

Fourteen other negotiating areas were also in limbo. Carla Hills, the U.S. chief negotiator, estimated that a full package of results in all 15 negotiation areas would be like writing a check for $17,000 over 10 years to every family of four in the world. On the downside, if the political response to the GATT breakdown was protectionism, U.S. politicians would find it easier to blame lost jobs on Japan or the EC, and protection would deepen the recession further.

At this writing, whether GATT will achieve a compromise remains uncertain. In January 1992 a further compromise document was floated by the GATT Secretariat in Geneva. However, it was rejected by the EC, and a crucial meeting between President Bush and EC leaders in April 1992 ended in disagreement.

In concluding this history, are there obvious lessons to be drawn from such complex events? The first, and most pervasive, lies largely behind the political debates themselves: the impact of technological change on surplus production, and hence on commodity policy. Lurking behind the machinations of farm policy is a relentless process of technological change, which has driven this policy even as it has been driven by it. Especially between 1940 and the present, both a mechanical and a biological revolution have led to major reductions in the hand labor required on most types of farms, increasing the number of acres that could be managed by a single farmer. Biological innovations in plant breeding and chemical innovations in pest and weed control have led to higher and higher crop yields. Wheat yields increased from 15.3 bushels per acre in 1940 to 38.1 bushels in 1985; corn from 28.4 bushels in 1940 to 118 bushels in 1985; cotton from 252.5 pounds per acre to 630 pounds in 1985. Similar gains were made in milk production (USDA various issues). Farming methods, and hence production efficiencies, in 1992 do not even remotely resemble those prior to World War II.

The rapid pace of this change has had numerous impacts on farm policy as well as on farming itself. Two are dominant. First, farm policy has been forced to confront the chronic tendency of technology to outpace political decision making. In practical terms, the fact that the rate of technological innovation has outpaced the rate of institutional innovation is obvious in the repeated failure of domestic farm policy to control domestic production, and the necessity to seek additional domestic and foreign outlets for these surpluses. Second, the interaction of farm technological advance and the operation of the commodity programs has resulted in a flow of the benefits from those programs to fewer and fewer farmers on larger and larger farms.

The story has unfolded as follows. The early adopters of a new and improved technology reap profits from declining production costs; as more and more farmers adopt the new technology output increases, and in the absence of price supporting interventions by government, prices of the commodity fall and net returns for all concerned are squeezed. For the laggard farmers who were slow to adopt, their costs do not decline as prices fall, and one by one they fail and are forced out of farming, as if falling off a treadmill that is running too fast. The profits earned by the early adopters were used in the post–World War II years to purchase the land and other productive resources from those farmers who failed. In this way the number of farms declined, and the remaining farms operated by successful farmers grew in size.

With one important exception, the above theory of the treadmill describes what happened in the post–World War II years. That one exception was the price supporting action by government. Government programs protected farmers against falling prices as output increased. In this situation, profits to the early adopters of new and improved technologies did not decline, nor did they decline for many farmers who followed in the adoption of the new technologies, until profits were squeezed by rising costs as those farmers sought to expand their operations and land prices were driven up in the competitive bidding for that scarce factor.

In this complex process the farmer of average ability pleaded with his government for higher levels of price support to protect him, which when realized had the effect of providing a profit bonanza for the successful early adopters. The laggard farmers, who had failed to get their production costs down, remained in financial trouble and became prime targets to be cannibalized by their successful, aggressive neighbors. Thus, the price supporting actions by government, rather than slowing down the resource concentration process in farming, speeded it up, by providing large windfall profits to the successful early adopters of new and improved technologies.

A direct consequence of this resource concentration process has been a persistent rise in land values, interrupted in the 1980s by a land market crash when export markets evaporated in the face of a strong dollar. Throughout most of the post–World War II era, the income benefits of the farm price and income support programs have been capitalized into rising land prices as the successful, aggressive farmers bid the scarce factor, land, away from their less successful neighbors. Thus, it could be said that the large, aggressive farmers made themselves wealthy as they took actions to make their operations even larger. But these large to very large farmers were not the only beneficiaries of the persistent rise in land prices. According to the USDA some 40 percent of the farmland in the United States was owned by nonfarm people and institutions in 1988. These nonfarmers included all kinds of people and institutions—retired farmers, relatives of the farm operators, small town businessmen, banks, insurance companies and others, including many urbanites. Thus, we see that the dynamic interaction of farm technological advance and the programs of price and income support have had the effect of increasing the wealth of many nonfarm people as well as certain well-placed farmers.

If a first lesson is that attempts to control production have failed, and that the interaction of farm technological advance and farm price and income support have led to rising land values as the productive resources of farming were concentrated into fewer and fewer hands, a second lesson is the incapacity of government to protect farmers through the complex machinery of price supports and acreage controls from the multitude of forces that raise and lower market prices. Despite the billions of dollars spent on supply-adjusting acreage retirements, price supports, and export subsidies, instability in both farm prices and gross revenues increased markedly over the period in which farm programs have been in effect. In the postwar period, more and more global price instability has been absorbed by U.S. farmers, in part because of the way U.S. policies are designed.

The tendency of the U.S. agricultural sector to become a "shock absorber" for world grain market instability results from a combination of factors. First, as noted above, in the early 1950s agricultural policy in the United States moved toward a system of price supports for grains and oilseeds, combined with acreage retirement and storage schemes designed to absorb excess production. In essence, the United States has accumulated inventories in periods of excess supply and reduced them in periods of excess demand. As "stock manager to the world," it has absorbed a disproportionate share of world price instability (see Sutton 1988).

Second, the European Community (EC) emerged during the 1970s from importer status to become an exporter of its own growing surpluses. Stimulated by high internal support prices, the EC expanded production yet continued to isolate its farmers from world price fluctuations. The policies of the EC, in contrast to those of the United States, shifted the burden of supply adjustments from the internal EC market to the world market as a whole.

Third, the United States increased its dependence on grain crops traded in international markets. From 1962 to 1971, an average of 49.5 percent of U.S. wheat, 13.0 percent of U.S. corn, and 31.1 percent of U.S. soybeans flowed into international trade. By 1971–1983, these proportions had increased to 58.4 percent for wheat, 27.0 percent for corn and 39.4 percent for soybeans. The land area planted to wheat, corn, and soybeans increased 54 percent between 1970 and 1981, while the proportion of total U.S. farm production value accounted for by these three export crops increased by 50 percent, from 16 to 24 percent of total (Sutton 1988; Runge, Houck, and Halbach 1988).

A third lesson, related to the first two, is that agricultural policy is less and less capable of protecting farmers from influences outside the domain of the farm bill itself. The internationalization of agriculture makes exchange rate and interest rate policies of equal or greater importance to the array of commodity policy instruments. This lesson is amply demonstrated by the experience of the 1980s, in which commodity price supports were insufficient to protect hundreds of farmers from near or total bankruptcy due to the impact of export market declines and asset devaluations. Houck (1986), for example, found that from 1962 to 1985, while overall changes in international grain prices maintained a steady level of instability, the proportion of this instability absorbed by U.S. producers jumped dramatically. Using econometric techniques, Myers and Runge (1984a, 1984b, and 1986) found significant increases in domestic U.S. farm price and gross revenue instability from 1962–1971 to 1971–1983. Using a variety of measures Sutton (1988) recently concluded that from 1973 to 1984, "U.S. producers were subject to a greater rise in price variability than producers in any other country." When the sources of the United States' grain market instability are divided into supply and demand side components, clear shifts in the direction of increased demand side causation are found from the 1960s to the 1970s and early 1980s.

All of these studies note that most of the U.S. demand shifts during the 1970s and 1980s originated from the export rather than the domestic market. Supply interruptions at home from drought and planting changes were of lesser importance as a cause of instability in this period than popularly assumed. In short, increased integration of the U.S. farm economy with world economic and political forces has led a greater share of international market instability to be reflected in domestic U.S. agriculture.

Fourth, and perhaps most obviously, the capacity of the U.S. Congress and executive branch to respond flexibly to the rapidly changing conditions of world markets is beset by all of the well-known inefficiencies of democratic decision making. The committees of the Congress cannot hope to decide on policies that remain essentially unchanged for years at a time, yet are robust enough to respond to international markets too. But neither is Congress willing to concede to the executive the power and authority to make rapid adjustments that may harm their constituents. The result, as in so many other areas of policy, is incremental adjustments which continually lag behind the conditions of the market (Rapp 1988). If the history of commodity policies is one of ever greater complexity, and ever diminishing effects, at ever greater costs, it is important to understand more specifically how these policies are designed.

Notes

1. This section draws heavily on Cochrane (1984).
2. Base acres refer to the number of acres enrolled with the USDA eligible for payments for growing a particular commodity, such as corn or wheat. In recent years this base has been a moving average of previous years' plantings. This number is an accounting unit, not a specific acre of land on a farm.
3. Nonrecourse loan refers to the mechanism that USDA uses to provide cash advances to farmers, which may then be repaid either in cash (at subsidized rates of interest) or in-kind, by surrendering the crop to the government in lieu of the loan itself. Because the government has no recourse to the loan principal, it is designated a "nonrecourse" loan. This mechanism accounts for a large share of the surplus commodities acquired by the government in times of low commodities prices.
4. This section relies heavily on Cochrane and Ryan (1976).
5. This discussion and that which follows dealing with the PIK program is based in part on Schnittker (1983).
6. "Real" rates are the nominal, or market rate of interest, less the rate of general price inflation.
7. The classic treatment of these capital market and exchange rate effects is Schuh (1974).
8. Permitted acreage is base acreage less the acreage set-aside under the Acreage Reduction Program. See Chapter 4 on "How the Commodity Programs Work" for more details.

References

Cochrane, Willard W. 1984. "Agricultural Policy in the United States—A Long View." In *Benjamin H. Hibbard Memorial Lecture Series*. Madison: Department of Agricultural Economics, College of Agricultural and Life Sciences, University of Wisconsin.

Cochrane, Willard and Mary Ryan. 1976. *American Farm Policy, 1948–1973*. Minneapolis: University of Minnesota Press.

Coughlin, C. C. and K. C. Carraro. 1988. "The Dubious Success of Export Subsidies for Wheat." Federal Reserve Bank of St. Louis, *Review*. 70(6): 38–47.

Houck, James P. 1986. "International Grain Market Price Instability: A Review of the Evidence." Department of Agricultural and Applied Economics, University of Minnesota, unpublished manuscript.

Myers, R. J. and C. F. Runge. 1984a, May. "Instability in North American Grain Markets II: Soybeans 1962–1983." University of Minnesota, Hubert H. Humphrey Institute of Public Affairs Working Paper.

_____. 1984b, May. "Instability in North American Grain Markets II: Wheat 1962–1983." University of Minnesota, Hubert H. Humphrey Institute of Public Affairs Working Paper.

_____. 1986, January. "The Relative Contribution of Supply and Demand to Instability in the U.S. Corn Market." *North Central Journal of Agricultural Economics*. 7(1): 70–78.

Rapp, David. 1988. *How the United States Got into Agriculture: And Why It Can't Get Out*. Washington, D.C.: Congressional Quarterly Inc.

Runge, C. Ford, James P. Houck, and Daniel W. Halbach. 1988. "Implications of Environmental Regulations for Competitiveness in Agricultural Trade." In John D. Sutton, ed., *Agricultural Trade and Natural Resources: Discovering the Critical Links*. Boulder and London: Lynne Rienner Publishers.

Runge, C. Ford and Daniel Halbach. 1990. "Export Demand, U.S. Farm Income and Land Prices, 1949–1985." *Land Economics*. 60-2.

Schnittker Associates. 1983, April. *The Crisis in Agricultural Policy*. Washington, D.C.

Schuh, G. Edward. 1974, February. "The Exchange Rate and U.S. Agriculture." *American Journal of Agricultural Economics*. 56(1): 1–13.

Sutton, John D. (ed.) 1988. *Agricultural Trade and Natural Resources: Discovering the Critical Links*. Boulder and London: Lynne Rienner Publishers.

U.S. Department of Agriculture. 1981. *A Time to Choose: Summary Report on the Structure of Agriculture*. Washington, D.C.

_____. Various Issues. *Agricultural Statistics*. Washington, D.C.

Wallace, Henry A. 1967. "For a Domestic 'Ever Normal Granary.' " From *The Century of the Common Man* (1943) in McGovern, ed., *Agricultural Thought in the Twentieth Century*. New York: Bobbs-Merrill Co.

4 How the Commodity Programs Work

Corn and Wheat

The Agricultural Adjustment Act (AAA) of 1933, as amended in 1936 and thereafter, introduced payments for idling land which remain the principal features of the corn and wheat program. The current array of policy instruments applied to these crops and other feed grains consumes a large percentage of federal commodity program outlays (Table 4.1).

The basic programs amount to a commitment by the government to buy the farmer's crop if it cannot be sold, and to guarantee a payment based on a fixed "what ought to be" (target) price. This is the broad protection affording by the "Social Contract" with agriculture. In return for such protection from market swings, the farmer is typically required to remove a portion of his acreage from production. This *quid pro quo* is best divided into two parts. First is the *quid*: the payment to the farmer is based on the relationship between the market price, loan rate, and target price, resulting in a "deficiency payment." The decision to seek this payment is voluntary; the farmer must declare his intention to participate through a "sign up" process before the planting season. The system works as illustrated in Figure 4.1. At the base of the block defining government payments is the acreage on which the farmer is entitled to receive such support. This "base" is established by planting a *specific* crop, such as wheat or corn, over a specified number of years or by buying land with an established base in these crops. "Corn base" is thus literally an *entitlement* to receive government payments, which if corn is *not* planted, erodes over time unless otherwise guaranteed.

Under 1990 provisions "flexible base acres" became a part of the commodity programs. The triple-base program allows producers to "flex" 15 percent of their crop base acreage to other allowed crops while protecting the base they are paid on. However, the triple-base program excludes all fruits, vegetables, potatoes, and dry beans from eligibility. Crops

Table 4.1. Corn and wheat program outlays

	1977	1978	1979	1980	1981	1982	1983	1984	1985	1986	1987	1988	1989	1990
Corn outlays (in billions)	$0.40	$1.70	$0.87	$1.26	$−0.67	$4.28	$5.72	$−0.93	$4.40	$10.52	$12.05	$8.23	$2.86	$2.64
Corn outlays as percentage of total farm programs	11	30	19	46	0	37	30	22	25	41	54	66	27	39
Wheat outlays (in billions)	$1.90	$0.84	$0.31	$0.88	$1.54	$2.24	$3.42	$2.54	$4.69	$3.44	$2.84	$0.68	$0.05	$0.58
Wheat outlays as percentage of total farm programs	50	15	9	32	38	19	18	35	27	13	13	5	.5	9

Source: U.S. Department of Agriculture (Printed in Rapp, [1988], p. 34) and USDA/ERS (various issues).
Note: Fiscal years.

planted on this 15 percent are not eligible for deficiency payments. This new flexibility allows farmers to use their management skills to produce the highest-return crop on 15 percent of their historical base acreage without losing eligibility for government payments.

In Figure 4.1, the base is 100 acres of corn. Recall that base acreage is an accounting unit, not an identifiable 100 acres of land. Fifteen percent of the base acres in this case is 15 acres, termed "flex" which can be planted to any crop other than a fruit or vegetable, including corn.

At the top, left-hand side of the figure is the target price. This "what ought to be" price is largely determined in the Subcommittee on Wheat, Feed Grains and Soybeans of the House Agriculture Committee and the Senate Agriculture and Forestry Subcommittee, although it may be haggled over throughout the farm bill process. In the example, it is set hypothetically at $3.00 per bushel. Once set, as in the 1985 farm bill, it is typically less flexible than other features of the commodity programs, and becomes Congress's "political price," guaranteeing protection to their corn and wheat growing constituents.

At the bottom left-hand side of the diagram is the loan rate, set hypothetically at $2.00 per bushel. The loan rate is an effective minimum price. It is the amount which the government, through the Commodity Credit Corporation (CCC) of USDA, agrees to loan the farmer (at subsidized interest). If at the end of a specified period (typically 9 months), the farmer cannot get better than $2.00 per bushel in the marketplace, he

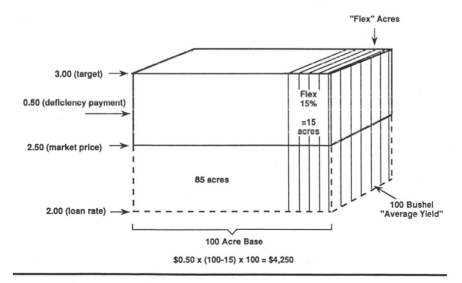

Figure 4.1. How deficiency payments are calculated (without acreage reductions)

can give up the crop and keep the $2.00 per bushel loan. Because the government has no recourse to the cash loan, and must accept the crop itself in lieu of payment, this is called a "nonrecourse loan." Because the farmer can do no worse than $2.00 per bushel, the loan rate is effectively a minimum price guarantee. At harvest, the market price may be higher than the loan rate, and the farmer can sell his crop and repay the loan. Whether he repays the loan in cash or in kind, he receives a "deficiency payment." The difference between the target price ($3.00) and the loan or market price (whichever is higher) determines the deficiency payment received from the government. Here we assume a market price of $2.50 and a $.50 deficiency payment.

The final dimension of the entitlement to farmers is the historical record of yields, determined by records kept, like base acreage accounts, at county offices of the federal Agricultural Stabilization and Conservation Service (ASCS). Under the 1985 law, the farmer may either accept "county average yields" or prove that his yields exceed the county average, raising his deficiency payment. "Proving up" yields has been an important strategy for aggressive program participants. The higher these average yields, the higher the payment received. Under the 1990 farm bill, yields were "frozen" for the life of this bill. Here the average yield is hypothetically 100 bushels per acre.

Together, average yields, base acres, and deficiency payments determine the amount received by the farmer if he elects to "sign up" for government price supports. To sum up, a farmer with a 100 acre corn "base" has, over a period of years, established this base acreage as an accounting unit with U.S. Department of Agriculture offices. If he elects to sign up for the "corn program" in a given year, he receives a deficiency payment equal to the difference between the market price (or loan, whichever is higher) and the target price set by the government, calculated on this acreage base (less "flex" acres) multiplied by average yields.

Together, these elements define a "block" of income to which the hypothetical farmer is entitled when he signs up for commodity price supports. The base of the block is given by his 100 base acres (less "flex" acres) the side by the $.50 deficiency payment; the length by the 100 bushel average yield. In the absence of acreage controls, this block would appear as in Figure 4.1, and the calculation would be

$$\$.50 \times (100 - 15) \times 100 = \$4,250.$$

Now consider the *quo*: in any year, the government may decide that it will require the farmer to reduce the amount of acres planted to corn. This "set-aside" decision will be a function of several variables. Based on existing conditions, and before each season, the USDA must forecast what the supply/demand balance will be in world markets. As one of the world's largest corn and wheat producers, this is especially difficult, since it is U.S. government decisions plus weather that largely determine this balance. If the government guesses too low, and supplies exceed demand, prices will fall and deficiency payments will rise, leading to high commodity program spending. If it guesses too high, and supplies fall short of demand, prices will skyrocket. While farmers may be pleased, the general consuming public will not be.

Along this razor's edge must be determined the amount of base acreage on which corn *cannot* be grown, the Acreage Reduction Program, or ARP. This is the cost to the producer of receiving the benefits of income protection via the deficiency payment. His income entitlement is reduced by the percentage of base required by the government to be left idle.[1] Consider the modified block in Figure 4.2 below.

In this case, the 20 percent ARP reduces the income entitlement by 20 acres (20 percent of base acreage), which must be "set-aside," and planted to some other approved crop. The effect is to reduce the deficiency payment by

$$\$.50 \times 20 \times 100 = \$1,000$$

Total deficiency payments, assuming 15 percent "flex" acres, are thus reduced to:

$$\$4,250 - \$1,000 = \$3,250$$

The "saving" is to government budget outlays. Budget savings dominate supply control as the true objective of ARPs. The reason they are less effective in controlling supply is straightforward. The more corn that can be produced on the remaining 65 acres, the higher overall receipts will be. This creates a powerful incentive to (a) retire low productivity acres in the ARP; (b) increase yields through intensification of production on the land remaining in corn.

A number of key points must be kept in mind as one considers this basic policy approach. First, it commits, sight unseen, billions of dollars of federal funds to an entitlement program, the actual cost of which is largely unpredictable from year to year, forcing guesswork on the part of both farmers and the government. Farmers must decide whether to sign up at all, or whether to forego the bureaucratic complexities in return for higher risks in the marketplace. The federal government must decide what level of payments will induce what percentage of corn base to come into the

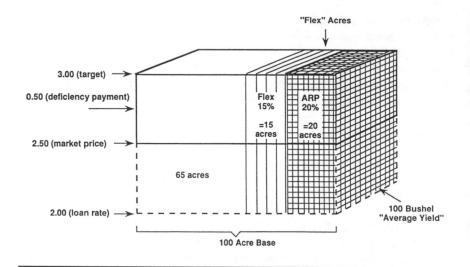

Figure 4.2. How deficiency payments are calculated
(with acreage reductions)

program, obligating payments, and then must turn around and decide how much of this base to take *out* of production. In the end, total payments are nearly always substantially different from projected ones, making commodity programs an open-ended, potential budgetary nightmare.

Second, the programs encourage the cultivation of those crops that are most heavily protected through high target prices, whether or not they are in market demand. The preservation of "base" encourages corn to be grown year after year, discouraging crop rotation practices that naturally improve soil fertility, and raises reliance on chemical fertilizers while reducing diversified farming operations. Raising average yields so as to garner larger deficiency payments becomes an end in itself, further encouraging investments in chemical- and yield-enhancing inputs that would be less profitable in the absence of artificial price supports.

Third, because a larger base represents a larger entitlement to government protection, farmers are encouraged to expand their base either through increasing corn or wheat acreage or, more easily, by buying other farms which come complete with corn or wheat base. This interacts with technological incentives to increase yields and to lower per-unit costs. Because the biggest farmers receive the biggest commodity payments and income supports, bigness is encouraged, together with heavy investments in land, chemicals, and equipment, all in quest of larger entitlements to a flow of government subsidies.

Chronic overproduction is thus encouraged, despite acreage reduction programs. Attempts to reduce production by "setting aside" corn base are largely frustrated, as they have been for over 50 years, by farmers capacity to retire the least productive land first, and to increase yields on the land that remains. While often defended as conservation improvements, even if not particularly effective supply control devices, there is no guarantee that acres lower in productivity will also be especially prone to environmental damages. In many areas of the country, it is high productivity land that is most subject to erosion and run-off. Ironically, the acreage reduction program encourages these acres to be farmed even more intensively than before. In "building corn base," it has also made curious sense for the farmer to plow up low productivity acres and bring them into cultivation so that they are available later to be set aside. This does little to enhance U.S. global competitiveness.

In 1985, the new farm bill departed from previous legislation by moving to dramatically lower loan rates while keeping target prices high—the compromise set up by the dual objective of income protection and export promotion. The floor price of U.S. corn and wheat to foreign buyers was effectively set by the loan rate. Hence, lowering loan rates and tying them to market conditions was important in improving U.S. export competitiveness, which had languished under the much higher loans of the 1977 and 1981 farm bills. However, lower loans also meant higher deficiency payments, leading to the massive costs of 1986 and 1987, before export markets and prices began their recovery.

Under the 1985 bill, wheat and corn loan rates were allowed to drop substantially from $2.55 a bushel for corn in 1985 to $1.92 in 1986, to $1.82 in 1987, $1.65 in 1989 and $1.57 in 1990. Wheat loan rates fell from $3.30 in 1985 to $2.40 in 1986, to $2.28 in 1987, $2.21 in 1988, $2.06 in 1989 and were at $1.95 in 1990. Target prices, meanwhile, remained high. In corn, the 1985 farm bill froze them at $3.03 through 1987. They were at $2.84 by 1989 and $2.75 in 1990. In wheat, they were frozen at $4.38 through 1987 and were $4.10 in 1989 and $4.00 in 1990. Chronic surpluses led ARPs to expand from 10 percent in corn in 1985 to 20 percent in 1987, with a 15 percent paid diversion on top. In wheat, ARPs rose from 10 percent in 1985 to 27.5 percent in 1987, with no paid diversion. Despite these large set-aside requirements, farmers could hardly afford not to sign up, given high deficiency payments and low market prices. Participation of farmers with base acres in the corn program rose from 69 percent of corn base in 1985 (compared with 29 percent in 1982) to 90 percent in 1987, 87 percent in 1988, 80 percent in 1989 and 76 percent in 1990. In wheat, participation rose from 73 percent of wheat base in 1985 (compared with 48 percent in 1982) to 88 percent in 1987, 86 percent in 1988, 78 percent in 1989 and 80 percent in 1990.

Two additional efforts were made to control burgeoning supplies in the late 1980s. As noted above, provisions of the 1985 bill were brought to bear that paid volunteering farmers 92 percent of their deficiency payments, yet allowed only 50 percent of corn base to be planted to corn. In 1987, this "50-92" provision was expanded to a "0-92" plan, which paid volunteers 92 percent of their benefits to plant no corn at all. This program represented a clear move in the direction of eliminating the linkage from payments to specific crops, or what was widely called "decoupling" payments from production. This effort was given additional attention in a bill introduced by Senators Rudy Boschwitz (R-MN) and David Boren (D-OK) to "decouple" payments entirely. While popular with economists, and consistent with the U.S. proposal to GATT, "decoupling" raised many of the problems that had plagued previous attempts (such as the Brannan Plan) to directly support producer incomes, undisguised by the complexities of loan rates and target prices (few nonspecialists discerned the decoupling of "0-92"). In addition, the Boschwitz-Boren scheme phased out its proposed "equity payments" rapidly over time, making decoupling appear a Trojan Horse to many producers, for whom the 1985 farm bill had proven quite profitable.

During 1987, 1988, and 1989, farm income rose steadily as federal payments streamed into the countryside. As exports resumed, a major drought hit North America in the summer of 1988, driving prices to new highs. Since higher prices meant lower deficiency payments, Congress reasoned that they had "saved" money on commodity programs, thus allowing a generous program of drought relief. Drought relief became the new battle cry in Congress, and a $3.9 billion drought aid package was passed in 1988, followed by a $900 million package in 1989. Like the "0-92" program, these expenditures were further evidence of congressional willingness to pay farmers large direct transfers, although the drought provided a different justification for doing so.

Starting with the 1991 crop year some of the basic mechanics of the farm program will be different. The 1990 legislation supplanting the 1985 farm bill basically moved a further increment in the direction of "decoupling." First, the market price used to determine the deficiency payment rate will be calculated on a 12-month average of the market price versus the previous 5-month average, likely resulting in lower payments. Second, the loan rate for the nonrecourse loan program will be set differently. The loan rate could previously be set between 75 and 85 percent of the 5 year moving average market price. Under the 1990 legislation the loan rate cannot fall below 85 percent and cannot be set more than 5 percent lower than the previous year's rate. However, the 15 percent "flex" acres reduce total payments, and allow farmers to plant a wider variety of crops.

The consequence of large government payments, reinforced by steadily increasing market prices, was a series of near record years for average farm incomes after 1985. Contrary to the images of disaster that continued to fill nightly news reports, net farm incomes rose from $32.2 billion in 1985 to $38.0 billion in 1986, $47.1 billion in 1987; $45.7 billion in 1988, and $46.7 billion in 1989. The distribution of incomes, as we shall describe below, leaves a less satisfactory impression. Much of this increase was attributable to government payments, including drought assistance, to corn and wheat producers.

Soybeans

Until the 1990 farm bill, the soybean program was often cited as a model by advocates of more market-oriented policies. Unlike corn and wheat, there were no target prices for soybeans, and no acreage-reducing set-asides. There was, however, a loan rate, set at $5.02 per bushel for 1986 by the 1985 farm legislation, which had been allowed to fall to $4.77 by 1988, and $4.53 by 1989.

Soybean producers, however, threw in the towel in the 1990 bill and sought the protection of a marketing loan, which amounted to a full export subsidy equal to the difference between the loan and market prices (see the section on Rice and Cotton below). However, the loan rate was set at $5.02 with a two percent service fee reducing the rate to $4.92, so low as to do the soybean grower little good. Having compromised their market oriented principles, the soybean growers failed to bring home much of a prize.

However, the operation of the soybean program was not independent of the corn and wheat programs. Soybeans, like most corn and some soft wheats, are used as a feed ingredient for livestock. In addition, as a nitrogen-fixing legume, soybeans are often planted in rotation with corn. As a substitute feed ingredient, and as a substitute for corn across growing seasons, the price of soybeans is affected by the price of corn and wheat, and hence by the government programs which support these prices.

High corn support prices, in particular, discourage the planting of soybeans, reducing their supply and their use in rotation. At the same time, higher corn and/or wheat prices make soybeans a more attractive alternative as a feed ingredient. The combined result of reduced supply and increased demand for soybeans is to raise their price, making them less competitive in global markets, where the United States once was preeminent as a soybean exporter. Soybean exports fell from 23.8 million metric tons in 1979–80 to 18 million metric tons in 1988.

The influence wheat and corn programs have had over soybean and oilseed production decisions was expected to be tempered with the institution of the triple-base program in 1991. The primary consequence of the program was expected to allow production of soybeans and other oilseeds on "flex acres." In the past, farmers were reluctant to plant these crops for fear of losing their "historical" base acreage. The triple-base allowed farmers to expand production of these crops somewhat (by 15 percent) without seriously jeopardizing their future eligibility. Whether these changes will be sufficient to introduce greater diversity into cropping patterns remained an open question, since the advantages to a typical farm of the 15 percent "flex" in the direction of oilseeds appears marginal.

Rice and Cotton

Rice and cotton both depend on a target price, loan rate and deficiency payment scheme, involving the same *quid pro quo* of payments for acreage retirement applied to corn and wheat. However, the total number of participants is much smaller, and the benefits are more concentrated regionally. In the southern and western states where rice and cotton are grown, the programs are skillfully defended by their congressional delegations (Rapp 1988). The 1985 farm bill froze target prices for cotton at 81 cents a pound in 1986, and allowed total reductions of only 10 percent until 1990, with additional reductions to 76 cents in 1988. ARPs were capped at 25 percent of cotton base. Rice target prices were allowed to fall from $11.90 per hundredweight in 1986 to as low as $10.71 in 1990, with ARPs as high as 35 percent of base. While these ARP requirements may seem severe, they mask the most significant feature of the rice and cotton program innovated in the 1985 farm bill—the same marketing loan extended to soybeans in 1990.

Using their senior positions on the House and Senate Agriculture committees, representatives of cotton and rice growers were able to provide this new twist on the loan rate concept in 1985. Rather than forfeiting their crops to the government, rice and cotton farmers would simply pay back the loan at the market price. If this price was lower than the original loan rate, they could keep the difference. No payment limitations were imposed on these marketing loan payments, such as those applied (in principle) to wheat and corn. These provisions led to massive windfalls for some producers, with payments ranging into the millions of dollars.

The marketing loan effectively allowed rice and cotton prices to seek world market levels, arguably stimulating export competitiveness, although exports in cotton increased from 1.1 million metric tons in 1985 to only 1.3

in 1988, and in rice from 1.96 million metric tons to 2.30 in 1988, hardly a dramatic turnaround. Nonetheless, the popularity of the marketing loan to producers (largely due to unlimited payments) led to calls by soybean growers for similar treatment realized in the 1990 bill. Demands by corn and wheat producers for the same sort of programs were met in part through a provision in the 1990 bill under which a marketing loan could go into force for corn and wheat if the GATT talks broke down. If the marketing loan was actually extended to those producers it would, by some estimates, increase total agricultural spending to levels unseen even in the highest spending years of the Reagan administration.

The planting decisions of cotton and rice producers were also affected by changes in the 1990 bill. First, the triple base program affected the acreage and deficiency payments of cotton and rice producers. Furthermore, set-aside acreage under the ARP will be treated differently than in the past for cotton and rice. Producers will be allowed to plant minor oilseeds or experimental or industrial nonprogram crops on the set-aside acreage.

Sugar

The U.S. sugar program is the most concentrated benefits package in the array of commodity programs, with more money flowing to fewer producers than in any other (legal) crop. While loan rates, target prices, and deficiency payments have been used in the past, current sugar policies are based on an overtly protectionist scheme of import quotas, tariffs and fees, designed to limit imports. This scheme dates in large part to the Sugar Act of 1934, although the current program was set by the 1981 and 1988 farm bills, amended slightly in 1990. It consists of a price-support-loan program, a minimum support price, and a market stabilization price, similar to a target price.

The key to the program is the import quota, limiting the inflow of sugar that can be produced in the Caribbean or the Philippines at about 5 cents a pound from entering U.S. markets, where the price is supported at nearly four times that level. The supposed virtue of the program has always been that it is run at "no cost" to the taxpayer. By law, if the loan rate is 18 cents a pound, prices *must* exceed this price. To push prices in the domestic market up, quotas choke off imports, cornering the U.S. market for domestic producers. As in the corn and wheat programs, if market prices fall below the loan, the crop may be turned over to the government. The 1985 farm bill prevented this because the market support price was legislated at 21.37 cents a pound, and import quotas were set in order to squeeze the domestic market to achieve this price. Without this program,

U.S. imports would be large enough to actually raise *world* prices a penny or two.

However, in response to the 1989 GATT ruling on U.S. sugar policy (see below), the absolute quota system was replaced with a "tariff rate quota" in October 1990. The Tariff Rate Quota (TRQ) is a "two-tier tariff instrument." The first tier consists of a low tariff for imports up to a specified quantity. In fiscal 1990–91 this low rate was .625 cents per pound on 2.315 million tons. The second tier is a high tariff rate on additional imports; 16 cents per pound on additional imports for fiscal 1990–91 (Barry 1991). To conform with GATT articles the TRQ is not an absolute import restriction.

While taxpayers may not pay subsidies to sugar growers directly, consumers are transferring huge amounts to sugar producers by paying artificially inflated domestic prices, while U.S. import quotas deny income to poor farmers in sugar exporting countries. Benefits to sugar producers are concentrated among fewer than 10,000 growers, dominated by five corporations producing 90 percent of the cane in Hawaii and two growers producing 50 percent of the crop in Florida. In addition to cane growers, sugar beet growers in the Northern Plains, including the Red River Valley of Minnesota and the Dakotas, have also reaped large benefits. The annual cost of a program run at "no cost" to the taxpayer is estimated at $1 to $1.5 billion in higher consumer prices (Rekha 1989).

In 1989, the import quota used to keep domestic sugar prices high was found to be illegal under the General Agreement on Tariffs and Trade (GATT). A GATT panel established at the request of Australia to look into the practices concluded that the United States "cannot justify the maintenance of quantitative restrictions on the importation of sugar," which are inconsistent with GATT Article XI:1, calling for the General Elimination of Quantitative Restrictions (GATT 1989). The U.S. delegation to GATT had little choice, in light of the overall U.S. position in GATT, but to accept the report. The result was the "tariff rate quota."

Even in the face of this GATT ruling, the sugar program largely escaped any substantial trade liberalization in the 1990 farm bill drafting process, suffering mainly at the hands of budget balancers. Sugar processors are to be assessed a one percent "market service payment" to offset the deficit and appease other commodity groups taking larger cuts. On balance, many sugar growers feel they are no worse off, and possibly even better off, under the 1990 bill.

A final dimension of the U.S. sugar program worth noting is the indirect effect of sugar prices on the competitiveness of sweeteners manufactured from high fructose corn syrup. These sugar substitutes would be far less price competitive for the soft-drink industry, where the bulk are consumed, if sugar was priced closer to world market levels. Corn sweeteners are now estimated to account for about 6 to 7 percent of U.S. corn production, mortgaging this aspect of the corn market to the entire apparatus of protection provided the domestic sugar industry. Corn interests are thus an important political factor in any reform of U.S. sugar policy.

Dairy Products

Whereas other commodity programs acquire surplus production through the nonrecourse loan mechanism, the dairy program authorizes direct government purchase of surpluses. "Milk equivalents" (butter, cheese, dry milk) are purchased from dairy cooperative processors at prices predetermined by Congress and redistributed as food assistance through various relief programs. Dairy producers thus receive their "milk checks," but not deficiency payments, as in other commodity programs.

The 1985 farm bill set the dairy support (purchase) price at $11.60 per hundredweight in 1986, $11.35 in January 1987, and $11.10 in October 1987. In 1988 it stood at $10.60 and remained there in 1989 (Rapp 1988). In 1990 the farm bill restricted the support price for milk from falling below $10.10/hundredweight for several years. Producers were also assessed 5 cents/hundredweight the first year; and a higher rate that could rise substantially for producers that expand production during the next four years. This latter provision provides a mechanism for extracting payments in the event supply exceeds demand, and may be exercised if output continues to drift upward.

The 1985 legislation also authorized "whole herd buy-outs," in which producers bid for the opportunity to send their entire herd to slaughter, and agreed not to produce again for five years. The program was in effect from 1985 until April 1986 and led to the slaughter of 1.3 million of the nation's 11 million dairy cows, although replacements caused the net decline to be less. Payments for the buy-out came from assessments to farmers. All producers that continued to produce milk paid the assessments. These assessments were deducted from the price received. Assessments were .40 cents/hundredweight from April through December, 1986 and .25 cents/hundredweight from January—December, 1987. In 1987, receipts from the assessment paid $684 million of the total $1.8 billion cost. Milk production fell from 13.2 million pounds in 1985 to 6.7 million pounds in 1987, which was still insufficient to mop up the excess supplies (Rapp 1988). Faced with continuing technological progress and increasing production per cow, dairy surpluses are a persistent issue, leading critics to claim that the buy-out was no more than a very expensive band-aid. Especially if farm programs reduce support for corn, wheat, and soybeans, it will be difficult to avoid land and feed from flowing into increased dairy production.

In addition to milk price supports, the dairy industry is one of over 40 agricultural groups receiving some form of assistance through federal "marketing orders." Federal milk marketing orders allow cooperatives to charge higher prices for fluid (Class I) milk compared with milk going to manufactured products, which receives the basic support price. Besides this difference in support price, there is also a regional disparity in the price paid to milk producers. This difference is defined by a little-known series of concentric circles drawn out from a central point in the upper Mississippi Valley: Eau Claire, Wisconsin, originally determined to be the lowest cost reference point for dairy production. In theory, since the costs of producing fluid milk further from the Wisconsin/Minnesota "milk shed" were higher, fluid milk producers in far away places like Arizona, Florida, and Texas should receive higher levels of support to assure a steady, healthy supply of fluid milk for their communities (California actually maintains its own set of orders). Despite rapid technological advances in the transport of milk and changing supply-demand conditions in various producing regions, these price differentials remained in place, exceeding the cost of transportation from Eau Claire for reconstituted milk. They have contributed to a form of protection for large, factory-farm dairies in the South and West. Cattle are seldom allowed to taste fresh grass, and are fed concentrated feeds, creating major environmental problems of manure disposal.

However, because of the concentric circles defining the marketing order, the only members of Congress now opposing them are in the upper Midwest. There are currently 42 of these orders, regulating 70 percent of all milk produced in the United States, with most of the remainder regulated by the states (Hammond 1991). Political support for the marketing orders grows with each concentric ring outward from Eau Claire. Because of the apportionment of House seats according to population density, and the heavy population levels on or near the East and West Coasts, the prospects for changing these orders remain dim, despite the fact that they are largely artifacts of an earlier era.

In 1990, the dairy marketing orders were the subject of federal hearings, which coincided with a major lawsuit brought in Federal District Court by representatives of the upper Midwest. The lawsuit and hearing together contested whether the price differentials enforced by the marketing orders were necessary to cover the costs of milk production, and whether they contributed to the orderly marketing of milk in various parts of the country.

The domestic supports provided to the dairy industry are also under attack in trade circles. As in the case of sugar, dairy products are protected from foreign competition by import quotas, which insulate the domestic market. These quotas admit manufactured dairy products equivalent to about 2 percent of domestic production. As in the case of sugar, these import quotas are the subject of criticism in GATT, and are inconsistent with the U.S. position there on agriculture, although they remain exempted from GATT law under a special waiver negotiated in earlier trade rounds. Because the dairy industry is heavily subsidized in other countries, notably the EC (leading to similar problems with surplus production), U.S. dairy producers anticipate that removing these quotas without reforming world dairy policies could lead to a flood of butter and cheese into the United States drawn from the mountains of surplus in other countries (Gardner 1989). Dairy products, particularly nonfat dry milk, have also been important export promotion tools. Public Law 480 and the Export Enhancement Program (EEP) authorized under the 1985 farm bill both have made substantial use of surplus milk powder to promote U.S. trade interests as a form of subsidy.

Tobacco and Peanuts

The tobacco and the peanut programs each offer acreage allotments and marketing quotas designed to provide legal monopolies for the production of these crops to a few growers. These allotments have a high value, and raise the price of the land on which these commodities are grown.

Tobacco (designated a "flue-cured" and "burley") has been supported in essentially this form since 1933. Nonrecourse loans are offered through producer groups, which serve as clearinghouses for government payments and store tobacco in approved warehouses. In principle, the allotments and quotas are then orchestrated to prevent excessive surpluses from accumulating, driving prices below the loan. Despite nearly universal participation in the program (due to heavy penalties for noncompliance), high loan rates and technological change have both encouraged increasing yields. In the early 1980s, surpluses rose to levels that threatened the viability of the entire program, leading in 1982 to the imposition of assessments on growers to cover losses. Assessments continued to grow each year until 1986, when emergency action was undertaken to stem these rising costs. Price supports were lowered and cigarette companies agreed to share the cost of the program, in return for the right to buy up existing surplus stocks of tobacco for as little as ten cents on the dollar (Rapp 1988). The companies now also will help determine the price of tobacco and the extent of foreign imports, converting legal monopolies by growers into a legalized monopoly/monopsony relationship with the large manufacturers that dominate the cigarette industry. This arrangement was made part of permanent law in 1986.

Peanut programs have remained basically unchanged since 1948, when Congress set high domestic prices by imposing production controls through allotments, marketing quotas, and import controls. Imports controls are set at zero, totally preventing imports from entering U.S. markets. As with tobacco, producer associations serve as clearinghouses for farmers. The 1988 loan rate was set at $615.27 a ton *if* the grower holds an allotment, and $149.80 if he does not, in which case his peanuts must be exported or used for nonfood uses. The USDA also directly acquired surpluses, converting them into oil, meal and peanut butter widely used in federal food assistance programs.

As in the case of the sugar, dairy and tobacco, domestic U.S. peanut growers are insulated from world markets. The program closes off access to potential importers, mostly in developing countries, through nontariff barriers (quotas). In 1989, the United States supplemented its proposal to GATT by proposing "tariffication" of those quotas, converting them into tariff equivalents that could be successively lowered over time. The result would be to make them much more obvious, or "transparent," barriers to trade. The proposal has been met coolly by the growers of these commodities.

A final observation relevant to the tobacco and peanut programs is that, much like rice and cotton, they represent regional interests which continue to give farm policy a strong southern flavor.

Honey, Wool and Mohair

Three relatively minor commodities that also are considered part of the commodity programs are honey, wool, and mohair. Honey producers are eligible for marketing loans similar to those paid rice and cotton producers, equal to 59 cents a pound in 1988. Despite the bucolic, small farm image of beekeepers, it is striking that Congress felt compelled in 1985 to impose a $250,000 limit on payments to individuals benefiting from the program. Yet in 1987, it determined that a quarter of a million dollars was too strict a limit, and removed it (Rapp 1988). However, in 1990 the payment limit was mandated to fall to $125,000 over four years.

Wool and mohair are also heavily subsidized through direct payments, equal to a "topping-off" payment over and above market prices. In 1988, support prices were $1.78 a pound for wool and $4.95 for mohair. These supports were complemented by an import duty on foreign wool, designed to give domestic producers an advantage. Payment limits were established for wool and mohair of $250,000 in 1985 but were to be reduced to $125,000 over four years starting in 1991.

Conservation Reserve Program (CRP)

While not strictly a commodity program, the Conservation Reserve Program (CRP) authorized under the 1985 farm bill, and reauthorized in 1990, deserves to be treated in the same space, since one of its substantial objectives was to reduce surplus supplies especially of corn.

Under the CRP, participating landowners agreed not to produce on highly erodible cropland for ten years in exchange for an annual rental payment. During periodic sign-up rounds, landowners submitted bids to the USDA indicating the acreage they would retire and the amount per acre they would be willing to accept annually in compensation. The USDA then selected the lowest bids in the multi-county pool in which the farm was located. Retired lands were to be managed to reduce erosion to tolerance levels—usually by planting a cover of perennial grasses, and in some cases trees.

But the CRP was designed to do more than reduce erosion. Surplus reduction was also supposed to occur, through what has been called the "base bite" (Tall and Runge 1988). Under the 1985 farm bill, each acre entered into the reserve proportionately reduced a farm's aggregate acreage base over the ten years of the contract. This base reduction, in turn, reduced the amount of land that the farmer was permitted to plant to program crops and so reduced the deficiency payments farmers received on those crops. Production and government outlays were both scaled back.

Unfortunately, even if the CRP ever reaches its ultimate goal of 45 million acres, it will only modestly affect commodity supplies. For example, if past sign-ups are extrapolated, the full CRP will reduce annual corn production through the base bite by only 435 *million* bushels. This compares with 1987–88 corn surpluses of 2.3 *billion* bushels.

A product of the Gramm-Rudman deficit era, the CRP also featured budget reduction in its array of objectives. The base bite effectively rented a portion of the landowner's acreage base for the ten years of the contract, thereby reducing the commodity payments for which the landowner was eligible. This, of course, created a major disincentive to CRP participation, especially in the Corn Belt where each acre of CRP entry could cost a farmer from $150 to $200 in foregone net cash returns. Periodic "bonus payments," like those offered for corn in the February 1987 CRP bidding round, were recognition of the need to entice CRP entry by additionally compensating farmers for the substantial opportunity cost created by the base bite.

CRP program costs were to be minimized by the bidding process itself. Since the opportunity cost of CRP parcels presumably varied from landowner to landowner, the government could get the cheapest conservation benefits by taking the lowest bids. As things turned out, however, the only genuine bidding occurred among first round participants who did not know that the USDA had decided to put an upper limit on accepted bids in order to prevent outlandish payments.

These caps remained essentially unchanged in subsequent rounds. As this knowledge became widespread, the distribution of bids received converged to the cap level in each pool. The cap rate in effect became the going price for cropping rights on fragile land, and low-end bids disappeared. Any cost-saving potential of a bidding process was lost.

The 1990 farm bill attempted to rectify some of these problems by adding special programs to complement the CRP targeted to critical environments such as watersheds and wetlands (see Chapter 5). However, many of the basic problems of targeting and cost ineffectiveness continued to beset the conservation programs.

Conclusion: Five Problems of Commodity Policy

In concluding this analysis of U.S. commodity policy, we wish to stress five overriding problems that have afflicted it. Having looked behind the imagery of farm policy and described how the programs work in reality, it is important to define clearly what problems need to be solved if a realistic reform agenda is to be built. These problems are in large measure *inherent* in the design and implementation of the programs, and are thus difficult to reform through surface or incremental improvements.

Before reviewing these problems, it is worth keeping in mind that despite their pervasive influence, most aspects of the commodity programs are currently voluntary. No forces other than the market and political influence leading to program benefits *compels* farmers to participate. And many agricultural commodities, especially livestock prices, are not supported by the government (although the feed grain programs obviously have indirect effects). Thus, not all farmers are covered by the commodity programs, and not all those eligible for coverage actually opt for it. But in recent years, the generous benefits of participating in the programs have made voluntary sign up levels very high.

The first problem the programs have continually struggled to overcome is to find an appropriate basis for this *coverage*: should eligibility to receive assistance be based upon being a farmer or farming a unit of land, on gross or net income, or farm sales? In many of the programs, the solution has been to define an entitlement in terms of base acres or allotments tied to specific crops (an accounting unit of land), often in combination with records of average yields over time. The problems with this definition of entitlement have long been apparent, yet no satisfactory alternative has emerged. It is our view that some alternative definition of coverage is necessary, if the programs are to overcome the charge that they pay farmers to be big, and to get bigger, in order to be eligible for larger program payments. We shall argue in Chapter 6 that divorcing base acres from specific crops must be combined with strict and enforceable limits on total payments per farmer.

Second, we find that the design of the commodity programs, in combination with technological change, has led to increasing *concentration* of farm assets in fewer and fewer hands. While this process has occurred in part due to "natural" economic forces, it is a delusion that the concentration of bigger and bigger farms held by fewer and fewer owners has not been promoted and aggravated by the commodity programs themselves. These programs send very clear signals to farmers to enlarge the base acreage or allotment entitlements that define current eligibility for program benefits. If this concentration has a "natural" dimension, so be it, but it is our view that deliberate social policies should not contribute to more and more regressive payments and concentrated industry.

Third, we find that the commodity programs work insidiously to undermine the quality of the natural *environment*. They do this in several ways. They encourage specialization in crops that receive the highest levels of price supports: corn, wheat and cotton. These crops are also the most erosive. Specialization, and the continued cropping of land without fallowing or diversification, is encouraged in order to retain the crop-specific base acreage entitlements. The programs also promote excessive applications of chemicals and fertilizers in order to increase average yields, again in order to hold onto payment entitlements. "Set-asides" fail to target the land most sensitive to environmental damages as that most in need of rest. Indeed, acreage reduction programs actually encourage farmers to cultivate their nonretired acres more intensively. The Conservation Reserve Program (CRP) despite its title, has been side-tracked in part into supply control as an objective, undermining its capacity to do the most good for the environment at least cost to the taxpayer. In short, the quality of the rural environment has been degraded by the structure and rewards of the commodity programs, which have even prevented a laudable attempt such as the CRP from accomplishing its objective.

A fourth problem with the programs, most especially their acreage reduction features, is that they undermine American *competitiveness* in a global marketplace. Less productive land is, of course, the first set aside. But acreage reductions lead the United States to be "stock manager to the world," contracting acreage in times of surplus (as in the 1980s) and expanding in times of shortage (as in the 1970s). This forces a large share of global market adjustments onto the shoulders of American farmers. Other competitors, such as the EC, have been only too happy with U.S. set-asides and supply control efforts, since they raise world prices and allow high-cost, less competitive production the shelter to expand. The loss of global export market share is thus in large part a result of conscious policy choices in the United States to try to support prices and incomes by acreage reductions, which have nonetheless been frustrated by farmers' ability to take low productivity acres out of crops first. This type of policy, originally conceived for a relatively closed domestic market, makes no sense in a global marketplace, and only encourages attempts to seal off domestic borders through import access restrictions. It is as if the American taxpayer was indirectly subsidizing the expansion of farms in France and Germany, leading to a process of farm enlargement in Europe not unlike that in the United States.

Fifth, despite over fifty years of effort, domestic commodity programs have proven less and less effective at reducing *instability* in farm prices and incomes. Over the last twenty years or so, as American agriculture has become increasingly international, farm prices and incomes have become more and more unstable, and less and less amenable to manipulation through domestic commodity programs.

Together, it is our view that redefining program *coverage*, reducing pressures for farm asset *concentration*, improving the rural *environment*, enhancing American agricultural *competitiveness*, and reducing farm price and income *instability* define an agenda for reform. In order to fully define this agenda, however, we must go beyond the commodity programs, casting our net to include a variety of other programs that affect the rural environment and figure prominently in the politics of agriculture and rural development. These programs are the subject of Chapter 5.

Notes

1. USDA may also pay farmers to remove additional acres, over and above the ARP. Such "paid diversions" would add to the ARP in Figure 4.2, so that, for example, 22 percent of base could be set-aside in total, equal to 20 percent mandatory (ARP) reductions and a 2 percent paid diversion. The payment for diversion would supplement the deficiency payment received.

References

Barry, Robert. 1991, January 23. "The U.S. and World Sugar Markets in Transition." Paper presented at Fifth Annual Agribusiness Outlook Forum. Piper, Jaffray, and Hopwood. New York City, New York.

Gardner, Bruce. 1989. "A Framework for Analyzing Commodity Programs." University of Maryland: unpublished paper.

General Agreement on Tariffs and Trade. 1989, July. "United States Accepts Ruling on Sugar Quotas." *Focus GATT Newsletter*. 63: 2.

Hammond, Jerome W. 1991. "Federal Milk Marketing Orders Adversely Impact the Upper Midwest: Remedies are Needed." *Minnesota Agricultural Economist*.

Rapp, David. 1988. *How the United States Got Into Agriculture: And Why it Can't Get Out*. Washington, D.C.: Congressional Quarterly Inc.

Rekha, Mehra. 1989, Winter. "Winners and Losers in the U.S. Sugar Program." *Resources*. Resources for the Future, Washington, D.C. 94: 5–7.

Taff, Steven J. and C. Ford Runge. 1988, First Quarter. "Wanted: A Leaner and Meaner CRP." *Choices*.

U.S. Department of Agriculture/ERS. Various Issues. *Agricultural Outlook*.

5   The "Other" Programs

Domestic Food Programs

Food programs in the U.S. Department of Agriculture have a long history. They have been around as long as the more glamorous commodity programs; in fact, they came into being as a complement to the commodity programs as a means of disposing of some of the more perishable surplus products generated by those commodity programs. But even though the food programs have been considered as stepchildren in the USDA, it is important to note that this view and practice has changed in recent years. The federal government spent about $23.7 billion in fiscal 1990 on domestic food and nutrition assistance programs.[1] Federal spending on these domestic food assistance programs will certainly rise above this level in the 1990s.

THE FOOD STAMP PROGRAM

The largest of these programs, the Food Stamp Program, accounted for $14.8 billion in fiscal 1990. The Food Stamp Program provides low-income participants with food stamps which they can use just like cash to purchase food in local food stores and markets. The program is available in all 50 states, the District of Columbia, Guam, Puerto Rico and the Virgin Islands. In 1990, some 19.3 million persons participated in the program, with monthly benefits amounting to about $59 per person. By any standard, the Food Stamp Program is a very large program, and it is appropriately targeted to the poor and the needy of the nation.

CHILDREN'S PROGRAMS

The U.S. Department of Agriculture operates five programs to provide meals and snacks to pre-school and school age children. The programs are the National School Lunch Program, School Breakfast Program, Special Milk Program, Child Care Food Program and the Summer Food Service Program. Federal expenditures on these five programs totaled $5.3 billion in fiscal 1990, with the National School Lunch Program accounting for about $3.2 billion of that total. Federal expenditures on these programs have increased significantly since 1983, and are projected to continue to increase in the future. Participation in the National School Lunch Program during fiscal 1988 approximated 24 million children, of which approximately 40 percent received free meals and another 7 percent received meals at a reduced price (USDA/ERS/CED 1990a). The Child Care Food Program, which provides meals and snacks to pre-school children in public and private child care centers, is the fastest growing child food and nutrition program. Participation in this program increased from 376 million meals served in 1979 to 866 million in 1989, with federal spending levels increasing from approximately $160.5 million to $669 million over the same period. With the continued and expected growth in private day-care centers, this program is certain to expand in the decade of the 1990s.

The Special Supplemental Food Program for Women, Infants and Children (WIC) was established in 1972 as a pilot program and has grown into a major food assistance program. It was established to improve the nutrition and health of pregnant, breast-feeding, and postpartum women as well as infants and children up to the age of five years. In fiscal 1990 federal expenditures on this program amounted to $2.1 billion, with an average monthly participation of 4.6 million persons, of which 23 percent were women, 30 percent were infants and 47 percent were children (USDA/ERS/CED 1990a).

FOOD DISTRIBUTION PROGRAMS

There are three principal food distribution programs: the Nutrition Program for the Elderly, the Commodity Distribution to Charitable Institutions, and the Temporary Emergency Food Assistance Program (TEFAP). Federal expenditures on these direct food distribution programs have fluctuated dramatically between 1978 and 1989: from $96 million in fiscal 1978 to $1.4 billion in fiscal 1985 and then back to $489 million in fiscal 1990. The early increase resulted directly from the accumulation of stocks under the price support programs and their distribution under the expanded TEFAP. With declining governmental inventories in 1988 and 1989, the distribution of government-owned stocks under these programs has declined.

The Hunger Prevention Act of 1988 extended TEFAP through 1991.

But TEFAP will be a much different program in the future. To make up for the lack of government owned stocks, the TEFAP was authorized to purchase $170 million worth of stocks in the open market for distribution to needy persons. If funds are indeed appropriated to make these commodity purchases, TEFAP will be transformed from a surplus disposal program to a hunger combatting program. The long history of basing physical food distribution programs in the USDA on the availability of surplus government stocks will have been turned up-side-down.

PROGRAM EFFECTIVENESS

The question may be asked: How effective have these food assistance programs been? The answer to this question varies with the program involved, and it also varies with the persons or organizations making the studies. It is generally agreed that the Food Stamp Program increases the spending of low-income families on food significantly—by 10 to 25 percent. The nutrition effects of the Food Stamp Plan are much less clear. Some studies indicate no significant effect, others show some nutritional improvement.

The price and income benefits to farmers of the Food Stamp Program have been so modest that farmers generally have shown little support for this program. On the other hand, farmers have always been strong supporters of the physical food distribution programs. They like to see surplus stocks of butter, cheese, flour, rice and other commodities move into consumption, but they rarely consider how much commercial sales are displaced by these commodity donations.

It is generally agreed that the National School Lunch and School Breakfast Programs have improved the nutritional status of all participants, and especially those from low-income households. The Economic Research Service found that the demand for red meats, poultry, and milk rose significantly as a result of the school feeding programs.

The objectives of the Woman, Infants, and Children Program are to lower infant mortality rates, increase average birth weights and reduce the chance of subnormal infant development. Unfortunately the research results regarding the effectiveness of the WIC Program in achieving these objectives have been mixed.

In sum, we know that the domestic food assistance programs have been properly targeted on the poor, the needy and the hungry of the nation. The spending of the participants in the largest of the programs, the Food Stamp Program, on food has increased significantly, but by far less than the value of the stamps received by the participants. The nutritional benefits of the programs to participants are a matter of much debate, and seem to vary both with the type of program, and the researchers involved.

The most important thing that we don't know is—to what extent are there still hungry, malnourished people in the national population even though these programs have been in operation for several decades? The extent of hunger and malnutrition in the United States remains one of the most controversial subjects on the national policy agenda.

Given the magnitude of these programs in dollar terms, and the importance of the subject of food, nutrition and health in the thinking of many, if not most, Americans, food and nutrition policy are likely to continue to be linked to national farm policy. At a minimum we must think in terms of a national farm and food policy.

A LITTLE HISTORY

How did these food programs become a part of the U.S. Department of Agriculture? They began with the physical distribution of food stocks owned by the government to the poor and the needy in the 1930s. The stocks for distribution were generated by the various commodity price support programs. From that beginning the food programs have evolved and grown over the decades. The National School Lunch Program was institutionalized in the 1940s with the federal government making cash payments on a per-student basis to schools participating in the program, as well as the distribution of food stocks to participating schools. The Food Stamp Program was experimented with in the 1930s and 1940s and put in operation on a limited basis in the early 1960s. The other food assistance programs described in this section were developed and placed in operation in the late 1960s and early 1970s. But the important thing that happened in the 1970s was the expansion of these food assistance programs from small, limited-sized programs, to very large programs, involving federal government expenditures of $20 billion per year or more.

How did this happen? It happened because urban congressmen, now the overwhelming majority in Congress, made it clear to farm and rural congressmen that they could continue to have their farm price and income support programs only if they were accompanied by large food assistance programs targeted to low-income consumers—consumers who, for the most part, lived in urban areas. The now very large domestic food assistance programs are the price that farm and rural congressmen had to pay for their farm price and income support programs. So now the U.S. Department of Agriculture has become in fact, if not in name, the Department of Food and Agriculture.

RESEARCH AND SURVEILLANCE NEEDED

How can the urban congressmen who pushed these programs onto the USDA, and the taxpayers who pay for these programs, be certain that a Department created to help farmers is in fact administering these programs so as to achieve their stated objectives? The USDA has had much experience operating large scale programs, and can generally administer them so as to make them run smoothly and with a minimum of scandal and corruption. But a different question is being raised here: Are the programs doing what they are supposed to do? Are they eradicating hunger and malnutrition in the United States? To answer this general question two types of periodic studies are needed. First, the General Accounting Office (GAO), the congressional watch dog, needs to do periodic studies to ascertain whether the stated objectives of the legislation are being achieved, and if not, what should be done about it.

Second, a scientific research organization with expertise in health and nutrition, needs to conduct periodic studies to ascertain the extent to which hunger and malnutrition continues to exist in the nation, and to suggest ways of eradicating those pockets of hunger and malnutrition. From the knowledge gained from these two types of studies, the Congress could first improve and strengthen the legislation authorizing these food assistance programs; and second, issue directives to the USDA for achieving the stated objectives of that legislation. These food assistance programs have grown too large, and become too important a part of the welfare landscape of the United States, to be given a secondary role in a national farm policy.

Foreign Food Assistance

A BRIEF REVIEW

The record of foreign food assistance by the United States is one primarily of commodity surplus disposal. When federal commodity programs were generating large and burdensome stocks, as in the middle and late 1950s and early 1960s, foreign food assistance programs became a leading vehicle for disposing of those stocks. But when stocks became short, as in the early and middle 1970s in the midst of a world food crisis, shipments under the various foreign food assistance programs were cut back severely. For example, the value of foreign food aid under Public Law 480 ran as high as $1.5 billion in the late 1950s and early 1960s; but in 1974 it fell to $867 million and then to $385 million in 1976. But when stocks became burdensome again in the 1980s, the value of foreign food aid shipments under P.L.480 rose again to $1.6 billion in 1985. Clearly, foreign food assistance in the United States has been driven by the need to dispose of surplus stocks held by the federal government.

The history of foreign food assistance since the end of World War II is a long and torturous one, with the specifics of various assistance programs changing over time—sometimes permitting the sale of food stocks to Less Developed Countries (LDCs) for their local nonconvertible currencies, sometimes not; sometimes emphasizing development in the recipient country, sometimes not; and sometimes emphasizing food donations by private charities, sometimes not (see Ruttan 1990).

CURRENT OPERATING PROGRAMS

In the late 1980s most foreign food aid shipments took place under one of four programs:

1.   Title I of Public Law 480, which provides for both long-term credit sales at low interest rates for certain designated countries to purchase specified commodities and for the sale of commodities to certain LDCs in return for their local, nonconvertible currencies;

2.   Title II, a donation program, in which commodities are distributed either through the recipient government or through private voluntary relief agencies, or through the World Food Program;

3.   Title III, the Food For Development Program, which allows local currencies generated under Title I to be used for development projects, and loans under Title I to be forgiven if specified measures to increase farm production and improve storage and transportation are undertaken by the recipient country;

4.   Section 416 of the Agricultural Act of 1949, also a donation program which was reactivated in 1982 to encourage the donation of dairy products, but which now includes all edible commodities held by the Commodity Credit Corporation.

Shipments of commodities under Title I of P.L.480 for 1990 were estimated at $849 million and under Title II at $673 million; no shipments are programmed for Section 416. Within the overall total of foreign food aid for the period 1986–88, shipments of grains accounted for approximately 55 percent; dairy, 5 percent; vegetable oils, 16 percent; and grain products, 13 percent (USDA/ERS/CED 1990b).

On the basis of historical experience, we can expect the specific content of these foreign food assistance programs to change every few years. And we can expect those changes to be in response to the surplus stock situation in the United States. Those programs will expand when the stock position of the Federal government becomes burdensome and contract when stocks become tight. The foreign food assistance programs will emphasize those commodities which are in greatest surplus. In the past that has most often been the grains, grain products and dairy products. To an important degree the foreign food assistance programs of the United States have not been geared to foreign food needs, but rather to the surplus disposal needs of the United States.

Consumer Food Protection

Protection of the domestic food supply, or food safety, has never had a high priority in the U.S. Department of Agriculture. The responsibility for a safe food supply for consumers has been, and continues to be, shared among numerous agencies: the many and varied state and local health agencies, the Food and Drug Administration in the Department of Health and Human Services, more recently the Environmental Protection Agency, and the U.S. Department of Agriculture.

FOOD SAFETY IN THE USDA

The one agency in the USDA with responsibilities in the food safety area is the Food Safety and Inspection Service (FSIS). The mission of this agency is to make sure that the nation's supply of meat and poultry is safe, wholesome and unadulterated. This agency has come under criticism from time to time with respect to its sampling procedures and its lack of inspection comprehensiveness; nonetheless, its record in providing domestic consumers with a safe, wholesome supply of meat and poultry products is a good one. The failure of the USDA in this area of food safety is not with the operation of the FSIS; it is with its lack of leadership in food safety and a failure to coordinate with other agencies. It will be noted that out of the myriad of food items consumed, the USDA is concerned only with the safety of meat and poultry products. And over the years when there has been some contamination problem with a given food product, the USDA has more often assumed the role of an advocate of the producers than it has the guardian of the safety of that product to the consuming public. Leaders in agriculture both in and out of government have been slow, even reluctant, recognize that the USDA has in fact become the Department of Food as well as Agriculture. The previous sections of this chapter make this clear; and, as a Department of Food, the USDA must assume leadership in this area of food safety for the public.

NUTRITION RESEARCH AND EDUCATION

The USDA has long been concerned with human nutrition research and education. Human nutrition research is conducted in the Agricultural Research Service; but it is interesting that in the 1990 Budget Summary of the USDA, the work in human nutrition is not mentioned although work in animal science, plant science, and soil and water is given prominent display. Also, it has been alleged from time to time over the years that research results in the human nutrition area have been suppressed or influenced by certain industry groups, notably the dairy industry. The USDA has been virtually silent on the issue of tobacco and health.

Nutrition education and survey work in the USDA is conducted by a small, independent service—the Human Nutrition Information Service. Why this educational work on human nutrition could not be combined with the research work in human nutrition in one reasonably large, independent service in the USDA is not at all clear. Perhaps the failure of agricultural leaders in and out of government to recognize that the USDA is now a Department of Food as well as Agriculture explains this anomaly, too. In such an independent service the work of nutrition research and education could be given a role commensurate with the magnitude of the operations of the food assistance programs.

Rural Development

THE CONCEPT

Rural development is an elusive concept that means different things to different people. In a generic sense it must refer to all income producing activities in a nonurban community or geographical area: farming, manufacturing, extractive industries, trade and services, the infrastructure, the educational system, and more recently the activities involved in retirement living. In the depression years of the 1930s, rural development was concerned primarily with helping financially strapped farmers, because most people living in rural areas were farmers, and most farmers were in financial trouble. Broadly speaking, two types of programs were developed in the 1930s at the federal level to help farmers:

1.   The Agricultural Adjustment Administration and Debt Restructuring Program to assist commercial farmers with adequate resources but who were in trouble because of low prices;
2.   The Resettlement Administration to help farmers living in poverty.

THE HISTORICAL RECORD

The Resettlement Administration and its successor agency, the Farm Security Administration, sought to help the poorest and most disadvantaged farmers and rural residents by shifting them to part-time communities where they could grow their own food and find jobs in new industries. Many of the programs of the Farm Security Administration were acknowledged to be experimental; but they were not communistic as some critics labeled them. In any event, these experimental efforts were terminated after World War II, and a more traditional agency, Farmers Home Administration (FmHA), was established to make loans to the poorest of poor and, later, to assume other developmental duties.

Perhaps the most successful and widely accepted developmental action of the New Deal in rural areas, was taken by the Rural Electrification Administration (REA). In 1933, before the REA was organized, 90 percent of American farms were without electricity. By 1941, some 35 percent of U.S. farms had electricity. By 1979, some 99 percent had electricity (Rasmussen 1985). The rural electrification program of the REA transformed farm and home life in rural areas.

World War II brought prosperity to the nation and to American farmers, and created an abundance of jobs in urban areas which absorbed most of the under-employed, surplus population of rural areas. In this economic atmosphere, questions about the quality of life in rural areas as well as economic opportunities were not being raised; and the need for rural development was forgotten. However, a new emphasis on rural development began in 1954 when a study by the Eisenhower administration indicated that rural poverty persisted in the midst of national prosperity, and that it would not be eliminated by an expansion of the commercial farm sector. The report argued that human and other resources would have to move out of agriculture. This, of course, was exactly what was happening. The farm population declined from 25 million in 1950 to 15.6 million in 1960, and the number of farms fell from 5.4 million to 3.9 million over the same period.

In this context the USDA launched in 50 designated pilot counties, under the leadership of the Cooperative Extension Service, a rural development program. Representatives of local agencies, USDA and other federal agencies and community leaders were organized into Rural Development Committees. By 1960 rural development work was planned or underway in 262 counties in 30 states under this committee arrangement.

On paper, a lot of rural development work appeared to be going on, and in terms of committee meetings, a lot was going on. But in terms of increased monies devoted to rural development work, very little was occurring. Each agency—local, state or federal—had to undertake any program agreed to in the Rural Development Committee out of its on-going budget. This would be a pattern that would be followed in the years to come. Some agency in the USDA would play an over-all coordinating role in the rural development effort. Action agencies in the USDA, other federal departments, and state and local organizations would take whatever program activities that it and the coordinating unit agreed upon, and the action agency could mount out of its on-going budget. Sometimes these actions by independent agencies were well-funded and involved large operations as under President Johnson's War on Poverty. However, sometimes these actions were minimal as in the Reagan administration.[2]

Each administration from 1960 to the present (1992) created some new administrative framework with the goal of abolishing poverty in rural areas. And each administration made some new, often exaggerated claims, regarding its efforts to end rural poverty. One of these efforts in the middle 1960s was short-lived, but for a few years it constituted a major effort. The Economic Opportunity Act of 1964 created a Jobs Corps, which employed young people recruited from among economically and educationally deprived Americans, provided for community action programs in urban and rural communities, and made loans to low-income rural families for projects that had a reasonable prospect of success. The 1965 Housing and Urban Development Act authorized the Farmers Home Administration to make loans to farm families to purchase farms, farm dwellings, and to improve farm structures. A Task Force on Agriculture and Rural Life in 1965 urged President Johnson to expand food programs in rural areas, establish a rural senior corps, help landowners over 65 maintain their farms, provide literacy training, extend medicare payments to all age groups and set up "opportunity homesteads" with training programs for disadvantaged rural residents. But none of these calls for sweeping changes was ever fully implemented. Escalating costs for the Vietnam War forced President Johnson to recommend sharp cuts in proposed programs of rural development as a part of his drive to cut federal expenditures.

One important result of these efforts in the 1960s was a far reaching study entitled *The People Left Behind*. It remains a superb statement on the conditions of rural poverty and what to do about it (National Advisory Commission on Rural Poverty 1976). The report made it clear that eradicating rural poverty would require a major and sustained effort providing for new employment opportunities, insuring minimum incomes, providing for improved educational programs, improved health services, and increased rural housing aid.

During the 1970s, rural America prospered (at least relatively), partly because farmers were doing reasonably well, and partly because other areas of the rural economy were growing. For the first time the economies of nonmetropolitan counties grew faster than metropolitan counties. The largest employment gains in rural areas were in the service trades, but employment opportunities also increased in manufacturing, mining and in recreation. In this context, the rural economy greatly reduced its dependence on agriculture. By 1980, only 702 out of 2,443 counties outside the metropolitan area were still considered to be heavily dependent on agriculture. Farm employment accounted for only about 13 percent of rural employment in 1980, and the rural farm population declined to some six million while the rural, nonfarm population increased to some 53 million (USDA/ERS 1988).

These population and employment trends continued into the 1980s. By 1984, over *90 percent of the rural population* did not live on farms. And employment in farming accounted for *only 9 percent of total employment in rural areas*. By any standard, rural people can no longer be thought of as farm people.

RECENT RURAL DEVELOPMENTS

But the prosperity experienced by rural America in the 1970s did not continue into the 1980s. Commercial agriculture was severely depressed in the first half of the 1980s. Nonmetro employment grew only a third as fast as metro employment in the period 1979–84—a reversal of the 1970s when nonmetro employment grew more rapidly. In 1986, nonmetro unemployment averaged above 9 percent, some 3 percent higher than the metro rate. And the nonmetro poverty rate was 18.3 percent in 1985 compared with 12.7 percent for metro areas. Thus, it should come as no surprise that the average per capita income in metropolitan counties was about $14,000 (in current dollars) in 1984, while in nonmetropolitan counties it stood at about $10,000 (USDC 1986 and USDA/ERS 1988). The air may have been a little cleaner in rural areas than in urban areas in the 1980s, but in almost every other respect rural areas were at a disadvantage in comparison to urban areas.

Given these economic conditions in rural areas in the 1980s, how has the federal government responded in the way of a rural development program? In response to initiatives by the Carter administration, the Congress passed the Rural Development Policy Act in 1980. This act created the position of Under Secretary of Agriculture for Small Community and Rural Development to head up work in rural development in the USDA, and to take the lead in coordinating interdepartmental efforts in this area. The act directed the secretary of agriculture to prepare a comprehensive rural development strategy, and to submit an up-dated version annually to the Congress. The strategy report is to include an analysis of the impact of the budget on rural development, a review of previous strategies, and recommendations for needed new legislation.

The Rural Development Policy Act was signed on September 24, 1980, and Ronald Reagan was elected president in November of that year. A new era in national rural development policy began in 1981. The philosophy of the Reagan administration was that rural development is a process that is best left to state and local governments and to the private sector. The result has been massive inaction in this area. With the exception of its rural development strategies reports (documents required by the Rural Development Policy Act of 1980) and bits of testimony before congressional committees, the Reagan administration made virtually no statements or new proposals with regard to national policies dealing with rural people and conditions. The Office of Rural Development Policy (an outgrowth of the 1980 act) in the USDA was eliminated in 1986 for lack of funding. Later agency communication and coordination was shifted to a White House Task Force on Rural Communities.

Although the leadership and coordinating role of the USDA in rural development was reduced to the minimum permitted under the 1980 act, work in rural development continued in the USDA during the Reagan administration in two agencies: the Farmers Home Administration and the Rural Electrification Administration. The Congress protected certain programs in these agencies through its power to authorize programs and appropriate funds to support them.

The total budget of the Farmers Home Administration (FmHA) in 1990 was some $8.0 billion. Of this total, funding for farm credit type loans amounted to approximately $4.2 billion, of which the largest share was guaranteed-type loans. In the 1990 farm bill, direct loans were cut by 75 percent and guaranteed loans were to be augmented by an unspecified amount. Farmers Home is moving out of the business of making direct loans to farmers as fast as it can.

Under the original legislation authorizing the FmHA, it was empowered to make loans to farmers of family-size units who could not get credit from conventional sources. Such credit involves ownership loans to enable individuals to buy farms; loans to individuals of inadequate farms to enlarge or develop their farms; loans to help low-income farmers to improve their farming operations; emergency loans to eligible farmers for losses from natural disasters; and soil and water conservation loans to assist farmers in developing or making proper use of their land and water resources. But a major criticism of the FmHA has been that it, in fact, has made loans to established farmers who could have obtained credit from conventional sources; and, it has ignored its mission to assist low-production, low-income farmers to become viable commercial farmers.

One of the largest and most successful operations of the FmHA has been its rural housing loan program, in which loans are made to low-income families to acquire housing in the open country, small rural communities and small towns of not more than 20,000 population. In 1990, nearly $2.3 billion was expended in support of this rural housing program.[3]

Finally, the FmHA has a small program, labelled Rural Development Programs, to assist rural communities to diversify and sustain their economies. Its funding levels in this area in 1990 were as follows: water and sewer facility loans, $425 million; community facility loans, $118 million; business and industrial loan guarantees, $95 million; water and sewer grants, $209 million; and other grants and loans, $19 million.

The Rural Electrification Administration makes direct loans and loan guarantees to borrowers who provide electric and telephone services to rural areas. The budget for such loans and guarantees amounted to $2.0 billion in 1990.

AN APPRAISAL

Over the years there has been much rhetoric about the need for an effective rural development policy and a set of programs to implement it. However, that policy and set of programs has never emerged. In the 1960s, under President Johnson's War on Poverty, a lot of money was spent to eradicate poverty in rural areas, but much of that money was not spent wisely or effectively. Then it ran out in the late 1960s. In the 1970s, with no clearly defined rural development policy, but with both national and farm prosperity, rural areas developed on their own with considerable success in the area of nonfarm enterprises. In the 1980s, with a severe farm depression and an essentially negative federal policy toward rural development, rural areas have once again become a backwater in the national economy with higher than average unemployment, relatively low per capita income, and disadvantages in education and health services. In this context, the USDA with its newly authorized under secretary for rural development has provided weak leadership and a set of minimal operating programs.

Congress authorized the creation of a new Rural Development Administration (RDA) in the 1990 farm law. The Bush administration in the budget proposal sent to Congress in February 1990 moved to activate this new Agency. Some of the programs in the Farmers Home Administration, for example, the Business and Community Loan and Grant Programs, will be lifted out of that agency and placed in the new RDA. The 1990 law further authorizes the secretary of agriculture to transfer other USDA programs into the new RDA. But it is important to note that the budget proposal the Bush administration sent to Congress cuts the funds available for water and sewer waste disposal to rural communities by 22 percent in 1992. This does not suggest an auspicious beginning for the new Agency. It suggests once again that recent administrations are more interested in "talking a good game" than in really promoting development in rural areas.

Natural Resources and Environment

SOIL AND WATER

The Soil Conservation Service (SCS) was established in 1935. It has the responsibility for developing and carrying out a national soil and water program in cooperation with landowners and other land users, with community planning agencies, regional resource groups and with other federal, state and local government agencies. Over the years it has been one of the most successful agencies in the USDA in terms of program acceptability and program accomplishments.

Its largest program, with a funding level of $396 million in 1990, and with a proposed budget of $424 million in 1991, provides technical assistance to landowners and operators in locally organized and operated conservation districts. About 3,000 such districts covering more than 2 billion acres were in operation in 1990.

Beyond this technical assistance work with individual farmers in established conservation districts, SCS has responsibilities under the Food Security Act of 1985 to work up plans for handling some 160 million acres of cropland that has the potential to erode well above acceptable levels, including plans for land that will be going into the Conservation Reserve. SCS also has the responsibility for determining which lands are subject to the "sodbuster" and "swampbuster" provisions of the Acts of 1985 and 1990.

The SCS has numerous other responsibilities:

- The conduct of a national soil survey, county by county.
- The conduct of snow surveys in the western states.
- The operation of plant material centers to assemble, test and encourage the increased use of plant species in conservation programs.
- River basin surveys and investigations.
- Watershed planning in small watershed projects.
- The Great Plains Conservation Program to promote greater agricultural stability in the Great Plains Region.
- Water resources management studies and surveys for local units of government.

How the SCS is able to carry out these varied and wide-ranging programs effectively on its limited budget of some $728 million is not clear. Perhaps it skimps in certain areas. Perhaps it has a well established system of program priorities. Or perhaps its program mission should be restricted. But this latter course of action does not seem likely with the growing pressure to plan for better and more efficient use of scarce water resources. What seems more likely is that its budget will be increased in the years to come to enable it to better address its resource protection responsibilities.

The Agricultural Conservation Program (ACP) provides cost sharing of up to 80 percent by the government with farmers to carry out specific conservation measures on their farms. These measures include such things as liming cropland, building water storage ponds and terracing. This program, along with a Forestry Incentive Program and the Water Bank Program, are administered by the Agricultural Stabilization and Conservation Service (ASCS). And they are among the most controversial programs administered out of the USDA. Almost every administration from 1960 to the present has recommended the termination of these programs. But the Congress keeps putting them back in the budget in the appropriation process. Federal administrators seek to terminate these programs because it is argued that farmers, the rich as well as the poor, are paid to undertake farming practices that they should be doing as a part of their normal farming operation. The Congress argues that incentives are needed to induce farmers to undertake these kinds of good conservation practices. And so the battle continues between the Congress and different administrations, with the current administration calling for the almost complete termination of these programs in the 1990 budget.

The Conservation Reserve Program (discussed in Chapter 4) was authorized by the Food Security Act of 1985 to conserve and protect soil and water resources on highly erodible cropland. It is administered by ASCS with technical assistance provided by SCS. The program, by means of ten-year contracts with participants, establishes and maintains a cover of grass or trees on the land under contract, implements a conservation plan for the farm, reduces the acreage base of the farm and forbids the grazing or harvesting of crops on land in the reserve. The goal of the program was to enroll 40 to 45 million acres of highly erodible cropland in the reserve by 1990. The 1990 farm bill extended enrollment to 1995.

The 1990 farm bill also established three new environmental programs to supplement the CRP. First, is the Wetlands Reserve Program (WRP) that calls for the enrollment of up to one million acres to be paid for easements of 30 years or longer. Priority is put on wetlands that enhance bird and wildlife habitat. The WRP is also established to help fund the restoration of wetlands by farmers before the lands are enrolled in the program. Second, is the new Water Quality Incentive Program (WQIP). The program helps producers develop and implement farm management plans that protect water quality and improve wildlife habitat. Producers can receive up to $3,500 a year in incentive payments and $1,500 in cost share assistance on approved plans; additional monies are available if the plan improves wildlife habitat. The enrollment goal set for this program is 10 million acres by 1995. Third, is the Integrated Farm Management (IFM) program where farmers submit three- to five-year plans for their farms which combine overall productivity with profitability. The plans must prevent soil erosion, maintain or improve soil fertility, conserve and protect water and interrupt pest cycles. Through the life of the plan 20 percent of base acreage, which is preserved, must be committed to a resource-conserving crop. Three million acres is the enrollment goal for 1995.

FORESTRY

The Forest Service is a large operating agency in the USDA which administers the National Forest System of 191 million acres with an annual budget of between 2 and 3 billion dollars. The Forest Service has multiple, and often conflicting, mission objectives. Those objectives include:

- The protection and conservation of forest land, open spaces and wilderness areas for future generations.
- Regulating the grazing of sheep and cattle on the national forests.
- The production and sale of timber.
- Providing recreation for American citizens.
- The protection of wildlife.
- Protecting watersheds.

Over the years, the Forest Service has been criticized for emphasizing certain of these objectives at the expense of other objectives. In the early years of the Service it was severely criticized by western cattle and sheep men for its emphasis on the first objective; in the 1980s it has been severely criticized by environmentalists for its emphasis on the second and third objectives at the expense of almost all its other objectives. Certainly the protection of the environment in the National Forest System has been given a low priority in the 1980s.

It is probably the case that the Forest Service will never be able to satisfy all of its diverse constituencies. However, with the increased interest and concern of an affluent urban population with outdoor recreation, the protection of the environment and resource protection, it seems clear that the Forest Service will be forced to give a higher priority in the future to its mission objectives in these areas.

WESTERN WATER

In the 17 western states there are between 40 and 50 million acres of land under irrigation (estimates vary with the definition of irrigated land, and the year in which the estimates were made). In those states irrigation accounted for about 90 percent of the consumptive use of water. This irrigated land in the 17 western states (which also accounts for between 80 and 90 percent of all irrigated land in the United States) was developed in part by private parties, in part by state and local governments, and in part by the federal government (Frederick 1988). Laws governing the ownership and distribution of water are almost exclusively state laws, although in the decade of the 1980s the Supreme Court of the United States held that water is an article of commerce and therefore is subject to congressional regulation. The fact, however, that the earliest state laws were based on the common law doctrine of riparian rights, which gives owners of land adjacent to a stream or lake the rights to use that water bordering on their property, rights that are inseparable from the land, renders the development of markets for the sale and distribution of water extremely difficult. The complex of common law and state laws, differing from state to state, further renders the development of an effective national water policy most difficult.

At the national level the Bureau of Reclamation in the Department of Interior was established in 1902 to promote the development of irrigation in the arid and semi-arid West. The bureau provides full or supplemental irrigation to some 11 million acres, and of the total water supplied by this agency over 90 percent of it is used for irrigation (Frederick 1982).

Although it was intended under the original reclamation law that irrigators would pay for the construction of the projects (exclusive of interest charges) as well as for the operation and maintenance of the projects, the subsidies to irrigators on these federal projects have been enormous. It is estimated that more than 90 percent of the capital costs of the federal project have been subsidized. Farmers lucky enough to receive water under these federal projects have reaped a bonanza. For example, farmers on the west side of the San Joaquin Valley of California, in the Westlands Water District (a Bureau of Reclamation project) pay less than 10 percent of the delivery cost of this irrigation water; on average users of Bureau of Reclamation Water in California in 1980 paid $3.50 per acre foot, while users of irrigation water in Kern County provided by the State of California, on a mostly unsubsidized basis, paid $28.62 per acre foot (Frederick 1982).

The inequitous situation with respect to the distribution of irrigation water leads to at least two difficult problems. First, who shall receive this highly subsidized federal project water? And this problem breaks down into two parts:

1. Which geographical area shall be the beneficiary of a major project?
2. Do all farmers within a project, regardless of size, receive the subsidized water in whatever amount they may require?

The geographical location of projects is no longer a hot political issue, since most of the best project sites have been utilized. But the question of whether large farmers should receive irrigation water at the same subsidized rate as small farmers has been and continues to be a hot political issue. Under the original Reclamation Law of 1902, farmers could legally receive this subsidized irrigation water on only 160 acres. But from the inception of the Bureau of Reclamation water projects, large farmers found ways, legal or illegal, around the 160 acre limitation. Supporters of the family farm ideal fought the circumventing practices of the large farmers in the courts and in the Congress for 80 years, and finally lost the war in 1982. In that year the Congress, bowing to the pressure from the large farmers, raised the acreage limitation to 960 acres. This enlarged acreage limitation still does not satisfy the thirst of many large farmers for government subsidized irrigation water, and they continue to subvert the acreage limitation of the law by various legal manipulations.

The second problem is concerned with the conservation of water, or the lack of it, in Bureau of Reclamation Projects. The second problem probably has greater significance for the economic development of the 17 western states than the first. It arises out of the fact that irrigators fortunate enough to receive subsidized water in federal projects have almost no incentive to conserve it. Not only is their water cheap, but farmers who make an effort to conserve project water risk losing their rights to that water. And under existing rules federally subsidized water cannot be sold by farmers or an irrigation district at a profit. Consequently changes in the price of water outside a federal project have little meaning for, or implications for, the use and distribution of water within a project.

The above problems, and the solutions found to them, are of critical importance to the economic development of the 17 western states and the nation because as Kenneth Frederick (1988) states:

> Water has become a scarce resource and it is sure to become scarcer as demands for water and the services it provides grow and as valued supplies are degraded or lost through contamination or depletion.

Scarcity alone is not cause for alarm, and need not result in shortages, *if* there is a market, or markets, to allocate the product, or input, among competing demands. Most important inputs in agricultural production are scarce to some degree and are allocated among the competing demands for them through the operation of markets. But water, once considered a free good, is not priced and rationed through a system of markets where competition reigns; it is priced and rationed through a maze of local, state and federal regulations and rules overlaid by a myriad of common law court rulings. Further, most of the legal and institutional arrangements that currently govern the use and distribution of western water evolved over a long period in which there was relative water abundance. Now these institutional arrangements are ill-suited to induce irrigators and other users with first rights to water to conserve that increasingly scarce resource, and to allocate it among competing demands in accordance with an economic rationale.

This situation involving (1) an increasing scarcity of water and (2) the absence of effective markets to allocate it, places increasing pressure on public bodies, local, state and federal, to develop policies and management practices that avoid shortages and misuse of water resources. In this context it seems reasonable and appropriate for the federal government to take the lead in developing a water policy for the nation that will lead to an efficient and equitable use of that increasingly scarce resource.

REGULATION OF CHEMICAL USE

The responsibility for regulating the use of chemicals on farms falls almost entirely outside the U.S. Department of Agriculture.[4] At the federal level it resides in two agencies: the Environmental Protection Agency (EPA) and the Food and Drug Administration (FDA). But increasingly regulatory activities controlling the use of chemicals on farms has shifted to the states. California's Big Green Referendum of 1990 is a case in point; it provided for the ban of any chemical that has been linked to cancer, even in trace amounts, but was defeated. Such referenda are likely to reappear.

Regulations governing the use of chemicals at both the federal and state levels have taken the form of prohibitions against the use of certain chemicals. The laws at the federal level which provide the legal basis for prohibiting the use of certain chemicals include the Federal Insecticide, Fungicide and Rodenticide Act (FIFRA) and the Federal Food Drug and Cosmetic Act (FFDCA). Together with the Clean Water Act, as amended, these laws are the primary means by which agricultural chemicals are restricted from use. Unfortunately, the treatment of agricultural chemicals under all three has been unclear and at times contradictory. Under FIFRA,

for example, EPA is supposedly responsible for determining what constitutes legitimate pesticide use, and for regulating the marketing of pesticides
through a complex registration process. The EPA's Special Review Process
takes from 4 to 8 years to complete. Despite these requirements, nearly 600
active ingredients used in nearly 50,000 commercial pesticides have not
undergone EPA review, leading many states to take unilateral actions
restricting certain chemicals.

An important factor missing from EPA's approach to pesticide
regulation, the pace of which was noticeably slowed during the 1980s, is that
such regulatory slowdowns actually deter private firms from bringing more
environmentally benign pesticides to market. In a strange reversal of
mission, EPA has in effect constrained the ability of the private sector to
respond to market demands for more environmentally benign chemicals. As
the National Research Council noted in 1987, "In some cases, new
compounds that are safer than the existing products they might replace have
been denied registrations while more hazardous products remain on the
market" (National Research Council 1987). An additional consequence of
the current regulatory climate is to encourage research seeking to make
crops more pesticide or herbicide resistant. While environmental groups
have objected to this research, it is at least partly a response to current
EPA regulatory practices, which constrain the registration of more
environmentally benign technologies.

The other major regulatory law affecting agricultural chemicals is the
Federal Food Drug and Cosmetic Act. FFDCA prohibits "any legal use of
any pesticide which concentrates in processed food and is shown to present
a cancer risk." This standard has been called into question on a variety of
grounds, not least that it becomes increasingly binding as our ability to
detect risk becomes more sensitive. At some point, the detection of a new
substance may show demonstrably lower risk levels than many natural but
nonregulated substances, yet still be prohibited. In response to these and
other inconsistencies in the enforcement of FFDCA regulations, the Board
on Agriculture of the National Academy of Sciences has recently issued a
report calling for a total reexamination of the standard-setting process, so
as to concentrate pesticide regulation where risks are demonstrably highest.

The third main area of environmental regulation impinging on
agriculture is the Clean Water Act, as amended. Under 1987 amendments
to the act, EPA is given authority to require states to submit groundwater
protection plans, which may include agricultural leaching of fertilizers and
chemicals including pesticides. These state plans, if enforced, may lead to
increasingly stringent restrictions on farm input use, although such
restrictions have yet to be widely felt. EPA has adopted a state-by-state
approach to such regulation, which leads to the devolution of responsibility

from federal to state agencies.

While arguably more efficient, in the sense that each state's problems differ, this approach relegates difficult decisions to state agencies with comparatively limited resources, and raises the distinct and important problem of a patchwork of different standards and regulations to which input suppliers will be forced to respond. In particular, a lack of state resources may contribute to a growing movement to tax fertilizer and chemical inputs, such as Iowa's recent tax on nitrogen fertilizers. These taxes will raise revenues, but also farm costs. Even more threatening to agricultural costs are the potential legal implications for farmers of holding them financially responsible for nonpoint source pollution (such as contaminated wells). It is possible that farmers may be found financially liable for damages resulting from nonpoint source pollution which was previously untraceable and is increasingly defined as a contestable damage under law. The 1990 farm bill strengthened farmer's legal responsibilities by requiring them to keep records of all chemicals used for at least two years.

In summary, environmental policies, such as FIFRA, FFDCA, and the Clean Water Act, as amended, each impose both direct and indirect requirements on farmers to comply with a variety of new and changing regulations. These regulations are not likely to ease in the future, instead they will become more numerous and more binding. Thus it is imperative that the process by which these regulations are arrived at and imposed on farmers be (1) speeded up, (2) made consistent with the latest scientific knowledge, and (3) effectively coordinated among the various federal and state agencies. If this does not occur the absolute need for control over the use of chemicals in agricultural production could become a regulatory nightmare in which farm production costs rise as farm technological advance is obstructed.

Science and Education

From its inception, the USDA has been deeply involved in the advancement of science, the development of new and improved technologies and educating farmers with respect to these scientific and technological developments. In fact, the principal activities of the USDA in its first 70 years of existence were in these areas, and its efforts in these areas were highly successful. The work of the USDA in science and education is currently conducted by four agencies: the Agricultural Research Service, the Cooperative State Research Service, the Extension Service and the National Agricultural Library.

SCIENTIFIC RESEARCH

The Agricultural Research Service (ARS) conducts fundamental and applied research in animal and plant production and protection; the conservation and improvement of soil and water; the processing, distribution and storage of farm products; and, as was noted earlier, in human nutrition. This work is carried out in 138 domestic locations, many of them in cooperation with state experiment stations, and in its national headquarters at Beltsville, Maryland. The research work of ARS on animal and plant production and protection has been highly successful since its inception and has enjoyed strong support from commercial farmers. But ARS has come under increased criticism (1) for failing to take into account the adverse consequences to the environment of certain chemical technologies; (2) for failing to focus on the technical needs of low-production farmers; and (3) for giving a low priority to research in human nutrition. The program mission of ARS in the future will need to be considerably different from what it has been in the past.

The Cooperative State Research Service (CSRS) is essentially engaged in two activities: (1) doling out research funds to state experiment stations and other governmental agencies in accordance with formulas prescribed by Congress; and (2) seeking to coordinate a nationwide system of agricultural research among the many state and federal agencies. Given the fragmented system of agricultural research in the United States, the work of the Cooperative State Research Service is absolutely essential, but the work of this agency is a thankless, never-ending one.

EDUCATION

The Cooperative Extension System is comprised of the Extension Service in the USDA as one partner (the federal partner); the 1862 land grant universities in 50 states, Puerto Rico, the Virgin Islands, Guam, American Samoa, Micronesia and the District of Columbia plus the 16, 1890 land grant universities and Tuskegee University as another partner (the state partner); and more than 3,150 county offices representing local governments as the third partner. All three partners participate in financing, planning and conducting the educational programs of the Cooperative Extension Service.

In this complex and unwieldy system, it is the mission of the Extension Service in the USDA to provide leadership at the national level in policy formulation, program development, management and organization, and representation to the public and governing bodies. Since the Cooperative Extension System is so complex and so unwieldy, the ability of the

Extension Service in the USDA to provide effective leadership in these areas has been minimal. Except in periods of great crisis, such as World War II, the Cooperative Extension Service wanders across the broad educational field, sometimes responding to problems and needs effectively, but more times responding slowly and ineffectively. In the early days of the Cooperative Extension System, when its almost sole objective was "extending" new and improved practice and technologies to farmers, giving direction to its work was easy, but today with multiple problems and multiple objectives, providing leadership and direction to the total system is an impossible task.

The National Agricultural Library with almost 2 million volumes is a great library. The only problem here is insuring that political leaders in the administration and the Congress keep it great by adequately funding it.

Farm Credit

The federal government has long been involved in assisting farmers in getting credit under favorable terms. The Federal Land Bank System was established in 1916, emergency mortgage relief of various kinds was provided under the Agricultural Act of 1933 and this was followed by the Farm Credit Act of 1933 which created an entire new system of farm credit.

THE FARM CREDIT SYSTEM

This system consisted of 12 land banks for making mortgage loans, 12 intermediate credit banks for making production and marketing loans, 13 banks for cooperatives for making loans to cooperatives, and the provision for production credit associations to provide an operating link between farmers and the intermediate credit banks. This system, loosely administered by the independent Farm Credit Administration, served commercial farmers reasonably well from 1933 to the middle 1980s, with the federal land banks providing farmers with about 20 percent of their long term mortgage credit and the production credit associations providing farmers with about 15 percent of their short term credit.

The federal land banks ran into serious trouble in the mid 1980s as the result of making too many mortgage loans at the inflated land prices of the 1970s. Many of their borrowers could not repay these loans in the depressed 1980s, with the result that some of the land banks faced insolvency. With this credit crisis, the federal government stepped in with the Agricultural Credit Act of 1987. This act did a number of things. It provided the system with the interest-free use of 4 billion dollars for five years. It required that the federal land banks and the federal intermediate credit banks merge. The banks for cooperatives must decide whether to consolidate. The regulatory powers and responsibilities of the Farm Credit Administration were expanded. The legislation established a federal agricultural mortgage corporation, or "Farmer Mac" to operate a secondary market for farm real estate and housing loans. And it established a whole set of borrower rights with respect to borrowers of nonperforming loans.

This legislation has given the farm credit system a new lease on life, but it is too early to say whether the farm credit legislation of 1987 has re-established the farm credit system on a viable basis. But if the 1987 legislation did not put the farm credit system back in a sustainable working order, we can be sure that there will be new attempts with new legislation. The Congress will not permit the farm credit system to fail—the economic survival of too many farmers is at stake.

CREDIT FOR LOW-INCOME FARMERS

The role of the Farmers Home Administration in rural development was discussed earlier. But what about the role of FmHA as a farm credit agency? Although those farmers who have obtained credit through the FmHA must be pleased that such a source of credit was available to them, it should be recognized that only a tiny fraction of the short- and long-term credit used by farmers in recent years was obtained through the FmHA. Further, the FmHA is presently moving as rapidly as Congress will permit away from making direct loans to farmers. It is the policy of FmHA as of 1989, to guarantee loans made by private institutions to farmers rather than make loans directly to farmers. The 1990 farm bill furthered this trend from direct to guaranteed loans. Certainly the FmHA is moving away from its mission of directly assisting low-production, low-income farmers. This raises the question of what role FmHA should play in the future, if any. If policymakers in the USDA are determined to convert the FmHA into another commercial credit institution, could not this function be transferred to a revitalized farm credit system? This would leave the Congress and rural leaders free to create an entirely new institution with a three-fold mission: (1) providing credit support for rural development projects, (2) providing supervised loans to low-production, low-income farmers, and (3) providing a new and ready source of credit to part-time farmers.

Still More Activities

Besides the major program initiatives described above, the USDA is engaged in a wide range of other activities. It collects, organizes and publishes statistics on every important aspect of farming, farm product processing, distribution and food utilization in the United States, and much of this same information for the world and key geographical parts of it. It conducts economic analysis of developments and problems in the food and agricultural sector; and it publishes a wide ranging list of outlook and situation reports as well as descriptive information on the operation of the agricultural economy. Three agencies—the Economic Research Service, the National Agricultural Statistics Service and the World Agricultural Outlook Board—do most of this work.

The USDA, representing American agriculture, is involved in numerous international activities. These activities are handled or conducted, for the most part, by the Foreign Agricultural Service (FAS). The FAS has responsibility for the development of foreign markets for U.S. agricultural products; for maintaining and expanding existing markets; for gathering foreign market and policy intelligence; and for trade policy activities during periods of multilateral and bilateral trade negotiations.

An Office of International Cooperation and Development (OICD) is responsible for cooperative international research, scientific and technical exchanges and liaison with international agricultural organizations.

The USDA undertakes a large number of animal and plant inspection and regulatory activities to protect the animal and plant resources of the nation from dangerous diseases and pests. It provides technical and management assistance to farmers' cooperatives. It establishes official standards for the grains. It conducts weighing and inspection activities to enforce those standards. Finally, it has all manner of administrative offices to provide overall planning, coordination and administration of the USDA's policies and programs.

Program Omissions

Although the USDA is engaged in a wide ranging set of activities, there are several gaping holes in this set of activities. In 1989, nearly 80 percent of the production units in agriculture classified as farms received more than half of their earned income from off-farm sources. In fact, the off-farm income of these units far exceeded their income from farming: the off-farm income of these units averaged about $29,600 in 1989 while the net income from farming averaged about $1,300. In other words, nearly 80 percent of American farmers in 1989 could and should be classified as part-time farmers (USDA/ERS 1991). Yet there is no agency or program in the USDA which focuses on the unique aspects of part-time farming. The credit needs, the technical needs and the management needs of this class of farmers are ignored at the federal level. The Extension Service in some states has in recent years come to recognize the important development of part-time farming and has initiated limited programs to assist part-time farmers. But at the federal level there has been almost no recognition of the growing importance of part-time farming.

As has been noted, the principal attention of Congress and the USDA has been directed to the needs and problems of commercial farmers with some lip service being paid to people living in poverty in rural areas. But the great development in the past two decades has been the increased numbers of farmers taking off-farm jobs and turning their farming operation into a side-line operation. Off-farm employment has become the important and steady source of income, and the farming operation is conducted at night and on the weekends to provide a supplemental source of income. The total product of these part-time farmers is not inconsequential; part-time farmers produce 10 percent of the total national farm product.

The facts are as follows. There are some 1.5 million plus part-time farmers in rural areas who produce 10 percent of the total farm product. However, at the federal level, almost no one is paying any attention to them—to their contribution to the quality of life in rural areas, to their contribution to the national product, or to their special problems. It is time that the USDA recognize that most of their farmer constituents are part-time farmers with a whole new and unique set of needs and problems.

Another area in which the administration, the Congress and the USDA have been program-deficient is the area of accident prevention in farming. Farming is the deadliest of occupations in the United States. In 1988, the death rate among farm workers was 48 per 100,000, nearly double the rate in mining, and much higher than in construction or manufacturing (Newsweek 1989). Farming has also the highest rate of poisonings, skin diseases and respiratory conditions due to the common exposure of farm workers to toxic agents. However, commercial agricultural interests have to date been successful in preventing the Occupational Safety and Health Administration (OSHA) from becoming involved in farm safety inspections and regulation. The excuse given by a leading farm organization: "The last thing [farmers] want to do is get encumbered in a lot of paperwork." Obviously, it is time for some agency of the federal government to become involved, very involved, in farm safety work.

MIGRANT FARM WORKERS

Migrant farmworkers are people who move frequently, who follow the crops, and who are often away from their home base for weeks or months at a time. There are tons of data and information about these people: their numbers, their personal and family characteristics, their working conditions and their poverty. Still, confusion abounds. Philip Martin (1988) describes it as a "harvest of confusion." For example, the estimated number of migrant farm workers ranges from 100,000 to 1,000,000 depending upon the definition of migrant farm workers used, and the agency doing the counting.

Martin tries to bring order out of this confusion by classifying migrant farm workers into three groups: solo men, migrant families, and skilled migrants (Martin 1988). He then describes these groups as follows:

> Most important are the crews of 20 to 30 immigrant men who are assembled by a crew leader or labor contractor and transported from farm to farm. These young solo men have no families or leave their families behind as they move from farm to farm to harvest crops. As immigrants with little education, an inability to communicate in English, and limited job information and skills which confine them to farmwork, they are vulnerable to unscrupulous labor contractors or crew leaders who (over)charge them for jobs, transportation, and food and housing.
>
> The migrant families memorialized in John Steinbeck's *The Grapes of Wrath* are the focus of most migrant assistance programs. The stereotypical migrant family packs up its belongings and follows the ripening crops from south to north; along the way, migrant assistance programs provide education and health care for the children and legal services and employment assistance for their parents. The number of migrant families has been declining because there is less temporary family housing available; because many farm employers prefer to hire solo men; and because many migrant families who previously would have migrated have found local farm or nonfarm employment.
>
> The third group of migrants is the least studied. Migrant workers also include more skilled and better paid workers who operate grain combines in the midwestern states or apply chemicals to crops in the western states. These workers do not satisfy the migrant stereotype because many are skilled white men, but they satisfy the migrant definition as persons who stay away from home overnight to do farmwork.

Strictly speaking, migrant farmworkers and their problems do not fit under this section of *Program Omissions* since, as Martin points out, at least 19 federal programs administered by 5 different federal agencies provide some form of assistance to migrant farmworkers (Martin 1988). In many of these cases, however, the assistance provided is not specifically targeted to migrant farmworkers and relates to them in only a tangential fashion. And in still more cases, these programs of assistance are related to migrant farmworkers in a "hit and miss" fashion: sometimes assisting a poor, illiterate family to find suitable housing, sometimes not; sometimes protecting workers from unscrupulous labor contractors, sometimes not; and sometimes insuring that school age children attend school, and sometimes not.

Thus, we argue, for at least two reasons, that migrant farmworkers and their many problems should be included in this section of program omissions. First, the USDA does not have any major program of assistance targeted to the needs of migrant workers. The USDA has often spearheaded the establishment of programs to import alien workers, typically from Mexico or the Caribbean to help farm employers to harvest their crops. But never to the knowledge of the authors has the USDA spearheaded an effort to assist and protect the workers doing the hard, stoop labor. Second, so long as there is no overhead agency with the staff and the authority to coordinate the diverse efforts of 19 programs from five different federal agencies, the needs of migrant farmworkers are going to be met in a haphazard fashion. This is especially true of the poor, illiterate workers who fall in Martin's first two categories. These people would require an ombudsman to help them find the relevant program, in the correct agency office, in the right town or city, to deal with their specific problem at a particular time.

With respect to migrant farmworkers we have the unusual situation in which the specific needs of a group of people at the bottom of the income scale have been recognized and efforts made to deal with those needs. But for the most part, those efforts have not been successful and the workers and their families remain in a permanent under-class, poverty condition. Why is this so? There are several reasons. First, the work is hard and unskilled, and will never pay high wages. Second, many of the programs designed to protect the workers, for example, the provision of adequate housing and insuring that school age children attend school, are inadequately funded and are poorly monitored and supervised. Third, the programs are not properly coordinated so that migrant workers and their families can take advantage of all the programs of assistance that are available to them. Fourth, neither the Department of Agriculture, nor the Department of Labor, the two federal agencies most directly involved, have taken the leadership in developing an overall program that deals with all the economic and social needs of migrant farmworkers, or in developing an overhead coordinating agency with the capacity to pull together the diverse programs available to these people. Thus, we continue to have in this phase of agriculture a situation which was once called the "harvest of shame" and is now called the "harvest of confusion."

Summing Up

The federal government, operating primarily through the U.S. Department of Agriculture, has a wide variety of programs, other than the commodity programs, to assist farmers. As we have seen, it now has some major programs to assist consumers, avoid hunger in some cases and to improve their diets in many more cases. The USDA is also moving, sometimes haltingly, and sometimes rapidly, into the resource and environmental protection area. Thus, while the USDA gives the highest priority to the needs and problems of commercial farmers, the Department is changing—has in fact changed—over the past two decades.

The food assistance programs have become the largest programs in the USDA in most years—certainly this is true if the foreign food assistance programs are lumped together with the domestic programs. There is still much room for improvement in these programs, particularly with respect to the foreign food assistance programs and research and education in human nutrition. However, without doubt, the food programs represent the direction of the future.

The resource protection and environmental programs have much further to go than the food programs and more obstacles to overcome in the USDA. The problem here is that society now understands that it must take action to protect the environment but it has not yet found the courage to meet the cost of doing so. Society is still twisting and turning looking for some cheap or cost-free way to protect the environment. But to date no one has found that cheap or cost-free way, and costs of cleaning up the environment mount.

When the problem is obvious and can be localized on individual farms, as in the case of soil erosion, the federal government with broad support from farmers has done a reasonably good job. The record of the Soil Conservation Service is excellent; but the record in protecting the national forests which belong to all of us leaves much to be desired. The federal government has found that harvesting timber on the public domain is a cheap and easy way to provide employment and to increase government revenues.

The record of the federal government, and the USDA in particular, in the area of rural development is dismal. There has been much talk and many reports written on the subject, but little effective governmental action. In the 1940s and 1970s, when the national economy was operating at high levels, rural areas were drawn into the national prosperity and did reasonably well. But in less prosperous periods, the development of rural areas has lagged and most rural areas have become economically depressed areas.

The farming aspect of rural development has been helped by the growing number of part-time farmers with reliable, steady off-farm incomes. But this development in turn presents a new challenge to policymakers in Congress and the USDA—what kinds of programs should be developed, if any, to assist part-time farmers? In short, the rural landscape has changed and is changing drastically, but leaders in the USDA and the Congress have been slow to recognize these changes.[5] The rural landscape in the 1990s is dotted with many new industries, many, many part-time farmers, and still a lot of people, mostly nonfarm people, living in poverty. Is the USDA going to be a major player in the development of rural America in the 1990s, or is that role going to be taken over by some other federal agency or unit of government?

The commercial farm traditionalists in the Congress and the USDA have done some changing with the times in the past two decades; they are going to have to do a lot more in the 1990s. They must come to recognize that commercial family farming is no longer a way of life; it is basically a business. The farming business is only one part of the rural landscape, and in many rural areas it is no longer the dominant business.

Notes

1. All federal program expenditure data for 1990 presented in this chapter are taken from the category "Program Level" (USDA 1990).
2. For an excellent historical discussion of Rural Development efforts in the United States, see Rasmussen (1985).
3. FmHA administers several rural housing programs, primarily providing direct loan programs for single-family housing and rental housing, as well as rental assistance to low-income tenants in FmHA rental housing projects. The typical family being served by the single-family housing program has an annual income of about $12,000. Those served by the rental housing program have incomes of about $8,000. The interest rate on these types of loans can be subsidized to as low as one percent. The average interest rate paid by single-family housing borrowers is 4 percent (USDA 1990).
4. This section is based on a report by Jared R. Creason and C. Ford Runge (1990).
5. For a wonderful discussion of the changes that have taken place, and are likely to take place in the rural heartland see the piece by Alan Bird (1990).

References

Bird, Alan. 1990, Spring Quarter. "The Rural Heartland in the '90s: A New Way of Life or Lagging Earnings." *Choices*.

Creason, Jared R. and C. Ford Runge. 1990, July 16. *Agricultural Competitiveness and Environmental Quality: What Mix of Policies Will Accomplish Both Goals?* University of Minnesota: Center for International Food and Agricultural Policy.

Frederick, Kenneth D. 1988, November. *Water Resources: Status, Trends and Policy Needs*. Discussion Paper ENR 88-02. Washington, D.C.: Resources for the Future.

Frederick, Kenneth D. with James C. Hanson. 1982. *Water for Western Agriculture*. Washington, D.C.: Resources for the Future.

Martin, Philip L. 1988. *Harvest of Confusion: Migrant Workers in United States Agriculture*. Boulder, Colorado: Westview Press.

National Advisory Commission on Rural Poverty. 1976, September. *The People Left Behind*. Washington, D.C.: U.S. Government Printing Office.

National Research Council Board on Agriculture. 1987. *Regulating Pesticides in Food: The Delaney Paradox*. Washington, D.C.: National Academy Press.

Newsweek. 1989, December 11. "Danger on the Job." P. 43.

Rasmussen, Wayne D. 1985, October. "90 Years of Rural Development Programs." *Rural Development Perspectives*. Washington, D.C.: USDA/ERS, 2(1).

Ruttan, Vernon W. 1990, July 10. "Food Aid: Surplus Disposal, Strategic Assistance Development Aid and Basic Need." St. Paul, Minn.: University of Minnesota: Department of Agricultural and Applied Economics, mimeo.

U.S. Department of Agriculture. 1990. *1991 Budget Summary*. Washington, D.C.: USDA.

U.S. Department of Agriculture/ERS. 1988. *Rural Economic Development in the 1980's: Prospects of the Future*. Rural Development Research Report Number 69. Washington, D.C.: USDA/ERS.

_____. 1991. *Economic Indicators of the Farm Sector: National Financial Summary, 1989*. ECIFS 9-2. Washington, D.C.: USDA/ERS.

U.S. Department of Agriculture/ERS/CED. 1990a, April–June. "Recent Trends in Domestic Food Programs." *National Food Review*. Washington, D.C.: USDA/ERS/CED.

_____. 1990b, July–September. "Food Assistance." *National Food Review*. Washington, D.C.: USDA/ERS/CED.

U.S. Department of Commerce/BEA. 1986. *Local Area Personal Income 1979– 1984*. Washington, D.C.: USDC/BEA.

6   A Proposed Food, Farm, and Rural Policy for the 1990s

In this chapter we propose our own alternatives to current agricultural policy. Before developing the specifics, a few general remarks on the thrust of these alternatives may be helpful. First, the policies we propose will be seen as very different from current practices in several ways. Most fundamentally, we propose to slow, and ultimately, stop government from paying large commercial farmers the lion's share of commodity price and income supports. Consistent with the principles of more equitable distribution of government spending and majority rule, we seek to wean the largest farmers from their current reliance on government price and income support.

We are under no illusions that the major beneficiaries of these subsidies will whole-heartedly endorse our proposals. In 1989, for example, the 627,000 commercial farms each grossing over $40,000 per year received payments totalling $9.2 billion for an average of just over $14,600 per farm (the 39,000 farms each grossing over $500,000 per year had payments averaging approximately $32,000 per farm); whereas the 1,544,000 farms each grossing less than $40,000 per year received payments totalling $1.7 billion for an average of some $1,100 per farm (USDA/ERS 1991).

By redirecting these subsidies to support policies of greater benefit to the taxpaying majority, as well as to a large number of farmers who do not receive much government support, we believe that we are reorienting agricultural policies in the public interest. In Chapters 7 through 10 we will discuss the economics and politics of this reorientation, specifically showing that although our prescription may be a bitter pill to some, it is still a viable political and economic strategy. The reason: the biggest, wealthy farmers can survive and prosper without large subsidies, freeing valuable resources for much needed innovations elsewhere. By liberating and redirecting these resources, we believe our proposal can capture the support of a broad cross-section of rural and urban residents.

Despite substantial reforms, our proposal will not eliminate government from agriculture or the rural sector, nor is it intended to. We aim to maintain an income safety net for commercial farmers, develop a price stabilization scheme and enhance the economic role of smaller and part-time farmers as well as nonfarm rural residents. In this sense, we are more in the tradition of progressive activism than laissez-faire, and doubt that "getting government out of agriculture" is a realistic approach to public policy. The 1980s have shown that those who call for getting government out of the nation's economy have actually increased its role, wittingly or unwittingly. Massive increases in government expenditures for military procurement, coupled with revenue losing tax reductions and resulting huge budget deficits will continue to stalk current and future taxpayers for years to come. We believe that the American public accepts government as a player in the economy. The question is: how good a player can it be? During much of the 1980s, government has been a fumbler on the field of public finance, and a double dribbler on the court of fast-breaking events in the global economy.

The redirection of government activities that we propose, while likely to somewhat reduce overall budget expenditures, is more a reorientation and reallocation than a cut-to-the-bone approach. The income safety net and price stabilization scheme developed here are intended to reduce substantially government payments to the largest farmers. This reform of the commercial farm and food sector is the first part of our program, and will reduce total spending on commercial agriculture, creating a farm policy reform "dividend." However, our other major initiatives will make use of much of this dividend elsewhere in the rural economy.

The second part of our proposal will be a substantially expanded program of resource conservation and environmental protection, allowing both rural and urban citizens to enjoy more fully the valuable natural resources in our rural areas, and to launch a full-scale attack on environmental destruction resulting from poor farming practices.

The third part will devote budget resources to a broad-based program of rural economic development intended to maintain and improve the lives of part-time farmers and the nearly 90 percent of rural residents who do not gain the majority of their income from farming. Coupled with natural resource and environmental protection, this program is intended to develop and enhance the human resources of small-town America, where nearly a quarter of our population still lives. Our goal is to make smaller towns and cities not only better places for urban cousins to visit, but places where people eager to regain a sense of family and community might prosperously remain or return to live.

The fourth part of our agenda is focused on the "other" programs affecting food needs of the poor, as well as the growing concern over food safety. It deals specifically with needs of the homeless, malnourished, and disenfranchised. It also calls for considerable expansion of regulatory responsibility in the area of food, health and safety.

In a fifth section we propose to increase substantially government support for research, education and extension directed to a wide variety of methods to improve the competitiveness of commercial agriculture, to reduce the negative environmental impacts of modern agricultural practices, and to create job opportunities in rural areas. This sort of human-oriented research and education, which declined drastically in the 1970s and 1980s as military research and expenditures mushroomed, is now again calling for attention.

Finally, we take note of the fact that the farming industry is a dangerous place to work. And in spite of much remedial legislation, many migrant farmworkers and their families live in poverty. Thus, we propose new legislation to promote safety in the work place, and a reorganization of federal programs from the Washington level down to the county level to assist farmworkers to gain their legal and economic rights.

The presentation of our proposal is organized generally as a "farm bill" would be, around a set of "titles" describing the programs and changes we envision. In many cases, we will refer to existing program functions, although not in the minute detail of an actual piece of legislation. This chapter will end with a summary of the main features of the program.

TITLE I: THE COMMERCIAL FARM AND FOOD SECTOR

As described in previous chapters, farm income for the largest commercial farms is currently supported for the field crops by a complex system of target prices, loan rates, deficiency payments, base acres and yields, marketing loans, quotas, production controls and various other devices that, one way or another, prop up prices and act to "short" the market by artificially restraining supplies. Some commodities are without this protection, especially poultry, pork, and beef, but even in the livestock sector the policies affecting grains and oilseeds have indirect effects by raising or lowering the price of poultry and livestock feed ingredients.

We believe that commercial farming in the United States is sufficiently productive and efficient to compete in the world economy without permanent price and income subsidies. There is, however, an instability problem for both producers and consumers that can have serious adverse effects on farm income. We therefore support an income stabilization mechanism. Further, in this age of mergers and acquisitions, an unhealthy lack of competition in the food processing and distribution area must be guarded against.

We propose to end the current system of price support, target prices and deficiency payments for the major field crops: corn, wheat, soybeans, barley, oats, cane, and beet sugar, as well as rice and cotton. In its place, we propose the following reforms. All existing individual field crop acres (including acreage devoted to soybeans, sugar, rice, and cotton) would be merged into a single "farm base," and payments would revert from commodity-specific to farm income stabilization payments. In effect, the farmer's base in any year is the sum of all crop acres farmed in previous years plus acres devoted to most conservation uses. This base can be maintained and expanded by continuing to grow any of these crops.

The 1990 farm bill moved the commodity programs toward greater flexibility in a manner similar to that which we will propose, but did not go nearly as far in the direction of flexibility as we will. The "triple-base program" established partial flexibility allowing 15 percent of base acres to be converted to a "farm base," although most crops such as fruits and vegetables are restricted from being planted on these acres. These "flex-acres" are not eligible, under the 1990 bill, for commodity-specific deficiency payments, but the chosen crop(s) can still receive nonrecourse loans.

There are three issues that will need attention in order to make this transition. First, provisions must be made to reassure producers of wheat, for example, that those farmers currently growing corn will not all suddenly turn to wheat (at least where it is feasible to grow both). This fear exists on the part of all the "program" crops currently protected by "base acreage" provisions. We would phase in the capacity to "cross over" from one program crop to another over a period of five years. For example, in year one, 20 percent of what had been corn base acres could be planted to wheat or any other program crop. In year two, 40 percent could cross over, and so on, until 100 percent of the farm base could be planted to other former "program" crops. This "phased flexibility" would allow markets and farm production patterns to respond, without imposing a "cold turkey" readjustment.

A second, and related, issue concerns nonprogram crops, such as dry edible beans, sunflowers, alfalfa, etc. Similar fears on the part of growers of these crops require a similar form of "phased flexibility." In the first year of our program, 20 percent of the new whole "farm base" resulting from the aggregation of previous base acres and other acreage would be allowed to "cross over" to what had been nonprogram crops. In year two, 40 percent could cross over, until 100 percent of the whole farm base could be planted to any crop imaginable, whether formerly a program or nonprogram crop.

The third and critical issue concerns how income stabilization payments would be calculated for the whole farm base, since (1) the payments could no longer be coupled to specific crops and (2) the payments are not intended to subsidize the enhancement of farm incomes over time. Related to these considerations is an underlying question of equity, since as long as payments continue to be made on a "farm base," the farmers with the largest base will continue to receive the largest payments.

Our reform would introduce an income stabilization payment, based on the relationship of the Index of Prices Paid to the Index of Prices Received for a regional "basket" of commodities. The calculation of this payment has several features that bear emphasis. First, the payment is intended to provide an income safety net in periods of *deteriorating terms of trade* for the farm sector. It does not exist to *support* farm income through good times and bad. It exists to *stabilize* farm income when prices paid out for feed, seed, fertilizer, interest on debt to plant a crop, and fuel costs are *rising* and/or prices received for the basket of regional commodities are *falling*. When the *terms of trade are improving,* the payments would disappear.

It would be useful if this income stabilization scheme could be based on a profitability index. But calculating such an index requires cost-of-production indices, and that in turn raises all kinds of questions. How are rising land values attributable to government program benefits to be treated? How are cost reductions attributable to technological advances to be introduced into the index? Most importantly, whose cost of production is to be used in calculating the profitability index? Should it be the cost of production of the technologically efficient farm with important economies of size or the medium to small farm that is less technologically efficient and with fewer economies of size or some farm in between?

To avoid these conceptual quagmires, our payment stabilization scheme, as noted above, is based on the "terms of trade" concept. This concept has pitfalls too. It is easy to fall into the "parity price" trap, wherein, over time, the Prices Paid Index greatly exceeds the Prices Received Index, because the former index takes no account of farm technological advances and economies of size. We avoid the parity price trap and the never ending debate about the proper base period for the two indices—Prices Received and Prices Paid—by comparing changes in those two indices year-by-year from the base of the previous year. From this comparison we derive a measure of the changes in the terms of trade for the year in question in comparison with the year preceding, which in turn indicates whether an income stabilization payment should be made to eligible farmers.

Specifically, we propose that a three-year moving average of Prices Received and Prices Paid be calculated annually by the USDA for the six main regions of the country (Northeast, Northcentral, Southeast, Great Plains, Mountain and Pacific Coast). For each of these regions, the percentage change in each of the indices in a given year from the previous year would be calculated. (It is also possible to calculate these indices for smaller geographic areas if finer distinctions in the types of agriculture practiced are needed.) Whenever the percentage measure of change for the Index of Prices Paid exceeded the percentage measure of change for the Index of Prices Received, a stabilization payment to eligible farmers would be triggered. In this day and age of electronic communications, it is reasonable to conclude that the stabilization payment arrived at for a given year, could actually be paid to farmers in the first quarter of the following year. And that is our recommendation.

It is important to note that the three year moving average value computed for each year for the indices of Prices Received and Prices Paid is the value employed in this scheme to compute that percentage change from year to year. This means that the trigger to either make, or not make, payments in a given year would be based on the pricing behavior of the previous three years, both with respect to prices paid and received. Thus, if the terms of trade deteriorated for two years, then improved for one, then deteriorated once again, payments would not stop abruptly in response to the transitory improvement, but only when the improvement was sustained for several years.

The above point, and the entire procedure for calculating changes in the terms of trade under our proposal may be reviewed in Table 6.1. The index values of Prices Received and Prices Paid in Table 6.1 are hypothetical; but they are also representative in a general way of the behavior of those two classes of prices. The index values of Prices Received fluctuate importantly and irregularly. The index values of Prices Paid increase steadily over time. Given the index values of prices Received and Prices Paid in columns 1 and 4 of Table 6.1, the three year moving averages of those indices are presented in columns 2 and 5. Given the three year moving average values for each year, the percentage changes in a given year from the previous year are presented in columns 3 and 6. In year 4, for example, the percentage change in the three-year moving average from year 3 to year 4 for the index of Prices Received is equal to .88; while the percentage change in the three-year moving average from year 3 to year 4 for the index of Prices Paid is equal to 1.047. *Whenever the value of column 6 exceeds the value of column 3, a payment is triggered.* In our example, the terms of trade have turned against farmers in year 4, and according to our proposal they are entitled to a stabilization payment. In the hypothetical time series of Prices Received and Prices Paid presented in Table 6.1, farmers would have been entitled to stabilization payments in 7 out of the 11 years for which computations were made (or in each of the years for which the percentage changes in column 3 are in boldface type).

Table 6.1 Hypothetical Illustration of Index Trigger System

| | Prices Received | | | Prices Paid | | |
Year	Index Value	3-Year Moving Average	Trigger[a,b] Value	Index Value	3-Year Moving Average	Trigger[a] Value
	(1)	(2)	(3)	(4)	(5)	(6)
1	100			100		
2	90			105		
3	80	90		110	105	
4[c]	70	80	.88	115	110	1.047
5	80	76.6	.95	120	115	1.045
6	70	73.3	.95	125	120	1.043
7	90	80.0	1.09	130	125	1.041
8	60	73.3	.916	135	130	1.04
9	50	66.6	.908	140	135	1.038
10	80	63.3	.950	145	140	1.037
11	90	73.3	1.157	150	145	1.035
12	100	90.0	1.227	155	150	1.034
13	110	100.0	1.111	160	155	1.033
14	120	110.0	1.1	165	160	1.032
15	110	113.3	**1.027**	170	165	1.031

[a]The value in year 4 of this column is the percentage change that the three year moving average of year 4 is of the three year moving average of year 3; and so on through the years.
[b]The boldface numbers indicate that stabilization payments would be made in those years.
[c]The trigger value for Prices Received in year 4 is less than the trigger value of Prices Paid, hence a stabilization payment would be made in year 4.

The question now arises: how would these stabilization payments be made to eligible farmers and how much would each farmer be eligible to receive? We propose that payments be made on a per acre basis on the farmer's whole farm base. The level of payment per acre should be set so as to reflect, as near as budget and program limitations permit, the declining revenue stream resulting from the deteriorating terms of trade in that agricultural region. We recognize that this payment level will be a political number. However, it can and should be prescribed by a hard and fast program limitation of a total payment per farm per year of $20,000; and by a *maximum* amount fixed in the federal budget each year available for distribution as farm income stabilization payments. We would set that figure at $7 billion.

The potential stabilization payment levels can be visualized in the following examples. A 500 acre "farm base" would translate into a stabilization payment for that farm of $5,000 if the per acre payment rate were set at $10.00; and, if the per acre payment rate rose to $40, the total payment to that farm would rise to the limit of $20,000. If there were 500,000 farms in the United States with a 500 acre "farm base" (which is a generous figure), the total federal expenditure for stabilization payments would amount to $2.5 billion at a $10 per acre payment rate; and, at a $40 per acre payment rate the total federal expenditure would be $10 billion (the latter figure exceeds our suggested budget restraint). Thus, given our proposed program constraints, the stabilization payment rates would most likely need to vary between zero and 40 dollars per acre. Further, since it is unlikely that the terms of trade would turn against farmers to the same degree in all six regions at one time, it is possible, even probable, that the payment rate per acre might be zero in one region, $10 in another region and $30 or $40 in another region. This scheme recognizes that there are important variations in economic conditions among farming regions.

Two important effects of this income stabilization scheme should be noted. First, although the program does not provide a permanent income subsidy to commercial farmers, it does protect farmers against dramatic declines in income. Thus, it should be much easier for commercial farmers to obtain production credit from private banks and the Farm Credit System under this program than would be the case in an essentially laissez-faire setting. The program eliminates part of the income risks from farming.

Second, the program greatly reduces the unpredictable aspect of agricultural program expenditures in the federal budget by placing a cap of $7 billion on the income stabilization payment expenditures. The commercial farm program part of the total agricultural budget is (1) reduced to reasonable proportions; and (2) made much more predictable from year to year than at present.

We recommend that this income stabilization program be administered through the existing Agricultural Stabilization and Conservation Service (ASCS) and its far flung county committee system. That agency has the experience and the capacity to administer the program efficiently. The handling of funds, decisions regarding per acre payment rates, and other financial matters should be undertaken in Washington by the Commodity Credit Corporation (CCC). It has great experience in these matters, but the double cap—the $20,000 payment limitation per farm and $7 billion federal budget limitation—places a double discipline on the board of the CCC in setting per acre payment rates for the years and in the regions that income stabilization payments are made.

Finally, to prevent attempts to manipulate acre and farm eligibility requirements under the income stabilization program, heavy criminal and financial penalties should be developed as a disincentive to such practices, enforced not by USDA but by the Department of the Treasury and Internal Revenue Services' special agents. Such abuses are felony fraud, and should be treated as such. The reason for this strict enforcement, outside of

USDA, has become abundantly clear from existing abuses of program payment limitations. In 1990, for example, one Nebraska family created a maze of farming entities on paper to get around the $50,000 annual payment limit, allowing them to qualify for more than $3.8 *million* in farm program price support payments from 1985 to 1990. The farmer involved divided his 24,000 acre holdings, spread over four states, into 15 farming entities in the name of friends, family and partners (*AgWeek* 1991).

Such occurrences are not rare. In Arizona, a similar division of 8,400 cotton acres led to 29 entities, each of which was eligible for a $50,000 payment. These entities were associated with tractor drivers, field hands and a friend of the farm owner's family that didn't even know the name of the farm operation she "owned." The General Accounting Office (GAO) of Congress has determined that from 1984 to 1988, farmers nationwide created some 9,000 additional subsidy payments, adding $4.2 billion dollars to farm subsidy costs in 1987 alone, by creative reorganization of farm units (*Arizona Republic* 1991). This abuse must be stopped.

In sum, this proposal creates an income safety net of up to $20,000 in times of deteriorating terms of trade for farmers, based on eligibility defined by each farmer's whole farm base. Program coverage thus extends to any owner of such a base in times of rapidly falling product prices or rising costs, but it is capped in terms of total cash payments per farm per year. In this connection, any farmer who so desired would be free to opt out of the program, lose his farm base, forego any stabilization payments, and be free to plant any crops on his former base. While the program does not initially divorce stabilization payments from specific crops grown, it slowly eliminates the most pernicious features of a base acreage linked to specific crops, allowing the participating farmer to phase into his operation those crops expected to be the most profitable. Different indices of Prices Received and Prices Paid would need to be calculated for the different regions, adapted to the mix of crops and type of farming operations for each region. However, in no region could the income stabilization payment per farm exceed $20,000.

In addition to this program, we would improve and expand the coverage and operations of the Crop Insurance Program currently operated by USDA. At the moment, this program is voluntary, and participation has been disappointing, averaging little more than 25 percent of those farmers eligible for coverage. An overriding reason for low participation is that the current commodity loans and deficiency payments are *already* a form of insurance and Congress is always ready to provide disaster payments. In 1989, the Commission for the Improvement of the Federal Crop Insurance Program reported that a sweeping overhaul was necessary to make it more attractive as a form of price and income protection. We endorse the findings of the commission, which argues that the program must be more attuned to the price and market conditions farmers face in any given year. We propose to make crop insurance, subsidized by the federal government as under the status quo, more widely available to all commercial farmers. Further, the Congress should make the commitment to refrain from disaster payments, except in the most dire circumstances.

In September, 1989, the General Accounting Office (GAO), the investigative arm of Congress, endorsed many of the crop insurance commission's findings, and argued for an expanded crop insurance program, with improved management capability, as the most constructive and cost-effective method of pooling and covering the risks of farming (GAO 1989a). Together, the commission's findings and GAO report provide an important agenda for reform. By making the crop insurance program more attractive (especially in light of our proposed elimination of deficiency payments), such an expanded crop insurance program should become less costly to farmers since risks will be more widely pooled. In addition to this expanded crop insurance coverage, the federal government should work with private insurers to develop an optional, all-risk farm income insurance program. Consequently, declines in farm profitability can be compensated at levels in excess of those provided by the government for those farmers willing to purchase additional insurance.

Before turning to questions of supply management, it might be useful to anticipate some of the objections and problems likely to be leveled at this approach. First, and most obviously, it proposes to eliminate government payments to farmers for individual crops, and to cap these payments at levels well below those today. This is because we do not believe commercial farmers with large farm bases are entitled to or need large payments from the federal treasury. Income *stabilization* should be the objective of farm policy, rather than perennial income support tied to specific crops. A second objection is that we have not eliminated the problem of payments tied to base, most particularly the tendency for such payments to be "capitalized" into the value of farmland. We accept this criticism, but have attempted to blunt it by imposing strict limits on such payments, as well as by making the linkage from support payments to land values explicit and transparent. The income stabilization payment explicitly provides a form of rent stability in periods of deteriorating market conditions. On balance, we expect this to lead to less "capitalization" than at present.

However, what is to prevent farmers from trying to carve up their units into separate farms, each of which is eligible for support up to a $20,000 maximum? The answer here is two-fold. First, we believe these levels of support are insufficient to make such manipulations attractive to most farmers, so long as payments are set in general to total less than $20,000 per farm. Second, we propose to make manipulations such as these even less attractive by treating them as felony charges, with criminal penalties and fines for conviction far in excess of the potential rewards. Enforced by the IRS, such evasion of the law (widely practiced today) constitutes nothing more or less than fraud, and should be treated as such.

Turning now to issues of supply control, we reemphasize that no nonvoluntary acreage restrictions of any kind would operate automatically as a part of these programs, except those targeted to environmental improvements or periodic interventions to control large surpluses, detailed below. In order to make these programs more efficient, we endorse the targeting scheme developed by Taff and Runge (1988) and proposed for the Conservation Reserve Programs (CRP) (see Figure 6.1). Under it, all land would be classified according to two basic criteria: (1) its vulnerability to various types of environmental damage; and (2) its productivity based on previous yields (see the four boxes in Figure 6.1). Three types of acreage diversion would then be allowed. The first two are environmental set-asides. On lands low in productivity but highly vulnerable to environmental damages, 10 year or permanent contracts modeled on the CRP would be offered to landowners to convert land to affirmative environmental improvements (Box 1, Figure 6.1). This land will be relatively inexpensive to retire and retiring it will not threaten global competitiveness because it is low in productivity. Second, on land that is higher in productivity but still vulnerable to environmental damages, three to five year contracts should be offered, with additional incentives to convert this land to uses (such as tree-planting) which protect the public from environmental damages over time (Box 2). Finally, and only after these two categories of land have been set aside, mandatory one-year unpaid acreage diversions would be permitted at the discretion of the secretary of agriculture in periods of commodity gluts, targeted *specifically* to higher productivity land (Box 3).

The purpose of this scheme, in addition to its primary emphasis on environmental improvements, is to discourage acreage restrictions as a device for supply control. It would restrict acreage diversion to periods of *excessive* supplies, and then *only* to acres of high productivity. These diversions would be mandated, and compensation to farmers would not be paid, making them last ditch responses to excess supplies. Since their objective is presumably to eliminate surpluses (raising prices), this alone should suffice as compensation, except that the acres would *not* be removed from the whole farm base. This stands in marked contrast to current programs, in which low productivity acres are the first to be diverted, and in which targeting for environmental goals, even in the CRP, has been obstructed by supply management objectives linked to program payment

Damage Potential

	high	low
high	3–5 years Box (2)	1 year Unpaid diversions Box (3)
low	10 years or permanent Box (1)	Other Programs Box (4)

Productivity Potential

Order of Retirement: Box (1) → (2) → (3) → (4)

Figure 6.1. Land categories and policy targeting

eligibility. By leaving higher productivity lands as the last to be retired, the program would ease the practice of surrendering competitive production to our international competition by making acreage diversion a last, unpaid, politically difficult resort for the secretary of agriculture. If the government actually desires to reduce surpluses, it should do so by mandating that farmers cease growing crops on productive land, rather than paying for the low-productivity acres that now enter set-asides.

Box 4 in Figure 6.1, designated as "Other Programs" refers to land that has no intensive agricultural use, hence is not targeted for any kind of agricultural retirement program. However, the land could have important uses in watershed protection or livestock grazing, timber growing or wildlife habitat. Other kinds of government programs could be involved to support those kinds of uses.

Payments under the 10 year or permanent and 3 to 5 year environmental land retirement programs would *not* be subject to the $20,000 limit on individual farm payments, nor would they be subject to the total $7 billion constraint on farm income support. The reason is precisely because the objective of this program is not income stabilization: it is to improve the quality of land and water resources. The eligibility of farmers to participate in these conservation programs is based on the vulnerability of their land resources to environmental damage. If this land is permanently retired from production and converted to conserving crops, such as perennial grasses or trees, it would cease to be a part of the whole farm base.

In the case of one year mandatory diversions, the secretary of agriculture would announce the proportion of whole farm base and number of acres to be removed from production. Since we assume that most environmentally vulnerable land (Boxes 1 and 2 in Figure 6.1) would already be retired, one year diversions would be targeted to Box 3, which would be relatively productive lands. Retirement would be for one year, during which the land would remain part of the whole farm base. As stated above, payments would not be made to farmers for taking this land out of production. Farmers who did not comply with the mandated acreage reduction would not be eligible for income stabilization payments.

As an additional stabilization component, we would propose the continued use of Section 32 funds to purchase perishable agricultural commodities (e.g., fruits, vegetables, poultry and other animal products) where market gluts are seriously depressing the prices of those products. Section 32 funds derive from the authority known as Section 32 of P.L. 320 passed in 1935, where 30 percent of all U.S. Customs receipts are allocated to the secretary of agriculture to encourage the export of agricultural products and to expand their domestic consumption. Consistent with other proposals in this chapter and past usage of Section 32 product purchases, we recommend that such products (1) be used in the domestic food programs of the USDA, (2) be donated to private charities in the United States and (3) be donated, where practical, to foreign food relief programs. But we would prohibit the use of Section 32 funds to subsidize commercial exports of agricultural products.

Having reduced government involvement in the commercial farm sector for the major field crops, we would alter the peanut, tobacco, wool, honey and mohair programs at this time only by actions taken at the border, as discussed in the pages that follow. Total payments to farmers producing these commodities would again be restricted to $20,000 per farm, and crop insurance would be revised as proposed. It is notable that the costs to the federal treasury of the programs for these commodities are insignificant. In addition, we believe that tobacco must be dealt with primarily as a health issue, not an agricultural policy issue.

Similarly, marketing agreements and orders for fruits and vegetables (and certain features of the orders for milk) would be left intact although crop insurance would again be revised and strict payment limits of $20,000 would again be enforced. The pricing and production features of such programs would be subject to the review and approval of the secretary of agriculture each year.

A final feature affecting the field crops concerns the handling of reserves—specifically grain reserves. Under current programs grain stocks enter into government storage and control, or into the Farmer-Owned Reserve, through the operation of the nonrecourse price support loan programs. Since nonrecourse price support loans for grains and oilseeds would be eliminated under our proposals, the government would cease to acquire grain stocks by this program device, and the Farmer-Owned Reserve would be phased out.

To help provide increased price stability in the food and feed grains sector, and to hold reserves for use in emergency shortage situations around the world, we would provide for a legitimate grain reserve program. This program would have the authority to make direct purchases of grain and oilseeds in periods of excess supply and release stocks through sales or donations in periods of excess demand, or extreme shortage. Although they have not been part of past reserves, we include oilseeds as part of our program. Their growing importance in national and international trade, and the importance of the United States as a reliable supplier of soybean products to world markets, justifies a reserve stock at a level of 6 million metric tons of oilseed products. In its trading operations the reserve program would seek to stabilize grain prices at or near the long-run *world* equilibrium price level, and as a consequence act to stabilize consumer food prices and the feed-livestock economy.

Since the grains are a part of a world-wide economy, this program would require the capacity to influence world grain prices. This means in turn that the program entity would need to be capitalized in an amount that would enable it to hold a reserve of grain stocks that averaged over time 50 to 75 million tons. Since this is conceived to be a price stabilization scheme, not a price enhancing scheme, and if donations constituted a small part of its activities, the program should not sustain major financial losses over the long-run.

To manage such an operation we would propose the creation of a Grain Stabilization Corporation with an appropriate staff and a governing board of seven members. The seven member board would be chaired by the secretary of agriculture (or his designate from the USDA). Other members of the board might include two representatives from government: the assistant secretary for economics from the USDA and the member of the Council of Economic Advisors with responsibility for the food and agricultural sector of the economy. The remaining four members should come from outside the government and represent the various sectors of the economy involved (farmers, domestic grain trade, international grain trade, consumers). The staff of this corporation should be full-time employees, but the board might meet once a week. The actions of this board with respect to the acquisition and disposal of grain stocks, would be analogous to the open market operations of the Federal Reserve Board of Governors in the monetary sector. Its goal would be to help keep a key sector of the farm economy running smoothly.

Dairy policy would be substantially changed. Price support for milk used in the manufacture of dairy products, and hence the whole structure of milk prices, would be eliminated. Since, however, the dairy industry would lose price support for milk under these proposals, milk producers should be eligible for income stabilization payments, like major crop producers, when the terms of trade turn against them. Thus, we propose that a stabilization payment program be established for milk producers by regions in which the prices received by milk producers are related to the prices paid by them. Producers in a particular region would receive payments when the terms of trade turned against them, as computed by a formula similar to that in Table 6.1, for that region. Payments would cease automatically when the prices-received, prices-paid relationship turned favorable. Payments would be made to producers on the basis of hundred weight of milk produced. The payment cap of $20,000 per farm per year would remain in effect, and payments to milk producers would be made from the $7 billion ear-marked in the agricultural budget for making stabilization payments to farmers.

The question now arises—What to do about the milk marketing orders which regulate the handling and distribution of fluid milk in all the important metropolitan areas? Since each of these orders facilitates price discrimination to some degree in those markets, a good economic argument can be made for eliminating them altogether. Further, modern technology has made it possible to ship fluid milk and its products long distances safely and economically; thus, the concept of individual "milksheds" around each metropolitan area is no longer a viable one. However these arguments do not take into account the structure of fluid milk markets. These markets are monopsonistic in structure. Many producers of a highly perishable product are confronted by a few large buyers (handlers and distributors of fluid milk and its products). As milk producers sought fair treatment in the 1920s and 1930s, these monopsonistically structured markets often became chaotic, and sometimes turned ugly with strife, turmoil and even violence. And this could happen again. Thus, we support the marketing order reforms proposed by Professors Edward Jesse and Jerome Hammond of the Universities of Wisconsin and Minnesota. The principal features of the Jesse-Hammond reform proposals include (Hammond 1990):

1.   For purposes of classification and pricing, two use classes will be employed. Hard cheeses, butter and nonfat dry milk shall be considered Class II products. Fluid milk and all other processed dairy products shall be considered Class I products.

2. One national milk marketing order will be established.
3. All dairy plants receiving Grade A milk shall be subject to the provision of the national Order.
4. Four regional zones shall be established for purposes of pricing Grade A milk and computing the blend price to producers.
5. The Class I price for each regional zone shall be the sum of:
    a. The national Class II price for milk.
    b. A price differential of $1.00 per hundredweight for all milk used for Class I purposes in the national Order. This is essentially pure revenue enhancement resulting from price discrimination. Such revenues should be distributed to all Grade A Milk producers equally.
    c. A utilization differential shall be based on the proportion of Grade A milk utilized by handlers in a given regional zone for Class I purposes. The purpose of this component is to encourage producers and supply plants to sell milk to fluid distributors. Current market wide pooling often discourages sales for fluid use.
    d. A transportation differential shall be based on the cost of transporting Class I milk from producers to the distributors using it. This component is to be redistributed both to plants and milk shippers who are actually incurring the costs of transporting milk for fluid uses. Its purpose is to encourage optimum assembly of milk for fluid uses.
6. The blend price paid to producers by each handler is based on the proportions of milk that are used (a) for Class I purposes, (b) Class II purposes by that handler and (c) the nationally pooled component of the Class I differential.

If all this seems complicated, it is. The complexities arise from the fact that milk is used to produce many different end products, and the prices of these end products yield different returns first to the handlers and processors of milk and second to the original milk producers. The Jesse-Hammond coalition proposals are aimed at reducing the pricing inequities that have grown within the milk marketing system over the years, and encouraging efficiencies in the production and handling of milk. But they still contain, as they must, a complex set of procedures for paying producers, as equitably as possible, in accordance with how their milk is utilized to produce end products such as cheese, nonfat dry milk, fluid milk, and ice cream.

The Jesse-Hammond proposals further take the position that there should be no impediments to, or discrimination against, the shipping of concentrated milk between local markets within a zone or between zones under the proposed national Order. With this we are in complete agreement. Milk concentrates for use in reconstituted fluid milk should be able to move freely within the national market.

One final question with respect to dairy must be resolved. Some milk producers also hold a crop base for producing corn and other grains. The question thus arises: Should these producers of milk and crops be permitted to receive stabilization payments on both types of commodities, when the price relationships call for such payments? We see no reason why a producer of both milk and crops should not receive payments on both types of commodities simultaneously, so long as the total payments to the farm do not exceed $20,000. The farmer should be free to produce whatever he wants, so long as his actions are legal, and receive stabilization payments on whatever commodities he produces, where such payments are authorized. The key control here is the $20,000 payment cap per farm, not what the farmer produces.

Before turning from domestic to international aspects of commodities policy, it is important to emphasize that food processing and distribution are increasingly dominated by concentrated industries, in which monopoly power has grown substantially. We would invigorate what have been lax government efforts to enforce anti-trust laws in the food processing and distribution area. We would extend this to include not only the "downstream" processing of grain and livestock, but the "upstream" supply of farm machinery, chemical inputs, fertilizer, and credit, so as to protect farmers and consumers from monopsony (concentrated buyers) as well as monopoly (concentrated sellers).

The final section of our first title deals with several key international dimensions of agricultural policy. First, consistent with the U.S. efforts to open world markets to agricultural trade through multilateral and bilateral negotiations, we would advocate that the general safety net approach that we have proposed for the United States be pursued by other GATT signatories, notably the European Community. However, we would *not* condition movements in this direction by us on the actions of others. We would convert current border measures protecting domestic agricultural products (including but not limited to sugar, dairy, peanut, tobacco, and wool and mohair programs) from quotas to tariffs, which could be more easily negotiated downward in future multilateral negotiations (see Appendix B). We would then implement unilateral 25 percent reductions in those tariffs in relation to the world market price, occurring at five percent intervals over five years.

Further tariff reduction in these and other protected sectors would occur only in concert with other GATT contracting parties. In short, unilateral conversion of quotas to tariffs would result in an initial tariff reduction, which would continue only when multilateral efforts assured a fairer international playing field for U.S. producers. Such a reduction would send a powerful signal to the world that the United States is prepared to open its markets to imports, without entirely sacrificing border protection for these commodities.

Consistent with efforts to reduce protection in all market economies, the use of export subsidies for agricultural products would be immediately stopped. These subsidies, notably the Export Enhancement Program, have been clearly shown to produce little in the way of export market expansion, and have been far less efficient as a mechanism of income support to farmers than direct payments would have been. Several recent studies (Paarlberg 1990; Coughlin and Carraro 1988; Bailey 1989) report that the cost per bushel of EEP has been $4.08 for wheat compared with an average market price at the Gulf of $3.16, implying that it would have been far more efficient to provide a subsidy directly to farmers and destroy the wheat than to have subsidized our exports to purchasing nations in this manner.

Indeed, the major beneficiary of such subsidies, apart from the large trading companies to which they have been paid, have been the governments that have demanded them as a condition of purchase, notably the former Soviet Union and China. As the formerly centrally planned economies open their trade to the West, there is far more to be gained from dealing with them on market terms than by continued subsidies. This does not preclude the development of long term trading agreements (LTA's), but such agreements should be explicitly based on the understanding that price subsidies will not be paid. And as Eastern Europe, the former Soviet Union and China become more integrated with the world economy, LTAs will become less necessary.

TITLE II: RESOURCE CONSERVATION AND ENVIRONMENTAL PROTECTION

Until recently very little attention has been given in the U.S. Department of Agriculture to the impact of intensive farming practice on the environment. The negative side effects of intensification—heavier applications of commercial fertilizer and the greater use of chemical weed controls—on the environment have been largely ignored or discounted. The Soil Conservation Service (SCS) has worked successfully with individual farmers in its Conservation Districts program, but in its work with the Conservation Reserve Program it has been frustrated by the CRP's conflicting objectives and limited budgets. The Forest Service has at times worked very successfully to protect and conserve our forest resources, but at other times has permitted their excessive exploitation. Overall, far less effort has been made by USDA as an agency to improve the rural environment than the public now demands.

We believe that USDA must establish a new set of priorities in the area of effective resource conservation and environmental protection. Such a reorientation is simply good politics. Each new public opinion poll gives greater weight to the felt demands of the American public for improved environmental protection, and their willingness to pay for these improvements through higher taxes, if necessary. In addition to being good politics, there is growing evidence that it is also good long-term economics. New methods of natural resource accounting (Repetto et. al. 1989; Faeth et. al. 1991) are now treating soil and water as assets subject to depreciation just like physical capital. When the true value of natural resources is calculated in terms of overall economic growth, farm production methods that are both more environmentally responsible, *and* more market oriented, rank better than conventional methods of production.

Achieving a more environmentally responsible agriculture, while retaining the market orientation of Title I, requires actions in eight main areas.

First, the Conservation Reserve Program must be both expanded and improved. Originally proposed to retire 45 million acres of erodible cropland for a 10 year period, the CRP has come under fire for spending too much to get too little in the way of environmental quality benefits (GAO 1989b). It is now unclear whether 45 million acres will be enrolled before the first of the 10 year contracts begin to expire in the mid-1990s. The issue is less how *many* acres are enrolled, than *which* acres are enrolled.

In large part, the CRP's problems have resulted from flaws in its design. The retirement of low productivity, highly vulnerable acres has not been a first priority. By adopting the dual targeting criteria for acreage diversion detailed in Title I above, the CRP should be directed primarily at those acres where the environmental payoff is greatest. By defining environmental vulnerability broadly, to encompass more than simply erosion potential, the CRP could be expanded to include areas vulnerable to groundwater contamination, loss of wildlife habitat, and wetlands. It could be further expanded by offering longer than 10 year contracts, and converting existing ones to permanent easements. In addition, acres that have not been actively cropped but which are clearly vulnerable to environmental damage should be eligible for permanent retirement from cropping, adding additional potential acreage. By concentrating on low productivity lands, total program costs could be held down.

Second, we suggest that the Wetlands Reserve Program (WRP), established in the 1990 farm bill, be structured the same way as our new CRP to protect our dwindling water fowl population, and to preserve wetlands as natural mechanisms of flood control and drought resistance. Before the 1990 farm bill the so-called "swampbuster" provisions threatened farmers who drained and plowed wetlands with total denial of commodity price supports. While seemingly tough regulations, the provisions have been very poorly enforced, and many exceptions are made by the local committees responsible for reviewing individual cases. Moreover, in periods of high commodity prices, foregoing future program benefits in order to bring additional land into production may seem to be a reasonable trade-off to many farmers. The 1990 farm bill, however, established graduated penalties for "accidental" violations, while intentional violations are still penalized with loss of payments.

We would propose a total moratorium on further wetlands drainage, and positive financial incentives under the CRP to enter existing wetlands into permanent easements where they will be protected for future generations. Additional payments should be made to restore former wetlands in relatively low productivity areas or on lands in zones highly susceptible to flooding. Only by such affirmative actions can wetlands be protected and expanded. Simply threatening to take away commodities payments has failed to provide this protection.

However, where wetlands drainage, sodbusting or other violations of conservation requirements occur, we would impose penalties based on the number of acres affected and the degree of damage. These penalties would be independent of farm income stabilization payments under Title I. A farmer would be assessed penalties based on environmental damages, whether or not he was participating in the income stabilization program. While the problem of inequitable penalties was partially addressed in the 1990 bill, we want to assure that these penalties would be divorced from the income stabilization safety net program altogether, and administered separately. Penalties are now smaller and more graduated for farmers who *accidentally* plow up highly erodible land or wetlands; between $750 and $10,000 on wetlands and $500 and $5,000 for drylands. We would eliminate the distinction between "accidental" and "intentional" damage, and assess the penalties whenever and wherever such damages occur on a *per acre* basis. The penalties would thus be proportionate to the damage done. We would favor enforcement of these penalties outside of USDA, preferably by the Environmental Protection Agency.

Third, we would provide budget support for a national effort to expand wilderness areas, national parks, and the national forests of the nation. Because these lands are administered by both the U.S. Forest Service of

USDA and the Bureau of Land Management and National Park Service of the Department of Interior, a successful initiative will require a joint, interagency effort. The expansion of these natural areas must preserve some in a pristine state, but must also acknowledge the legitimate public demand to use some as sources of recreation and supervised economic exploitation.

A large share of new government land acquisition and protection has been in Alaska. Greater attention should be given to demands for natural areas in the lower 48 states. Working in cooperation with schools of forestry and agriculture in the land grant system (see Title V), we would substantially expand research into the management and promotion of more diverse biological systems on these lands, such as replanting of harvested public timber with multiple species rather than single species forests, which tend to support a far narrower band of wildlife and plants.

Fourth, consistent with a general approach advancing greater biological diversity on both public lands and private agricultural acreage, we would develop an expanded program to protect existing wildlife and to reintroduce birds, fish and mammals depleted through activities of man. While such reintroductions are risky and difficult, because of the dramatic ecological changes resulting from agricultural and urban development, they can be successful if farmers do not perceive them as obstacles. Local farmers must be made an integral part of the process. This may include paying farmers and ranchers to assist in wildlife management, habitat improvement, or for losses due to changes in production possibilities.

Fifth, water is becoming an increasingly scarce and precious resource. Agricultural irrigation and drainage practices have permanently depleted water resources in the Ogalala aquifer, and elsewhere have contributed to excessive erosion and runoff of fertilizers and chemicals into rivers and streams, and have led to leaching of farm effluents into groundwater, which supplies 95 percent of rural water needs. Water subsidies in the West have contributed to distorted agricultural land uses, to water shortages in urban areas, and to serious environmental damages. These trends must be stopped. Implementing the changes outlined above will help encourage greater diversity in production and less damaging cropping practices because lands vulnerable to these damages will be less intensively farmed. But more affirmative actions will be required to maintain and improve water quality.

We would initiate a joint presidential/congressional commission to survey and evaluate the quality of existing water resources of the nation, to estimate future needs and requirements, and to develop a national water policy. This policy should focus on two main problem areas:

1.   Actions, or programs, needed to protect both surface and ground waters from pollution resulting from agricultural and other industrial

production practices.

2. Actions, or legislation, needed to effect a more efficient and equitable way of allocating scarce supplies of water among competing demands where supplies of water are increasing slowly, or perhaps even decreasing, and the demand for water is increasing dramatically as the result of increases in population and personal incomes.

If such a policy is not developed by this proposed commission and then enacted into law by the Congress, many parts of the nation are going to be confronted with critical water shortages by as early as the year 2000. And many parts of the nation are already confronted by polluted water supplies that are unfit for human consumption. The water problem has reached a critical stage in the United States.

Sixth, we would increase the opportunities for urban residents to remain in touch with rural and natural areas through a federal program to establish green belts and forest belts adjacent to all urban areas greater than 50,000 population. In addition to halting the encroachment of urban sprawl on productive and valuable farmland, and helping to support the maintenance of urban core amenities, such a program would guarantee access by all urban dwellers to unspoiled countryside.

Seventh, we would propose that all agricultural chemicals and fertilizers currently in use be the subject of a renewed set of tests undertaken by the Environmental Protection Agency (EPA) to determine their effects on human health, worker safety and the environment. Many of these chemicals have been "grandfathered" out of regulation because they were developed prior to current test requirements. They, and all newly developed chemical inputs, should be carefully scrutinized before approval. But there are problems with this straightforward recommendation. Given present review procedures in EPA the recommendation could not be carried out in "the next hundred years." Further, the scientific basis of many of the standards employed for approving or rejecting a given chemical substance have been called into question. These same arguments apply to the review procedures in the Food and Drug Administration (FDA).

Therefore, we recommend that the Congress direct the Office of Technology Assessment (OTA) to convene a working group composed of representatives from the federal agencies involved (EPA, FDA, and USDA), the scientific community, the chemical industry, environmental groups and farm groups to (1) examine and appraise existing chemical review procedures and (2) make recommendations to expedite the review processes and give them a more reliable scientific basis. OTA would chair this working group, provide the necessary staff and be responsible for the preparation of the reports to Congress. A preliminary report should be made to Congress at the end of one year, and a final report at the end of two years. These reports should provide Congress with the information base to pass legislation which streamlines and renders more effective the chemical review procedures in the EPA and FDA.

Eighth, in light of the large number of initiatives we have detailed, the Soil Conservation Service, the Forest Service and possibly a new environmentally-oriented service of USDA would, after appropriate reorganization, receive substantial increases in funding to carry out items one through six above. This is the first use to which we would put any farm policy reform "dividend" resulting from Title I. Soil, water, and forest resources would emerge as a central institutional mission of the Department of Agriculture. The ultimate foundation of American competitiveness is the natural resource base on which sustained productivity ultimately depends.

To carry out the initiatives outlined above, an overhaul and a reorganization of the USDA agencies in this area will be required in coordination with the Environmental Protection Agency. If the Soil Conservation Service is to provide staff work for the joint presidential/congressional commission on future water resources and play a larger role in the expanded and improved Conservation Reserve Program, it will require a significant increase in its budget. If the Forest Service is to give greater attention to the environmental needs of our forest land and less attention to timber harvesting, it will need new policy guidelines from the Congress. If the wetlands and the green belts initiatives are to go anywhere, a new agency with new leadership with new visions of the future will almost certainly be required to carry them out. If wildlife is to be reintroduced, protected and fostered by the Department of Agriculture, certainly a new agency will be needed to develop this new kind of husbandry in the USDA.

We recommend that the Congress direct the secretary of agriculture to appoint a task force of 15 members (seven of which, including the chairman, come from within the USDA, and eight of which come from outside the government and reflect the conservation and environmental needs of the assignment) to undertake the following four-fold task: (1) to indicate needed changes in existing programs of work, (2) to indicate completely new needed programs of work, (3) to indicate a desired organizational structure for this general area of conservation and environment, including the agencies that would be involved and broad programs of work that would come under each agency, (4) to indicate the general budget requirements for each agency. This task force should report through the president to the Congress in one year.

Before leaving these environmental initiatives, it is useful to emphasize that the environment is increasingly recognized as a global issue, beyond the control or authority of any single national government. Water and air pollution do not respect political or national boundaries. This fact, combined with the large role of trade in world agriculture, lead environmental policy to have global trade effects. If the United States decides, through the chemical registration process outlined here, to ban certain agricultural fungicides because they pose health risks, how can it prevent these same fungicides from being used in other countries, and the reimportation of tainted fruits, vegetables, or other products? And if farmers and consumers demand that such products be stopped at the border, is the United States acting unilaterally to violate its own calls to reduce agricultural protectionism?

These questions lead to a need for environmental policy to be structured with a careful eye on its international implications. Environmental protection cannot be allowed to become camouflage for trade protection. Yet if imports or exports are potentially harmful to human health and the environment, both the importing and exporting country should be notified, and if necessary the trade flow should be interrupted. We maintain that a basic principle guiding environmental policy should be to strive for higher standards in food, health and safety throughout the world, working through multilateral organizations such as the General Agreement on Tariffs and Trade (GATT) and the Food and Agriculture Organization of the United Nations (FAO). We will take up these issues in greater detail in Chapter 8.

TITLE III: RURAL DEVELOPMENT AND PART-TIME FARMING

The need for assistance to people living in rural poverty, as well as help for low-production and part-time farmers, is real. It is unrealistic to imagine that these producers will contribute the bulk of the nation's food and fiber supplies; such supplies will continue to be produced by large commercial growers. However, part-time farmers are important as suppliers of various specialty commodities (e.g., maple syrup, wild rice, some fruits, and nuts) and may also be more inclined to experiment with more environmentally benign crops or varieties. Active, productive, land-owning, part-time farmers in rural communities can also contribute to a higher quality of life in those communities. In addition to part-time farmers, many low-income residents prefer economic opportunities that allow them to remain in less expensive rural communities. These opportunities can be expanded through government action at relatively low cost compared with the cost of interventions in poor urban cores. Rather than heavy federal spending, we propose a program focused primarily on building and maintaining educational opportunities, information services, and loan and credit guarantees. It is our contention that all three are different kinds of "public goods." Education, information, and adequate credit are unlikely to be maintained in rural areas without government assistance. Once in place, however, they provide a basis for the private investment that must be the ultimate backbone of rural economic development.

Consistent with our calls for reorganization of USDA under Titles I and II, we would create two new agencies under Title III. The first is a new Rural Development Agency (RDA) authorized to provide small grants to needy families; to develop and operate an employment service in cooperation with county extension offices; and to make low-interest loans to counties, towns and villages for needed facilities such as water treatment plants, schools, and medical clinics and to take over certain of the successful programs of the Farmers Home Administration (e.g., the $2 billion rural housing program). The purpose of RDA small grants (less than $10,000 per family) would be to provide families living in poverty with job training, education, child care, and home and business improvement. These grants would be administered through local county committees, and would create a flow of funds to the primarily nonfarm rural poor. At the same time, county extension offices and multi-county economic development groups would be assisted in creating employment services designed to match local skills with local needs as well as employment opportunities in urban areas. Projects for construction of public or private facilities (e.g., repair of roads and bridges) that have gone largely unmet in many rural areas since the New Deal would be emphasized once again. Such projects would be partially underwritten by low-interest loans to incorporated units designed to provide this infrastructure. The grants, employment services, and loans provided by the Rural Development Agency would function together to build up the "human capital" of rural families, creating jobs and the demand for additional rural services less through direct government spending than through investments in rural people.

The second new agency we propose is a Part-time Farming Agency (PFA) in USDA designed to service the clear majority of rural residents who rely on farming for less than half of their income. Similar in spirit to the Rural Development Agency, its mission is not to subsidize these farmers directly (although they would remain eligible for "safety net" stabilization payments under Title I). It is to provide services missing from rural areas at present so that communities can diversify from sole or even primary dependence on farming, while retaining agriculture as an important part of individual and community portfolios.

It would do this in three ways. First, part-time farmers would be assisted in obtaining credit, a continuing need in all agricultural production, and a special need for smaller operations without substantial collateral. A special category of loan guarantee and interest write-down would be created by the Part-time Farming Agency, earmarked for part-time farmers, which would be extended to private banks and the Farm Credit System to leverage additional loans to these individuals. The objective is thus *not* the creation of a new credit agency, but assistance at the margin designed to prime the pump of private credit sources and the Farm Credit System to relieve credit constraints in this part-time farming category. Second, the PFA would provide technical production information to county agents tailored to part-time producers, and would assign special agents to county offices whose primary mission would be to work with part-time farmers. Third, the new agency would develop and share marketing information designed for these producers, allowing them to start and maintain marketing channels for specialty or nontraditional products with high value added, such as "organic" poultry or specialty cheeses.

Together a Rural Development Agency (RDA) and a Part-time Farming Agency (PFA) would account for an additional slice of any farm policy reform "dividend." However, these agencies would together serve to supplant the beleaguered, ineffective, and at times nearly bankrupt Farmers Home Administration (FmHA), which would be abolished under our policy proposals, saving many current expenses (and future bad loans) from being made. Current FmHA loans outstanding of over $40 million would be retired as soon as practicable, and agency salaries and expenses ($565 million in 1990) would be diverted for RDA and PFA use (USDA 1990).

In this connection, the reformed Farm Credit System is experiencing renewed success after a major overhaul in the late 1980s. We believe that the system should be carefully monitored in the 1990s to assure that it is servicing the needs of all rural residents, and not just those of large commercial borrowers. We believe that early in 1993, following the presidential election, a review of the system should be undertaken to assure that the reforms have been successful, and that the system has succeeded in broadening its base of borrowers and investments in a manner compatible with a well-diversified rural economy.

TITLE IV: FOOD PROGRAMS AND FOOD SAFETY

The "other" programs described in Chapter 5 have made improvements in recent years designed to meet many of the food needs of the urban and rural poor. Unfortunately, however, the programs have not reached many of the neediest, especially the homeless, the elderly and children of the poor. In foreign countries, U.S. food aid has resulted primarily from the need to dispose of surpluses, and has often missed its intended targets—the poorest nations and the poor within them, especially children. Apart from the need for reforms in these programs, there is another side of USDA programs targeted at consumers that is in critical need of improvement. This is the need for the Food Safety and Inspection Service to expand its coverage of products and to coordinate its work with the Food and Drug Administration, the Environmental Protection Agency and the Surgeon General to assure the public a safe, unadulterated food supply. We believe that four major policy initiatives are necessary affecting consumers at home and abroad.

First, we would continue the current food stamp program, school lunch program, and other food surplus disposal programs. However, we would expand the availability of food stamps to public and private care units for the handicapped, elderly and infirm, and would utilize part of the savings from farm policy reform in Title I to increase the types of food and nutrition content of school lunches administered under the school feeding programs. Especially in inner cities, optional high-nutrition school breakfasts and summer meal programs should be expanded, combined with special teaching sessions, to draw needy students into an environment in which education and nutrition are twin priorities.

Second, we would make strenuous efforts to assure that food programs reach deeper into the lives of the homeless, elderly, and preschool children of the poor, who may not be in contact with institutions through which food programs are typically administered. The Departments of Health and Human Services, Education, and private charities such as the Salvation Army and various church groups should participate in these efforts, establishing food and shelter stations in urban areas where temporary shelter and cooked meals are made available. We would also increase the capacity of cities, municipalities and private groups to take food to the homes of those who cannot travel to such facilities for help.

Third, in the foreign food aid programs, we would revamp Food for Peace (PL-480), so that its primary function is the provision of emergency food relief in areas of critical shortages, rather than surplus disposal on an on-again, off-again basis to areas where shortages may not even be present. The effect of such untargeted disposal is often the reverse of what is ostensibly intended: food prices are so depressed that local farmers are ruined. While it is unrealistic to suppose that commodity surpluses, when they arise, can be ignored, we believe that they should be used primarily to alleviate shortages that arise in the neediest parts of the world. In addition, food aid should be targeted to groups within recipient nations that need it most. This would make the administration of Food for Peace more complex, but would reduce the tendency for it to serve as a conduit for surpluses which, once out of sight, are out of mind. In short, we would sever the link between surplus disposal and foreign food aid. The best way to assure this is to reduce or eliminate bilateral food aid, and to work through multilateral agencies such as the High Commission on Refugees, the United Nations Children's Fund (UNICEF), and U.N. Development Program (UNDP) and private overseas charities to develop targeted programs of food assistance for those most in need within the neediest countries.

Fourth, we would create a high level interagency working group composed of representatives from the Food Safety and Inspection Service (FSIS), Food and Drug Administration (FDA), Environmental Protection Agency (EPA) and Surgeon General's Office, and chaired by a presidential assistant to develop a new agenda in cooperation with the private sector in which human health and food safety is given the highest national priority. In practical terms, this will require a regulatory structure (1) which tracks the use of chemical agents and food additives from their development in the laboratory to their use on the farm, through food marketing channels to the consumer; (2) which monitors and inspects *all foods* from the initial production stage to the final consumption stage; and (3) which has the authority to halt at once any unsafe practice. The public demands for human health and food safety justify this kind of unified structure. Private industry would also benefit from eliminating the bureaucratic layers, inconsistencies, and balkanized approach to regulations in this area.

The interagency working group on food safety should be directed to report to the Congress at the end of one year. Once this report is presented to the Congress and made public it would be up to the Congress working with the administration to take action with respect to the recommendations in the report. This report should do two important things: (1) evaluate the existing structure of research, inspection and regulation in the area of food safety and point up weaknesses, points of failure and blind spots in that structure; (2) recommend new agencies or reorganization of old agencies where needed and the assignment of work and action responsibilities among the agencies. The ultimate objective is to assure the American public that it is guaranteed a clean, unadulterated, safe food supply.

TITLE V: RESEARCH, EDUCATION, AND EXTENSION

As the previous titles in this policy reform package emphasize, we envision the role of USDA in the future to be far more oriented to groups outside its traditional clientele in commercial agriculture. This is likely to be enlightened self-interest from the point of view of USDA, since it is increasingly difficult to justify so huge an agency in the name of 300,000 or so mainly wealthy clients. Yet as it emerges in the 1990s as a department devoted to a wide range of needs in part-time farming, rural development, environmental protection, resource conservation, food programs, foreign emergency assistance, health and safety, and nutrition, it is important not to lose sight of the singular role of commercial farming. While we have proposed cuts in direct subsidies to commercial agriculture, we do not want to underemphasize its critical role as a highly competitive, export-oriented and income-producing sector of the American economy. We want commercial agriculture to survive and prosper as an essentially unsubsidized sector of the economy. And we believe that it can. But to do so it must build on its generous resource endowment and remain competitive in world markets.

Underpinning its continued competitiveness in global markets will be research and education designed to keep costs low and the quality of "human capital" in the food and fiber production system high. In addition, the growing environmental and health consciousness of the American public will require new methods of agricultural production that reduce its adverse environmental impacts and assure high levels of food purity and nontoxicity. These advances will not come without investments in research and technology that must be supported by federal funds to the experiment stations of land grant colleges and universities. In the Extension Service, the expanded role of the county offices in rural development and part-time farming will also require increases in support.

In our view, three vital research and education needs stand out as priorities for the 1990s. First, research into improvements in the efficiency of production at the farm level must continue if American commercial agriculture is to remain globally competitive. While the private sector has played an increasingly active role in this area over time, private sector priorities must continue to be augmented by public sector research for well-balanced advances in productivity over time. In addition to farm-level efficiencies, one important part of this research agenda concerns the utilization of agricultural output to develop new products. A recent example of such successful "downstream" utilization research is soybean-based ink for the printing industry. Another, more controversial, effort has been ethanol made from corn. Ethanol based fuels will be increasingly attractive as the price of alternative hydrocarbons based on petroleum products rises. We would continue to support the research and development of these fuel sources. However, we would make them part of a far broader research effort to promote conservation and energy efficiency throughout the U.S. economy. Without a broad effort, simple subsidies to ethanol will be inadequate in dealing with U.S. energy needs.

Second, a major shift must occur in land grant colleges' research and teaching and in USDA research grants, in the direction of improvements in environmental quality. This broad based shift in research priorities must include biotechnologies, biocontrols, chemical and fertilizer composition and application technology, integrated pest management, crop rotation practices, irrigation techniques and other areas that promise to protect yield increases and reduce adverse environmental effects of modern agricultural technologies. Similar support should be given to applied forestry and wildlife ecology, promoting approaches that can enhance the role of retired lands and wetlands as repositories of biological diversity. In the health and nutrition area, more research is needed on the health impacts of various farm chemicals and on the nutrition needs of the population in order to steer future production practices. We are just beginning to understand the role of improved nutrition in building strong, healthy citizens; this important work must be encouraged and expanded.

Third, the applied social sciences must develop and help implement local and regional strategies to promote rural development, part-time farming, and local infrastructure. Here, the role of extension will continue to be vital, and will need to be expanded.

The above research, education and extension priorities reflect the needed long run investments that will protect American agriculture's preeminent role as a food producer; and, at the same time, act to improve the quality of life that is increasingly demanded by the American public.

TITLE VI: FARM SAFETY AND MIGRANT WORKERS

With regard to the critical problem of safety on farms we would have the Congress direct the Cooperative Extension Service to develop, in cooperation with the Occupational Safety and Health Administration (OSHA), a national educational program of accident prevention in farming. The Congress should provide the Extension Service with the required additional budget money to first develop this educational program, and second, carry it out year after year. First, however, the Congress should lift the ban that prevents OSHA from doing accident prevention work in the farming sector, and second, direct OSHA to develop a full inspection and regulatory program that is applicable to the farming industry. The farming industry is unique in many ways; but it is also deadly. The federal government must assume the responsibility for making farming a much safer line of work.

The problem with respect to migrant farmworkers is not the absence of protective or assistance programs. It is the failure of existing programs to reach out to poor, illiterate workers and effectively help them raise their incomes and improve their quality of life. In programmatic terms, the problem is threefold: (1) insuring that the programs are adequately funded; (2) insuring that there is adequate staff to monitor the programs and provide the necessary guidance and regulations when called for; and (3) coordinating the various existing programs emanating from different agencies to make sure that the needs of the migrants are, in fact, met. Thus, we propose that the Congress direct the administration to establish a permanent working task force, a task force on migrant farmworkers, composed of members from the federal agencies with some involvement with migrant farmworkers to be chaired by a White House assistant. The charge to this task force in its first year should be fourfold:

1. Review the present mix of programs and determine where the programs are achieving their stated objectives, and where the mix is failing to properly protect and assist the migrants.

2. Recommend a revision of old programs, the establishment of new programs, and the development of new procedures for program coordination wherever appropriate.

3. Provide firm budget estimates of the program undertakings recommended in (2) above.

4. Select a lead agency, probably either the Department of Agriculture or the Department of Labor, to serve as the coordinating, and overall supervising, agency for the federal programs relating to migrant farmworkers.

At the end of its first year, the task force should report to the Congress on the four points outlined above. In succeeding years the task force should monitor the work of the various agencies involved and appraise the effectiveness of these programs, and report each year to the Congress on the progress achieved in improving the economic level and the quality of life of migrant farmworkers.

Based on the first year's report of the task force on migrant farmworkers, the Congress should direct the lead federal agency to establish, in areas of migrant workers concentration, centers which house all of the diverse federal assistance programs under one roof. At these centers the lead agency should perform a coordinating role in which a continuous effort is made to see that the diverse programs adequately meet the needs of the migrant workers. In this connection it is recommended that the lead agency provide an ombudsman service to migrant clients, so that these clients, who are likely to be illiterate and hesitant to approach any government agency, be directed to the program in that agency that meets their specific needs at that particular time. It is important to recognize in the design of programs of assistance to the poor and the downtrodden, that those people must have assistance in finding the entrance way to the very programs set up to help them. Thus, we emphasize the need to establish procedures at the local level which can and do reach out to migrant workers and direct them to those programs which were established to guarantee their legal and economic rights.

These centers could provide other important functions. Labor contractors could obtain valuable information at such centers about rules and
regulations that have a bearing on their business of hiring and employing
migrant farmworkers; such centers might also develop into something
approaching an employment agency or a town hiring hall. Farm businessmen could also find such centers useful in providing information about legal
and illegal hiring and employment practices. In sum, these centers could
become important information centers to benefit everyone involved in the
use of seasonal migrant farmworkers: the workers themselves, the interme-
diary labor contractors, and farmers and business interests.

Summary

The overall thrust of our proposed policy reforms is quite simple: we
propose to take away permanent subsidies from the already rich commercial
farm sector and replace them with income stabilization payments made in
times of deteriorating market conditions. Dividends created by this reform
would then be redistributed to growing priority needs. These include
environmental quality, rural development, part-time farmers, the urban and
foreign poor (especially children and the elderly), food health and safety,
research and education, and protection for farm workers. In many respects,
ours is a program of reallocation as much as it is a program of reform.

Together, these six titles of our proposed food, farm and rural policy
will have manifold consequences on both domestic and international
markets. As Appendix A to this chapter, we provide a side-by-side comparison of the 1985 and 1990 farm bill provisions and the program changes we
propose. We turn now to an analysis of the projected effects of these policy
changes, and to the feasibility of making them in the real world of political
and economic decisions.

Appendix A
General Features of Legislative Alternatives

	Food Security Act of 1985 (FSA)	Food, Agriculture, Conservation, and Trade Act of 1990	Cochrane/Runge
Crop Base Acreage	Five year average of acreage per crop.	Same as FSA with 15% of base designated as flexible[1] and not eligible for deficiency payments.	Whole farm base acreage including all acreage planted to current nonprogram crops.
Income Stabilization Payments	No income stabilization payments.	No income stabilization payments.	Made per acre when percentage increase in index of prices paid by farmers exceeds that of prices received by farmers.
Deficiency Payments	Difference between target price and market price or loan rate, whichever is higher, times acreage and yield.	Same as FSA except market price based on 12 month average, not 5 months.	No deficiency payments.
Marketing Loans	Cotton and rice producers repay loans at lower rate if world price falls below loan rate. Discretionary for wheat and feed grains.	Program extended to soybeans, sunflowers, flax, canola, rapeseed, and mustard seed.	No marketing loans.
Price Support Payments	Producers take out nonrecourse loans with the CCC, using commodities as collateral. Loan rate set between 75 and 85 percent of five year moving average market price.	Loan rate must now be set at no less than 85 percent of five year moving average market price. Rate cannot be set more than 5 percent lower than previous year's rate.	No price support programs except for peanuts, tobacco, wool, mohair, and honey.

[1]Flexible refers to acres that can be planted to program and nonprogram crops, excluding fruit and vegetables.

Appendix A (*continued*)

	Food Security Act of 1985 (FSA)	Food, Agriculture, Conservation, and Trade Act of 1990	Cochrane/Runge
Farm Program Payments Limits	Commodity program payments limited to $50,000 per person and $100,000 for disaster payments. Limits exclude loans and purchases, loan deficiency payments and inventory reduction payments.	Same as FSA, except payments to honey producers falls from $250,000 to $125,000 over four years.	Limit of $20,000 per farm regardless of the commodity or program. CRP and other environmental program payments not subject to limits.
Expenditure Cap on Total Farm Income Support Program	None specified	None specified	Cap of $7 billion.
Federal Crop Insurance Program	Subsidized insurance program on 50 crops varying by county.	Federal Crop Insurance Corporation to review new types of policies.	Expand and reform government program and develop an optional all-risk income insurance program with private insurers.
Supply Control	Acreage reduction, set-aside programs, and discretionary paid land diversion.	No change from FSA.	Secretarial discretion for one year acreage removal with no payments.
Market Stabilization of Perishables	Use of Section 32 funds to encourage consumption of commodities by purchase, export and diversion programs.	No change from FSA.	Continue use of Section 32 funds but prohibit subsidization of commercial exports.
Marketing Agreements and Orders	Allows producers to promote orderly marketing and to collectively influence price or quality of certain commodities.	No change from FSA.	Continue current status of orders (except for milk), yet prohibit using them to subsidize commercial exports.

Appendix A (*continued*)

	Food Security Act of 1985 (FSA)	Food, Agriculture, Conservation, and Trade Act of 1990	Cochrane/Runge
Disaster Payments	When substantial loss creates economic emergency and crop insurance is insufficient.	No change from FSA.	Payments will be replaced by the expanded crop insurance program.
Grain Reserves	Grains are put in FOR[2] and CCC under nonrecourse loan price support program.	No change from FSA.	Grain Stabilization Corporation makes direct purchases of excess supplies and releases stocks in periods of extreme shortage to stabilize prices at world levels.
Dairy Policy	CCC buys dairy products, supply is reduced through diversion and termination programs, and 42 marketing orders oversee distribution and pricing.	Same as FSA, except limit on government purchases and fees assessed on producers and processors.	Stabilization payments paid when increase in index of prices paid by farmers exceeds that of prices received. One national order is established.
Monopolies and Antitrust	Nothing specified.	Nothing specified	Increase government efforts to enforce antitrust laws in food processing and distribution.
Import Controls	Sugar and cotton quotas authorized.	Same as FSA.	Import quotas on all commodities converted to tariffs and all tariffs reduced 25 percent over five years.

[2]Farmer Owned Reserve (FOR) allows farmers to take out three year nonrecourse loans on stored wheat and feed grains. Grain is not released until market price reaches the release price.

Appendix A (*continued*)

	Food Security Act of 1985 (FSA)	Food, Agriculture, Conservation, and Trade Act of 1990	Cochrane/Runge
Export Subsidies	EEP and Export Credit Guarantee Programs subsidize sales with CCC commodities.	If no GATT agreement by June 30, 1992, an additional $1 billion is to be spent on subsidies and marketing loans are to be instituted on wheat and feed grains.	Terminate all export subsidy programs.
International Food Safety and Health Standards	Nothing specified.	Nothing specified.	Work through international agencies, like GATT, to harmonize standards.
Conservation Reserve Program	Convert highly erodible cropland to conserving, noncommercial use by offering annual rental payments.	Extends enrollment period to 1995. Expands list of eligible lands to windbreaks and shelterbelts.	Retire low productivity, high vulnerability lands and offer longer than ten year contracts and permanent easements.
Wetlands Conservation	Prohibit USDA program benefits to producers that convert wetlands to croplands.	Smaller penalties for violation of swamp-buster program. Creates Wetland Reserve Program to restore and attain long term easements for wetlands.	Moratorium on wetland drainage and provide positive financial incentives for permanent easements.
Wilderness Conservation	Nothing specified.	Provides cost share assistance for production plans which improve wildlife habitat.	Work with Department of Interior to expand wilderness areas, national parks, and national forests. Expand research into wilderness management.

Appendix A (*continued*)

	Food Security Act of 1985 (FSA)	Food, Agriculture, Conservation, and Trade Act of 1990	Cochrane/Runge
Wildlife Management	Authorized under U.S. Forest Service.	Same as FSA.	Work with farmers to protect existing wildlife and reintroduce birds, fish, and mammals.
Water Research and Management	Provide plans and assistance to state and local governments to protect ground and surface water quantity and quality.	Creates program that offers incentives to adapt production practices that reduce the release of agricultural chemicals.	Study and recommend how to protect surface and ground water from pollution and how to allocate water more efficiently and equitably. Joint presidential/congressional commission to develop national water policy.
Urban Environment	Nothing specified.	Education and assistance program created to assist forestry projects.	Establish green belts and forest belts around urban areas.
Chemical Standards	Nothing specified.	Farmers required to keep records on use of restricted pesticides.	Examine existing chemical review procedures and recommend more reliable and faster processes.
Rural Community Assistance	Changes criteria for receiving water and waste facility loans, and grants and guarantees loans made to nonprofit rural development and finance corporations.	Creates Rural Development Administration, expands grant program and waste disposal systems, and provides funds for rural communications networks.	Establish new Rural Development Agency (RDA) to provide small grants, develop and operate employment services and make low income loans for community facilities.

153

Appendix A (*continued*)

	Food Security Act of 1985 (FSA)	Food, Agriculture, Conservation, and Trade Act of 1990	Cochrane/Runge
Part-Time Farming Assistance	Maintains FmHA Small Farmer Training and Technical Assistance Program.	Nothing specified.	Establish Part-time Farming Agency to assist part-time farmers in obtaining credit, provide technical assistance, and develop and share marketing information.
Rural Credit	Requires more FmHA guaranteed loans, adds joint farming operations to FmHA eligibility, and studies need for insurance to protect Farm Credit Service (FCS).	Cuts direct FmHA loans by 75 percent and increases guaranteed loan program funds.	Abolish FmHA and transfer functions to RDA. Monitor FCS on its service to rural residents.
Food Stamps	Continues $14 billion program. Makes residents of public mental health units and centers for chemical dependency eligible and expands definition of disabled for eligibility purposes.	Continues program. Allows restaurants to accept food stamps in exchange for meal for homeless.	Continues current program and expands availability to public and private care units for elderly, infants, and handicapped.
School Lunch Program	Continues $5.2 billion program and Cash-in-Lieu of Commodity Letters of Credit programs.	Continues program with studies to determine cause of declining school enrollment and cost effectiveness.	Continue current program, increases types of food and nutrition content of school lunches and expand high nutrition school breakfast and summer meal programs.

Appendix A (*continued*)

	Food Security Act of 1985 (FSA)	Food, Agriculture, Conservation, and Trade Act of 1990	Cochrane/Runge
Food Distribution	Continues $736 million program, defines emergency feeding organizations, and calls for methods to distribute food stamps to the homeless.	Programs continued.	Continue current program and increase availability of food programs to homeless, elderly and the preschool children of the poor by constructing community shelters and kitchens.
Food for Peace	Makes commodities available through long-term credit, as donations for emergency relief and authorizes food for development projects.	Commodities to be made available on multi-year basis.	Reduce or eliminate bilateral food aid, work through multilateral institutions and charitable agencies to insure help to the needy and prohibit use as surplus disposal.
Other Foreign Food Assistance	Food for Progress created to support countries moving to market economies.	Food for Progress extended to assist middle income and emerging democracies through private volunteer organizations and nonprofit organizations.	Nothing specified.
Food Safety	Continues current inspection of meat and poultry, applies U.S. standards to imported poultry, and calls for study of product purity and inspection regulations.	Same as FSA.	Continues current inspections and creates regulatory structure which tracks use of chemical agents, monitors, and inspects all foods and halts unsafe practices.

Appendix A (*continued*)

	Food Security Act of 1985 (FSA)	Food, Agriculture, Conservation, and Trade Act of 1990	Cochrane/Runge
Agricultural Production Research	Continues National Agricultural Research, Extension and Teaching Policy Act and creates Technology Development Research Program to develop technology for use on small and medium-sized farms.	Increases in Agricultural Research Service Programs funds. Programs for Supplemental and Alternative Crops Research extended. Establish Agricultural Science and Technology Review Board.	Expand government sponsored research programs for a competitive commercial agriculture. Increase private sector role in production research.
Environmental Research	Creates Agricultural Productivity Research program which stresses low-input sustainable agricultural research.	Pilot projects on Integrated Pest Management are created. National Institute for Alternative Products is established.	Shift research priorities to improving environmental quality, including but not limited to low input sustainable agriculture.
Health and Nutrition Research	Calls for a plan for national food and human nutrition research program.	Funds authorized to establish at least one food science nutrition research center for the Southeast U.S. Pilot project created to better coordinate nutrition education.	Increase research on health impacts for farm chemicals and nutrition needs of population.
Applied Social Science Research	Develop and demonstrate technologies in home economics and increase research in transport of perishable commodities and overcoming market barriers.	Program established to research development of niche markets.	Develop and implement strategies to promote rural development, part-time farming, and local infrastructure.
Farm Safety	Nothing specified.	Nothing specified.	Direct OSHA to develop inspection and regulatory program and accident prevention program with Cooperative Extension.

Appendix A (*continued*)

	Food Security Act of 1985	Food, Agriculture, Conservation, and Trade Act of 1990	Cochrane/Runge
Migrant Farm Labor	Nothing specified.	Nothing specified.	Establish permanent working group and lead agency to coordinate programs and create centers in areas of migrant labor concentration which contain federal assistance programs.

Source: Information for the 1985 and 1990 farm bills from USDA. Cochrane/Runge information derived from Chapter 6.

Commodities Subject to U.S. Import Quotas and/or Tariffs in 1990

Commodities Subject to Tariff Rate/kg[a] (unless specified)			
Durum Wheat	.77¢	Buttermilk	.4¢/liter
Barley	.23–.34¢	Yogurt	20%
Corn[b]	.20–.98¢	Whey	.4¢–10%
Rice	.69¢–17.5%	Butter	12.3¢
Grain Sorghum	.88¢	Cheese	6–20%
Millet	.7¢	Eggs, in shell	3.5¢/doz
Wheat flour	1.1¢	Eggs, not in shell	12.1–59.5¢
Rye flour	.5¢	Sugar beets	88.2¢/ton
Corn flour	.66¢	Sugar cane	2.76¢/ton
Rice flour	.2¢	Cane and beet sugar	1.4606¢
Cereal grains (worked)	.1¢–10%	Other sugars	6–15%
Vegetable flour & meal	2.8¢–15%	Peanuts	6.6–9.35¢
Malt	.66¢	Tobacco	25.4¢–$6.45
Wheat gluten	4–8%	Wool[c]	5.5–28.7¢
Starches	.88–1.2¢	Cotton[d]	1.5–4.4¢
Linseed	.86¢	Lard	6.6¢
Rapeseed	.9¢	Tallow	.95¢
Cottonseed	.73¢	Cattle[e]	2.2¢
Soybean meal & flour	3%	Goats	$1.50/head
Hops	16.5¢	Poultry	2¢ each
Soybean oil	1.5–22.5%	Beef carcasses	4.4¢
Peanut oil	8.8¢	Processed beef	4–10%
Olive oil	5.7–8.4¢	Processed pork	2.2¢
Sunflower and safflower oil	2¢ + 4%	Lamb carcasses	1.1¢
Cottonseed oil	6.6¢	Lamb meat	1.1–3.3¢
Rapeseed oil	7.5¢	Poultry offal	11–18.7¢
Linseed oil	9.9¢	Leather	2.4¢–5%
Corn oil	4%	Vegetables[f]	.77–11.3¢ & 4.2–25%
Castor oil	3.3¢	Vegetables, dried[g]	.9–.11¢ & 5%–35
Sesame oil	1.5¢	Fruit[h]	.4¢–35%
Margarine	11¢–22.5%	Nuts[i]	1–37.5¢
Milk and cream	.4¢/liter–17.5%		

[a]Flat rates for a commodity range according to quality, as indicated for barley; rates also vary between flat and *ad valorem,* as indicated for rice.

[b]Does not include corn for seed.

[c]Does not include unimproved wool.

[d]Does not include cotton with staple length less than 28.575mm.

[e]Does not include pure breed breeding cattle or dairy cows.

[f]Does not include cowpeas, pigeon peas, or truffles.

[g]Does not include split peas, truffles, or cowpeas.

[h]Does not include bananas, fresh plantains, apples, pears, quinces, cherries, peaches, plums, or berries, except for strawberries.

[i]Does not include Brazil nuts, cashews, or chestnuts.

Source: U.S. Dept. of Commerce, Harmonized Tariff Code, 1989.

Appendix B (continued)

Commodities Subject to Quotas in 1990 Quantity Restricted in kg			
Milk and Cream	2,443,045	Animal feeds with milk	7,393,554
Dried milk	1,048,023	Peanuts	775,189
Butter and Sour Cream	864,999	Cotton	167,625,436
Cheese	111,227,205	Sugars, syrups and molasses	2.2¢/kg

Commodities with both Tariffs and Quotas in 1990			
Milk	Cream	Butter	Sour cream
Cheese	Peanuts	Cotton	Sugars
Syrups	Molasses		

References

AgWeek. 1991, April 1. "Nebraska Family Gets Caught in Farming Loopholes." P. 6.

Arizona Republic, The. 1991, April 7. "Farms Abuse Subsidies." P. A6.

Bailey, Kenneth W. 1989, December. "The Impact of the Food Security Act of 1985 on U.S. Wheat Exports." *Southern Journal of Agricultural Economics*. 21(2): 117–28.

Commission for the Improvement of the Federal Crop Insurance Program. 1989, July. *Recommendations and Findings to Improve the Federal Crop Insurance Program: Principal Report*. Washington, D.C.: U.S. Government Printing Office.

Coughlin, C. C. and K. C. Carraro. 1988. "The Dubious Success of Export Subsidies for Wheat." *Federal Reserve Bank of St. Louis, Review*. 70(6): 38–47.

Faeth, Paul, Robert Repetto, Kim Kroll, Qi Dai, and Glenn Helmers. 1991. *Paying the Farm Bill: U.S. Agricultural Policy and the Transition to Sustainable Agriculture*. Washington: World Resources Institute.

General Accounting Office. 1989a. *Disaster Assistance: Crop Insurance Can Provide Assistance More Effectively Than Other Programs*. 89-211. Washington, D.C.: GAO.

_____. 1989b. *Farm Programs: CRP Could be Less Costly and More Effective*. 90-13. Washington, D.C.: GAO.

Hammond, Jerome W. 1990, November 15. *Testimony for Hearings on Federal Milk Marketing Orders*, Irving, Texas. Department of Agricultural and Applied Economics: University of Minnesota.

Paarlberg, Robert L. 1990, Second Quarter. "The Mysterious Popularity of EEP." *Choices*.

Repetto, R., W. Magrath, M. Wells, C. Beer, and F. Rossini. 1989. *Wasting Assets: Natural Resources in the National Income Accounts*. Washington: World Resources Institute.

Taff, Steven J. and C. Ford Runge. 1988, First Quarter. "Wanted: A Leaner and Meaner CRP." *Choices.*

U.S. Department of Agriculture. 1990. *1991 Budget Summary.* Washington, D.C.: USDA.

U.S. Department of Agriculture/ERS. 1991. *Economic Indicators of the Farm Sector, National Financial Summary, 1989.* ECIFS 9-2, Washington, D.C.: USDA/ERS.

7 The Domestic Consequences of the Proposed Policy

Since the policy reforms set forth in the previous chapter are broadly conceived, reflecting a national agenda, people from many walks of life are affected. Too often writers of "policy analysis" talk only of programs and budgets, without mentioning the people who will be affected by them. Because people are the objects of policy reform, we believe they should also be its subjects. In this chapter, we consider the specific ways in which our proposals are likely to affect various groups of people.

As in any broadly conceived reform, different groups of people will be affected in different ways. Large commercial farmers are affected in certain ways, while smaller and part-time farmers are affected in other ways. Merchants along mainstreet and entrepreneurs looking for a favorable place to locate a plant in rural areas are likely to be affected by certain of our proposals, as unemployed rural youths and retirees living in poverty are affected by other features of those proposals. Timber companies and ranchers dependent upon grazing rights for their livestock in the national forests are affected by other parts of our program as are backpackers, hunters and bird-watchers. Food processing firms and their advertising affiliates are affected by still other program provisions, as are their customers, who will experience different effects if they are middle income consumers than if they are hungry people living in poverty. Directors of agricultural experiment stations and the researchers doing the work are affected by changes in research priorities, as are consumers of their research products—farmers, land use planners, food processors, nutritionists and medical practitioners. Bureaucrats in the Immigration Service and Occupational Safety and Health Administration (OHSA) are all affected in certain ways, as are poor, ignorant migrant laborers and part-time farm workers from the city. As we develop the domestic consequences of the policy reforms, we will try to bring the story to life by portrayals of how certain of those individuals are affected.

Commercial Farmers

In the last chapter we proposed a safety net for commercial farmers comprised of four parts:

1. An Income Stabilization Program.
2. A Grain Reserve Program.
3. An expanded Crop Insurance Program.
4. The continued use of Section 32 funds to purchase perishable commodities in times of market gluts.

The goal of this set of related programs—this safety net—is to protect commercial farmers from a sudden and unexpected drop in income due to a sharp decline in prices received by farmers relative to prices paid, or a partial or complete crop failure. In more general terms the goal of this set of related programs is the provision of a stable economic environment for farmers. Its purpose is not to provide a large and permanent subsidy for commercial farmers.

As we have stated elsewhere in this volume, commercial farmers in the United States have the natural resource base, the required transportation and marketing system and the research and extension support to enable them to compete successfully in the world market without a permanent income subsidy. But they do operate in a highly unstable industry in which uncertainty abounds. It is to assure greater stability, rather than a guaranteed income, that we proposed the safety net set forth in Chapter 6.

The operation of all four of these programs will require some expenditure of government funds, but not at levels approaching those of the 1980s. Payments to farmers under the Income Stabilization Program could in some years (especially in the transition to greater market orientation) run as high as $7 billion (total payments are capped at the $7 billion level). But because of the regional structure of the program we would expect payments to run below that maximum level even if the terms of trade generally are turning against farmers. And, of course, when the terms of trade are running in favor of farmers, no stabilization payments would be made.

The Grain Reserve Program would require a major appropriation of funds by the government in its initial phases. Such an appropriation would be necessary to provide it with the capital to acquire the grain reserve stocks to enable it to operate effectively in the world market. But since the operating goal of the Grain Reserve Program would be to smooth out world grain prices by eliminating temporary market gluts and shortages, the program, if managed conservatively, should not suffer losses over the long-run, as would be the case if it tried to hold day-to-day market prices above the long-run equilibrium price level. Stabilization programs get in trouble financially when they attempt to "stabilize" prices upward, not when they hold to a goal of smoothing out short-run market price gyrations around a concept of the long-run equilibrium price level.

There is one exception to the above conclusion. If the Congress asked the Grain Stabilization Corporation to act as its agent in making grain product donations to foreign nations experiencing food shortages or famine conditions, then the Congress should expect to repair the operating capital of the Grain Stabilization Corporation annually by the dollar amounts involved in the donations. Making donations of grain to poor nations experiencing crop shortages and/or famine would certainly be a logical function for the Grain Stabilization Corporation, but monetary losses attributable to such actions should not be charged against it as an operating loss.

The federal subsidy on the Crop Insurance Program should be expected to continue year after year, but the subsidy per insured farmer should decrease over time as experience is gained with an expanded program in which risks were pooled nation-wide. As of the late 1980s governmental subsidies ranged from $400 million in 1988 to $1.1 billion in 1990 under a limited program with the number of insured acres approximating 54 million in 1988. Under an expanded program total government costs should decline as crop risks are pooled, but rise as the number of insured acres increases.

Purchases of perishable commodities with Section 32 funds approximated $350 million in 1989 and 1990 (USDA 1990). It is reasonable to assume that purchases of perishable commodities for distribution under the various USDA food programs would continue in the 1990s at about that level. Thus, we gain some idea of what the budgetary obligations of the federal government would be under the proposed safety net for commercial farmers.

Offsetting the protection that producers would be receiving from the operation of the above four programs must be counted the loss of income that certain producers would sustain as a result of the elimination of the price and income support under the existing commodity programs. Producers of cotton, feed grains, rice, and wheat who had their incomes supplemented by substantial deficiency payments throughout most of the 1980s would no longer be the recipients of such payments. And dairymen whose incomes were supported by major dairy product purchase programs throughout the 1980s would no longer benefit from such programs. Thus, the incomes of producers of these products, could fall with the elimination of the traditional commodity programs and the initiation of the programs proposed in Chapter 6, *unless* certain developments occurred to counter those losses in income.

One such development might be an important increase in export demand. American farm policy is always seeking ways to expand exports, and the volume of exports depends to an important degree on events and conditions beyond the purview of this policy study (e.g., economic conditions in the importing countries, foreign exchange rates). But our policy proposals are certainly consistent with an expansion in the trade of agricultural products and would facilitate efforts in that direction by private traders and government trade negotiators. This would be the case, particularly, if our proposed policy reforms led to, or induced, trade liberalization policies in the EC and Japan. These and related ideas will be developed in the next chapter.

Another development might be the increased opportunity for producers of the program crops, such as cotton, corn, or wheat, to cut back their production of those crops under our proposed Income Stabilization Program and increase the net returns of their farming operations by diversifying into more profitable nonprogram crops. Increased flexibility in the planting of crops could result in higher yields, reduced costs and increased net returns.

In a report to the Oilseed Council of America, Abel, Daft, and Earley (1990) present a strong and convincing argument for increased flexibility in crop planting. They argue as follows:

> If farmers had genuine planting flexibility coupled with crop-neutral income protection, they could base their planting decisions solely on relative prices and the technical and management constraints under which each individual must operate, whether these be agronomic, financial, or environmental. But freedom to establish a rational cropping pattern is not provided under current policies, which have compelled farmers to plant target-price crops for the deficiency payments and base protection. . . .
>
> Policies that facilitate production flexibility would result in significantly lower production costs due to improved yields and lower input costs. Results from agronomic experiments in Iowa are fairly typical of Cornbelt experience and generally indicate that appropriate corn-soybean rotations increase corn yields by 5–15 percent, reduce fertilizer and chemical use, and reduce per bushel costs for corn by 30–40 cents. Benefits accrue to farmers in other regions of the country as well from better rotations that involve a more agronomically sound mix of soybeans and other oilseeds with target price crops—wheat, rice, feed grains, and cotton. The potential production cost savings are large and will improve both net farm income and U.S. competitiveness in world markets. For any equivalent package of program benefits, farmers could increase their net revenue by $1–2 billion if they had greater planting flexibility.

Still another development might involve changing over to a less intensive form of farming and increasing net family income in any one of several ways, or combination of ways: moving back into some form of livestock production; taking the sustainable agricultural production route with fewer purchased inputs; or working part-time off the farm. Some combination of these enterprise routes might reduce *gross* farm income but increase *net* family income. Increasing fertilizer and pesticide applications to maximize output may not be the way to increase net family returns in the future with or without the policy proposals of the authors.

The direct consequences of the policy proposals presented in Chapter 6 for commercial farmers are then the following. First, they would be operating in a far more stable and less risky industry than in a free market, but have almost all the flexibility, or freedom of operation, that a free market provides. Second, in a change from the existing commodity programs to the proposed programs of the authors, farmers in certain commodities such as cotton, dairy, feed grains and wheat could experience some diminution of income for a period of time. But our proposals are likely to compare favorably with proposed cuts by the administration and a coalition of urban representatives in the Congress bent on lowering the level of target prices and hence deficiency payments to producers of the program crops. Third, if, as it appears, the period of generous price and income subsidies to American farmers is winding down, could not commercial farmers more readily adjust their production, marketing and financial strategies in the flexible, yet stable, economic situation that we have proposed than in a situation of shrinking price and income supports under the traditional commodity programs? We believe the answer is definitely "yes." It is our position that when farmers must respond primarily to market conditions, rather than program benefits and constraints, they are best served by a stable economy in which resource adjustments are easily made. And that is the kind of farm economy which our set of proposals provides.

Certain friendly critics of our proposals from the commercial farm sector have suggested that our proposals might cause grain production in the United States to decline, because continued large subsidies are required to hold grain production at present levels. Without those subsidies producers would be required to cut back on purchased inputs such as fertilizers and pesticides and as a result production would fall.

We believe that this argument is fallacious for at least two reasons. First, we believe that government subsidies to commercial grain producers have been used primarily by those producers to expand their operations. In the process of bidding for additional land to expand their operations the subsidies have been capitalized into higher land prices. In other words, the continued subsidies to grain producers have not been necessary to maintain grain production at present levels, but rather have been capitalized into higher land prices in the competition for the scarce factor of production, land.

Second, any reduction in grain production resulting from a reduction in purchased inputs attributable to our program reforms would be more than offset by land brought back into production that had been withheld under various set-aside provisions of past commodity programs. In other words, the release of land for productive purposes from past production control schemes would more than offset any diminution in production resulting from a reduction in purchased inputs attributable to lost subsidy payments.

Consistent with our emphasis on people as the subject of policy analysis, we will consider the consequences of our policy reforms for the operators of three types of commercial farms: a huge cotton operation in the southern San Joaquin Valley of California, a large corn-soybean operation in the Central Corn Belt, and a medium-sized dairy operation in one of the Lake States. The business man operating the cotton farm, many thousands of acres in size, has in the late 1980s been the recipient of a wide range of government subsidies: price supports, deficiency payments, marketing loans, and irrigation water subsidies. If the deficiency payment and marketing loan subsidies for cotton were eliminated and the laws and regulations governing the distribution of government subsidized irrigation water were tightened and enforced, the income bonanza provided the operator of this great cotton farm by the federal government would be sharply reduced. If, further, environmentally approved regulations dealing with the application of chemical pesticides and fertilizers are instituted and the program changes recommended for dealing with migrant labor are put in place, we might expect to see some important changes in the size and organization of cotton farms in the lower San Joaquin.

Forced to operate without the benefit of major subsidies and within the bounds of approved environmental and labor practices, this huge cotton operation could well be broken up and sold off in units ranging from 160 to 640 acres in size, and be operated thereafter more in the mode of family farms. In this context there would be less reliance on hired, or migrant, labor, and more reliance on family labor; we might see custom harvesting enter the picture as has developed in wheat farming on the Great Plains; and we might see some fruit and vegetable farming substitute for cotton on these family sized units. We would expect to see operators of all units, large, small and in-between, looking to the agricultural college at the University of California at Davis, and to private firms for help in developing biological methods for controlling pests. Finally, with the certainty of target prices, price support loans and deficiency payments gone, we would expect to see operators of cotton farms spending a lot more time developing marketing strategies, and perhaps becoming much more active in organizing and operating successful marketing cooperatives.

Now let us consider a farmer operating a large corn-soybean farm in the central Corn Belt. Such a farm might be 1,200 acres in size and be operated by a father and son. In this case we would not expect that our policy reforms would have any consequence of importance for the size of farm. But we would expect that some important internal adjustment might result. With the elimination of the target price and deficiency payments for corn, and the institution of planting flexibility in the whole farm base, we would expect soybean production to increase at the expense of corn. And specialized crop farmers might once again think about developing a hog enterprise or a cattle operation to utilize some of the feed that they are producing. If located in Iowa or Illinois, this farmer would likely seek greater use of biological methods of pest control to substitute for toxic chemical ones, as regulatory restraints on the use of these chemicals increases. Perhaps most important, this farmer-businessman will have to spend much more time developing and executing marketing strategies. As a *quid pro quo*, he will spend much less time figuring out how to "farm the government."

The emphasis on management on these Corn Belt farms will shift away from choosing options under the government programs, to a whole series of business management decisions: choice of production enterprise, choice of production technologies, choice of kinds and amounts of purchased inputs, and choice of a marketing strategy. The large commercial corn-soybean farmer, to be successful under this restructured farm policy, will need to be a keen, astute business manager. But is this not what these farmers have always said that they wanted the chance to be?

The medium-sized dairy farmer in one of the Lake States, given our set of policy reforms, could well find himself operating in a expanding market. He, along with every other dairy farmer, would lose his support price for milk. But if the rules of the game were changed so that he could ship milk concentrates into southern and western markets where the price of fluid milk was no longer set at artificially high levels, then he could expect to expand his dairy operation. And with the price support programs no longer in operation for the feed grains, he could also expect feed grain prices to be favorable to an expansion of his dairy enterprise. Of course, this development does not represent pure joy for the dairy industry, since, unless there was expansion in the demand for fluid milk in the western and southern markets, milk production in those markets would have to decline. This dairy example illustrates how the location of agricultural production could change with a movement toward a market-oriented agriculture.

Part-Time Farmers

The largest group of farmers in American agriculture is part-time farmers. This is, however, a very heterogenous group. Virtually all that farmers in this group have in common is that their off-farm income exceeds their net income from farming. This explains in part why this group of farmers has received so little attention from the agricultural professionals and so little help from their government.

The farm production activities of part-time farmers in the United States range from the grains to citrus to cattle in the more traditional lines and from goats' milk to organic vegetables to wine-making in the more esoteric lines. The range of off-farm income producing activities of part-time farmers is even wider. It ranges from the skilled crafts such as carpentry and metal working to teaching, to truck driving, to real estate sales to county government employment. With such a diversity of interests both on and off the farm, it is next to impossible for part-time farmers in a county or a state to form an effective interest group to promote their welfare.

Once in a while a distinct group like the goat-milk producers in a state or region may be able to form an association or a cooperative to promote their interests; but this is the exceptional case. More often part-time farmers will tag along with the commodity association in which their production activity falls. But those associations are run by and for the large commercial farmers who pay little or no attention to the needs and interests of the smaller part-time farmers.

We have identified three groups of people in the part-time farming category that need some form of assistance: (1) urban dwellers who want to get into farming on a part-time basis; (2) under-employed "full time farmers" who are desirous of increasing their family income from some form of off-farm employment; and, (3) existing part-time farmers who wish to expand or improve their farming operation. The first group will require technical assistance (a) in choosing a farm production activity, (b) in developing that production activity once the production choice has been made, and (c) locating a market for their product. This first group may also require credit assistance, although urban dwellers who make the decision to go into some kind of farming will generally have access to the necessary financial resources.

The second group, the under-employed "full time farmers," probably will be thinking about staying with their existing production enterprise, not believing that they need technical assistance in production. In this they may be right; however, one reason that they are underemployed may be that their production methods are technologically inefficient. If so they will require technical assistance with regard to their farm production methods, and probably credit assistance to enable them to acquire and place in operation the needed improved technologies. But the greatest need of farmers in this group, probably for both husband and wife, would be for reliable information regarding off-farm employment opportunities, and in many, if not most, cases some form of job training to enable them to take advantage of those opportunities. A low-production, underemployed farm family, after all, cannot augment its income as a successful part-time farm family until some member of the family finds a productive, remunerative off-farm job.

The third group, the existing part-time farmers who want to expand, will almost certainly need credit assistance in some amount. Part-time farmers who seek to expand their farming operation, particularly in the more esoteric product lines, may also encounter marketing problems; thus, they may need assistance in developing a marketing strategy to deal with their expanded output.

To assist part-time farmers dealing with these many and diverse problems we have proposed the creation of a Part-Time Farming Agency to provide three principal forms of assistance. The first is assistance in obtaining credit. The second is the provision of technical production information. The third is the provision of relevant marketing information. We also proposed a Rural Development Agency (whose role will be discussed in greater detail in the next section), which could play an important role in helping low-production, underemployed farm families find remunerative off-farm jobs and convert their low-production operations into satisfactory part-time farming operations.

We believe that if the above agencies were adequately financed, in part from funds released from the elimination of the price and income support operations under the commodity programs, that there would be three important direct results for rural America. First, the number of part-time farms would stop declining in number and very possibly start increasing. Second, the total farm product of part-time farms in the United States would increase, and with it the farm income component of part-time farm family incomes. Third, the disposable income available to purchase farm supplies, household items, and family services in rural communities would be increased.

The indirect results of these developments in part-time farming would be equally important. We would expect the rate of population decline to slow down and possibly stabilize in rural communities where part-time farming became important both in terms of numbers and income generated. We would expect services such as health care and public education to improve in rural communities where part-time farming became important, as higher incomes and property values enhanced local tax bases. And we would expect the process of farm enlargement by already large commercial farms to slow down in rural communities where part-time farming became important. In sum, an expansion in part-time farming both in terms of numbers and output per farm should contribute to economic and social stability in rural areas.

Family life on a part-time farming operation is not easy. Nor will it become easy with the adoption of our proposed reforms. Let us consider the case of a family in which the husband works a regular day shift in a manufacturing plant in town and the family maintains a herd of about 75 beef cows on a farm of perhaps 100 acres in size. The husband will have to get up early in the morning to feed the cattle before he sets off to work in town, and then feed the cattle when he returns home at night. Assuming that part of the spread is cropland, the husband will need to work at night and/or weekends at both planting and harvest times. At calving time both husband and wife are likely to be up at night checking the condition of cows giving birth. The wife could have small children to care for, could help out with a garden (although farm gardens have gone out of style), could work at some part-time job, and most likely would keep the books, or accounts, on their farming enterprise.

The programs of the Part-Time Farming Agency could help this struggling family in numerous ways. It could help the family secure the credit to buy or rent a bull to improve the feeding efficiency, or meat producing quality, of their herd. It might also help the family purchase an additional 50 acres and thereby reduce their need to purchase feed for this herd. In conjunction with the Rural Development Agency, it might also assist them to expand the size of their house, and to modernize it, to meet the needs of their expanding family. Through these forms of assistance this part-time farming family would increase its income, raise its level of living, and become a more secure, stable part of the rural community.

The part-time farming family in which the wife works full time in town as a school teacher, or real estate agent, or secretary, represents a totally different situation. Suppose that this farming operation consists of 20 to 40 acres of fruit trees. In this case the husband will be heavily engaged on the fruit farm during peak periods of work—pruning and cultivating in the spring, perhaps spraying and irrigating in the summer, and picking fruit in the fall. During the quiet periods the husband, too, could work part-time off the farm. This family will encounter two critical problems in the fall: (1) where to find the labor to pick the fruit; and (2) where to market the fruit.

In some localities this family may belong to a fruit marketing cooperative which provides a solution to both of these problems. In other localities, particularly if the fruit growing enterprise is new, the family may experience extreme difficulty in arriving at a satisfactory solution to one or both of these problems. This is where the programs of the Part-Time Farming Agency could play an important role. This agency could work with some of the migrant labor agencies in locating the needed labor to pick the fruit. If this were a developing fruit growing region it could help this farmer and his neighbors organize a cooperative to both harvest the fruit and market it. Or it might advise this family on where and how to locate a road-side stand to sell their fruit. This part-time fruit farming case illustrates the various ways that an effective Part-Time Farming Agency could assist families with their production and marketing problems. With this kind of assistance, part-time farming, which is already important in terms of farm numbers, could become a prosperous and stable segment of rural America.

Rural Development

Rural development in America has been a difficult and halting process since farming ceased to be an expanding industry in terms of employment toward the end of the 1920s. It has proceeded most successfully in periods of rapid economic growth in the overall economy: in the 1940s and the 1970s, when the surplus rural population was readily absorbed into the urban work force. But even in those decades, pockets of poverty remained in rural areas composed largely of poorly educated adults, often in poor health and of a minority racial status (e.g., blacks, native Americans). And as we learned in Chapter 5, those people living in poverty in rural areas are, as of 1990, mostly nonfarm people; this has to be the case since 90 percent or more of the people now living in rural areas do not derive the majority of their income from farming. It is thus unrealistic to think about reaching and helping the great majority of the rural poor through the operation of the farm programs.

It has long been recognized that government programs with the goal of rooting out poverty in rural areas must have the capacity to reach out and assist poorly educated, poorly trained nonfarm people living in small towns and scattered across the countryside. But except in rare cases little has been done to help these people. We proposed in the last chapter the creation of a new Rural Development Agency with three principal functions. First, it would make small grants to families living in poverty to enable them to obtain job training, more and better education and home and business improvements; these grants would flow mainly to the nonfarm rural poor, since that is where most of the rural poor are to be found. Second, it would develop and operate an employment service in cooperation with the Extension Service and its many county extension offices. Third, it would make low-interest loans to counties, towns and villages for needed facilities such as water treatment plants, schools and medical clinics.

Our proposed new agencies—the Rural Development Agency and the Part-Time Farming Agency—would replace the Farmers Home Administration. We recommended that the Farmers Home Administration be abolished because its record in dealing with rural poverty has been so dismal over the years. The existing farm operating loan program would be transferred to the new Part-Time Farming Agency and the rural housing program would be transferred to the new Rural Development Agency. To deal effectively with the intractable rural poverty problem, we argued that these new agencies were needed with new leadership and with a new sense of purpose. *This new agency is going to require a greatly expanded budget.* The housing program which the RDA would inherit from Farmers Home Administration was operating at a program level of about $2.3 billion in fiscal 1990 (USDA 1990); it could make effective use of a budget twice that size. And the three poverty eradicating functions assigned to the new agency, which are largely ignored in the current programs of the Farmers Home Administration, would require major annual expenditures by the federal government. Eradicating poverty is a costly business. These funds are not likely to come purely from the "dividend" resulting from our reforms.

What would be the result of these poverty-eradicating programs for rural areas? If vigorously pursued over a ten-year period, and assuming the general economy does not slip into a major recession, they could greatly improve rural housing, significantly improve educational levels, provide job training for rural youth, help trained adults move to where the jobs are, and create jobs by creating incentives for light industries to move into communities with a literate labor force. The direct result of these developments would be increased real incomes for rural residents. The indirect result would be an improvement in the quality and availability of social services. And the expansion in part-time farming, as discussed in the previous section, would complement and buttress this development of rural areas.

Is this a dream? Yes, it is, but a dream that could be realized. There is an enormous pool of poorly educated, underemployed manpower in rural areas waiting to be brought into the mainstream of modern economic life. We have proposed a set of programs—really the social and physical infrastructure—to do just that. What we have proposed has been talked about since the middle 1950s. We argue that it should be done now—in the 1990s. And the costs, which are not minor, could be defrayed in part from savings from the reduced or eliminated traditional price and income support programs.

Related to these possibilities for improving family incomes and the quality of life in rural areas, are the contributions that would flow from the programs designed to improve worker safety and to protect and assist migrant farm workers proposed in Chapter 6. If the injuries due to machine accidents and the handling of toxic materials in farming operations were greatly reduced the quality of life in rural areas would obviously be much improved. And, if the slum conditions often associated with the labor camps of migrant farm workers, the undesirable conditions under which they work, the lack of educational opportunities for their children, and the poor state of health of many workers and their families were eradicated then obviously the quality of life in rural areas would be much improved. This, of course, is precisely what our proposals in Chapter 6 are intended to achieve. The rural development package cannot be considered complete until these latter programs are in place and operating effectively.

Many different kinds of people would feel the beneficial impact of these rural development programs. We will look at two very different types. Let us first consider a large family living in poverty in a run-down house in the country with a male head of household who earns a little income doing odd jobs, and with a teenage son who has dropped out of high school and is unemployed. If this were a typical rural family living in poverty, the family might also include a housewife and numerous smaller children. An effective rural development program could help this family in any one of several ways. First it could help the male head of household find a steady job perhaps working on the roads for the county, or perhaps working on a reforestation project in a nearby county, or perhaps driving a truck for a new plant opening in the community. Second, it could assist by making a small grant to the family to fix up the run-down house—perhaps putting a new roof on it, or perhaps adding a needed bedroom. Third, it could give a training grant to the teenage son to enable him to attend a trade school in a nearby city at which he would complete his high school work and learn a trade—perhaps become an auto mechanic, or perhaps learn to be an electrician. This son might return to the rural community from which he came, if a suitable job opened up there, or he could become a part of the urban work force. As job creation expanded, and if child care facilities were created through rural development activities, the wife might also find part- or full-time employment.

Let us consider next a business representative of an industrial firm who is looking for a place to locate a plant making parts for heating and air-conditioning units. He is looking for a location with an adequate supply of labor which is literate but not necessarily trained in this specific kind of manufacturing work, a good county road system not too far removed from an interstate highway, a town with a good school system, a functioning hospital and at least one medical doctor, preferably two or three. Finding such a community, the firm decides to locate a plant there, which provides

100 to 200 additional reasonably well-paying jobs to the community. This new payroll contributes to the volume of business on main street, enlarges the tax base of the community to support the school system and might provide the catalyst to change this town from a one- to a two-doctor town.

The rural development program could have played a determining role in this specific industrial development in any one of several ways. First, it could have helped the town construct an adequate, safe water system. Second, it could have helped the community build the local hospital which in turn induced the first doctor to remain in the town and the second to locate there. Third, the employment service operated by the Rural Development Agency could have provided the information about the potential, literate labor supply that convinced the representative of the industrial firm to locate a plant in that community. In sum, an effective rural development program could in many ways play an important, implementing role in bringing industrial development to a rural community.

There are also other beneficial effects of a strong rural development program. Both the part-time farming agency and the rural development agency will require staff in rural communities. And, if the small grants are used as we expect, there will likely be an increased need for instructors and other professional training specialists to locate in rural communities. These new jobs, funded from outside the local economy, will increase the local economic base. Those hired will also add to the underlying region's stock of human capital, helping to rebuild the leadership potential in communities which have suffered from continued out-migration.

The impact of the Cochrane-Runge program on Main Street cannot be determined simply be calculating the net change in local federal payments. Agricultural income, including commodity program payments, has a slightly smaller tendency to be respent in the local economy, reducing its multiplier impact on downtown merchants. A U.S. Senate study done in 1986 found that in the agriculturally dependent counties of southwestern Minnesota, for example, an increase in the commercial agricultural sector's income of $1,000 increased local spending on consumer goods and services by only $140, while an additional $1,000 in manufacturing income or transfer payments increased local spending by $190 (Stinson 1986). Thus, in appraising the consequences of the Cochrane-Runge proposals on rural communities there is evidence to suggest that the shifting of a like amount of federal expenditures from commodity programs to a rural development program would increase total spending in those communities.

The Environment

Many farm leaders and professional agriculturalists in government and out have tended to view environmentalists as belonging to the radical fringe of society. The senior author remembers the derision with which Rachel Carson's *Silent Spring* was greeted by most of the professionals in USDA in the early 1960s. The prevailing view among professional agriculturalists in the United States for the past 100 years has been: "It is our job to help farmers increase their yields per acre and output per worker and thereby become more efficient producers." There is nothing wrong with this view, so long as the product of these works is neutral with respect to other important aspects of the social and physical environment. But for the most part the impacts of their advice, or their technological improvements, on the physical environment were simply not considered. The physical resources of the nation were there to be exploited. So farmers, their professional advisors and citizens generally said, "We will exploit our abundant resources today with the means that we have; if these resources run out tomorrow, we will worry about it tomorrow."

There has been one important exception to the above mindset. Most farmers who have seen their top soil washing away, or blowing away, have decided that they must take action to stop it. Thus the Soil Conservation Service, working with individual farmers in soil conversation districts, has had considerable success in getting farmers to adopt soil conserving practices. And in recent years some farmers and some professional agriculturalists have begun to worry about the "water problem"—about contamination of groundwater, falling water levels, and the run-off of pollutants into lakes and streams.

But the agricultural community as a whole has been very slow to give serious thought to the important environmental issues of a modern industrial society, of which agriculture is very much a part. Commercial farmers and their leaders concerned with squeezing an additional bushel or two of corn or wheat per acre, or a pound or two of cotton, out of their land would rather not think about the great environmental issues of the day: the pollution of the land, water and air, the continued soil erosion in the United States and the horrendous soil erosion in the less developed world, the destruction of public forests and timberlands in the United States and with it the diversity of wildlife, the even greater destruction of forests in the less developed world, and the threat that global warming poses.

The greater urban community of the United States is not, however, oblivious to these environmental issues. Poll after poll indicates the deep concern of most Americans about these environmental issues. For example, a CBS News–*New York Times* poll in 1989 indicated that nearly 80 percent of the adult population of the nation agreed with, and only slightly over 20 percent disagreed with, the following statement: "Protecting the environment is so important that requirements and standards cannot be too high, and continuing environmental improvements must be made regardless of cost" (Hager 1990). Thus, we have argued that the USDA must arise from its deep sleep on these environmental issues as they relate to agriculture, and take the initiative in eight main areas. First, the Conservation Reserve Program should be expanded and improved. Second, an expanded wetlands program should be developed as a part of an enlarged CRP. Third, there should be a major effort to expand wilderness areas, national parks and the national forests of the nation. Fourth, there should be a general approach to advance greater biological diversity on public and private lands including specific programs to protect existing wildlife and to re-introduce species into areas that have been depleted through activities by man. Fifth, a special presidential/congressional commission should be established to study future water resources, water use, and pollution in the United States. Sixth, green belts and forest belts near urban areas should be established for the use and benefit of urban residents. Seventh, all agricultural chemicals and fertilizers currently in use should be the subject of renewed tests by the EPA to determine their effects on human health, worker safety, and the environment. Eighth, the Soil Conservation Service, the Forest Service, and probably a new environmentally oriented service, after an appropriate reorganization, should receive substantial increases in funding to carry out the seven initiatives outlined above.

The organizational structure and budget to carry out these initiatives will be the product of the task force recommended in Chapter 6. But it will be recalled that the task force membership will come partly from people within the USDA and partly from people outside the government, to study the environmental needs of the nation with respect to agriculture, to consider the seven initiatives that we propose, and then to make recommendations regarding needed areas of work, organizational structure and budget requirements. It would then be up to the Congress to direct the USDA to make such a study and see that its directives were carried out.

We can, however, comment on budget priorities, and sense of purpose in this environmental area. Some increase in budget will be required to support the expanded Conservation Reserve Program that we have proposed, and a major increase will be required, either through the CRP or some other environmental program in the USDA, to underwrite a significant increase in the wetlands of the United States. An expansion in the number of national parks and wilderness areas by the Departments of Interior and Agriculture out of existing public lands should be possible with relatively small budget increases. What is required here is the will to create these new parks and wilderness areas, and that must come from the president and the Congress. The creation of new, additional national forests from private or state lands, and green belts around large metropolitan areas will be a very costly business. Government expenditures to support this initiative could run into the billions of dollars. Such initiatives will require presidential leadership of the highest kind.

Getting the Forest Service to shift its priorities away from a primary emphasis on timber production to a much greater emphasis on protection of the forest environment will not cost government dollars, in fact it might save money, but it will require strong directives from the Congress. The concept of using the forest resources of the nation primarily to help protect the atmosphere, for watershed protection, for wildlife habitat and for recreation rather than to produce timber and provide grazing for sheep and cattle comes hard for the Forest Service.

In terms of government expenditures, the budget requirements for the joint presidential/congressional commission to study future water resources, water use, and water pollution would be minimal. But the program recommendations of that commission for protecting and managing the water resources of the nation in the future could involve costs running into the billions.

The budgetary requirements of a new agency in the USDA concerned primarily with protecting and improving the quality of the rural environment will depend upon the tasks assigned to it. If it is to be primarily a monitoring, research and extension type agency then its budgetary requirements would not be great. But if it were given the responsibility for increasing significantly the wetlands area in the United States, for planning and developing important greenbelts and parks near metropolitan areas and the development and management of new habitats for wildlife on both public and private lands, then the budget requirement for such an agency could again run into the billions of dollars.

What this discussion makes clear is that a serious commitment to the protection of the physical environment in rural areas, and to an improvement in its quality, will involve substantial costs to the government, part of which can be defrayed from savings effected through the reduction in, or the elimination of, the price and income support programs for commercial agriculture. But these costs cannot be incurred, nor can the priorities of the Forest Service be turned around and a new environmental action agency be put in place, until the American people instruct their elected representatives in Congress to direct the USDA to take these actions. An important environmental initiative will not come out of an agency that for 100 years or more has been concerned almost exclusively with the production needs of commercial farmers. The people must speak and direct the president and the Congress to give the USDA a new set of environmental priorities.

In the environmental area the people who could be affected by our proposals are countless. We will consider three widely differing situations and the people involved in each of those situations. First let us consider a situation somewhere in the agricultural heartland of the nation where the cultivated lands in the area drain into a stream which in turn flows into a string of lakes. At one time they were good fishing lakes, and a nearby small town drew its water supply from one of these lakes. But with heavy applications of nitrogen fertilizer and toxic chemical pesticides on the farmlands in the drainage system, the run off into the streams and lakes has so polluted them that game fish can no longer survive, and the water has become unsafe to drink, with the result that the town has had to drill a deep well to obtain a clean, safe supply of water.

With the proper control and management of rates of chemical nitrogen applications on these lands, and a partial shift from chemical methods of pest control to biological methods, the pollution of this drainage system could be reversed, the lakes be brought back to life, game fish re-introduced with a good chance of survival, and the water made safe to drink again. But this could only be achieved with a shift away from the current practice of heavy applications of chemical fertilizer and toxic pesticides—perhaps in the direction of low input agriculture, perhaps in the direction of greater use of biological controls, perhaps with lighter applications of chemical products applied so as to minimize the run-off problem. These are the directions in which our environmental programs should induce farmers to move. Both research and extension institutions should assist farmers in making these moves.

Let us consider next back-packers from some urban area in search of pristine wilderness in which to hike, camp, fish, watch the birds and take pictures of wild things. They may be seeking this adventure in the Allegheny Mountains of the East, or in the High Country of the Rocky Mountain West, or in the wilds of Alaska. But to achieve this adventure they must have a government and a set of agencies in the Departments of Agriculture and Interior that believe the public domain exists for more than timber harvesting, sheep grazing and the pumping of oil. The public domain also exists for these back-packers. But more importantly, it now must exist to help protect the biological diversity of this planet. The trees, the plants, the flowers, the fish and the wild animals that our back-packers want to observe in the wilderness need to be protected and preserved, in their own right, and most of them can only be protected and preserved in a wild or wilderness environment. Thus a major thrust of our environmental proposals involves an expansion in wilderness areas, national forests, national parks, as well as less pristine but still important greenbelts and parks near major population centers.

The third situation involves timber harvesting on the national forests somewhere in the Pacific Northwest. The Forest Service in recent years has taken the view that these forests exist primarily for the amount of saw lumber which they can produce, and to produce that lumber most efficiently the nation should pursue a policy of clear-cutting those forest lands. The timber companies and the loggers who operate, work and live in those areas hold the view that the timber is there to be cut and they have the "right" to harvest it. But the Forest Service, the timber companies and the loggers are wrong. Those lands and forests on them belong to all the people of the nation, as well as all those still to be born. Further, those forests serve many purposes besides timber harvesting—watershed protection, habitat for wild birds, fish, animals and plants, recreational places for citizens of the United States from Seattle to New York City, and now perhaps protection from global warming. Thus, the Forest Service can no longer take the view that selling lumber and logs to Japan to make card-board cartons and plywood should take precedence over providing a habitat for brown bears, spotted owls, and certain rare plants. And the loggers can no longer argue that, because "we live where we do," and know how to cut down trees, we should be allowed to keep cutting down trees as long as there are any left standing. The rights of the national society take precedence over the sale of lumber or logs to Japan, or the timber harvesting jobs of a relatively few loggers who happen to live near the great forest of the Pacific Northwest. We would be quick to add that, if our environmental proposals should be successful in slowing down or stopping timber harvesting operations in certain important areas of the Pacific Northwest, our proposals in rural development should provide these displaced loggers and mill workers with assistance in job training and in locating productive jobs in different industrial or service pursuits. It is not our purpose to discriminate against timber companies and loggers; it is our purpose to protect and preserve a valuable national resource and to diversify the rural economic base.

Consumers of Food

The diets of most Americans are relatively good—relative to other peoples' around the world and to the current state of nutritional knowledge. Outright starvation in the United States is rare, and malnutrition where it exists is at least as much a function of nutritional ignorance as of conditions of poverty. This reasonably good state of institutional affairs is the result of several factors. First, food is plentiful in the United States and its price is low relative to average per capita incomes. Second, information regarding good nutritional practices is widespread among a population that is reasonably literate. Third, the food programs operated by the federal government designed to reach the poor and downtrodden in the national society have been reasonably successful, but could be improved.

It is important to note that the policy reforms proposed by the authors reinforce the conditions outlined above. Our proposals for the commercial farm sector should result in plentiful supplies at stable prices. And we recommend a continuance of the existing food programs, with the only caveat that they should be monitored carefully to insure that they are achieving their stated objectives.

Nonetheless there are some gaps in the food and nutrition programs of the federal government. We would mention three. First, the existing food programs have failed in large measure to reach the homeless whose needs are great, but who may not fit into traditional welfare programs as well as certain vulnerable groups of people who cannot make their needs known: children of the very poor and some of the aged. Second, food safety provisions involving research, inspection and regulation are conceived and administered on a hit-or-miss basis in the United States. Third, foreign food assistance is driven in far too many instances by the surplus disposal needs of the nation rather than by the food needs of hungry and malnourished people in foreign lands.

Our proposals in Chapter 6 deal with each of the food problem areas noted above. We hope that a growing public opinion in the United States will support the development of programs designed to meet the food needs of the homeless. Reaching the children of the very poor and the non-institutionalized aged will be exceedingly difficult. We further hope that the growing demands of an aware consuming population for an unadulterated, healthy, safe supply of food will result in a major overhaul of our food safety laws and programs as recommended in Chapter 6. Our proposal that foreign food assistance be conducted primarily through international organizations and private charitable groups could run into difficulty. The pressure to dispose of surplus farm products in far away lands becomes intense at times, and many Americans and their congressional representatives love to see sacks of grain being unloaded in an African or Asian port stamped with the words "A Gift from the People of the United States." But we have made progress over the years in matching the food surpluses of the United States with the legitimate food needs of hungry people abroad. Our programs have become more sophisticated and have made increasing use of international organizations and private charitable groups with expertise in reaching the truly hungry in distant, inaccessible locations.

The food programs of the U.S. Department of Agriculture, as we have noted, have a good overall record for reaching the poor and vulnerable groups in society in need of food assistance. But they could be improved with respect to three groups of people: pre-school children in low income families, children who come to school in the morning either hungry or with nutritionally inadequate breakfasts, and the homeless who eat on a hit-or-miss basis and sometimes do not eat at all. In March of 1990, the Food Research and Action Center, a nonprofit group, reported that of a sample of 2,335 low income households, one in eight contained children under 12 who experienced food shortages. When extrapolated to the country as a whole, this represents 5.5 million children under 12. These households did not include children or adults who were homeless. Even the Women, Infants and Children (WIC) program, largely regarded as quite successful, is estimated to serve only 45 to 55 percent of those eligible for it. And the study found that among those interviewed, almost one-third of those participating in the WIC program said they were hungry (*New York Times* 1991).

In both middle income families as well as poor families, the morning rush to get to school on time often leaves children with inadequate breakfasts in terms of both quality and quantity. The serving of a breakfast snack, available for all students, comprised of fruit juice, a nutritious roll with an appetizing spread, and a serving of milk would go a long way toward dealing with this ubiquitous modern American nutritional deficiency. For students from very poor families, an even more adequate breakfast and school lunch should be made available.

The homeless, as the name implies, have two major problems: finding a clean, safe place to sleep, and finding three nutritious and appetizing meals each day. Common sense would suggest that the U.S. Department of Agriculture merge its budget for feeding the homeless with the budget of the Department of Housing for providing shelter to assist local agencies like the Salvation Army or the United Way to renovate buildings in cities to provide hostels for the homeless where they might find food and shelter. Such hostels would include dormitories for sleeping, washrooms and showers and kitchen and eating facilities as well as budgets to pay for rent, lights and heating, bedding and food supplies. By combining the budgets of these two departments to create hostels for the homeless the nation could begin to treat them in a civilized manner.

The average American consumer has a food problem too. What foods are safe to eat, and who can he or she trust to provide that information? Private labelling is a mess, and most advertising is not nutritionally informative. And government activity with respect to food safety is very uneven—very good in some areas, very poor in others, timely with respect to some things, late or nonexistent in others.

The proposals made in Chapter 6, if implemented, should help to correct this situation. The determination of the safety of all foods would be made by the appropriate governmental agency, and the responsibility of each agency for inspection, regulation, research and information would be established. There still remains the question: How is the average consumer to be apprised of this food safety information? We suggest that those persons in government with responsibility in the area of food safety will need to pay attention to two consumer related questions: (1) how better to reach consumers with the relevant information, and (2) how to win their trust, which to an important degree is lacking in the early 1990s. The first question can be dealt with through improved regulations governing product labelling and the establishment of a recognized and consistent method of issuing food safety information. The second question will then be dealt with over time, *if* the above processes turn out to be informative, timely and reliable.

Research and Education

An expanded, improved and more effective research establishment is absolutely essential to the success of our package of farm policy reforms. This is true for a number of reasons. First, for an unsubsidized commercial agriculture to compete successfully in the world market, it must be a highly productive agriculture. A favorable climate and bountiful physical resources are still important in this connection, but a highly productive agriculture in modern times must be the beneficiary of the most improved production practices and technologies, which only a first-class research establishment can provide. Thus, the future of an unsubsidized commercial agriculture in the United States will depend largely on the quality and productivity of its research establishment.

Second, if commercial farming in the United States is to remain competitive in the world market, and at the same time stop polluting ground and surface waters, using chemicals in ways that are injurious to farm workers, wildlife, and the atmosphere and applying chemicals to farm products that can possibly injure consumers, then a whole new wave of research must be undertaken that produces a set of production and marketing practices that can be substituted economically for the above mentioned injurious practices. For the research effort in this direction to be effective, two important things must happen: (1) there must be a substantial infusion of funds that is specifically ear-marked for this kind of research; and (2) there must be a growing awareness in the agricultural research community that this kind of research is important. It is doubtful that commercial agriculture in the United States can achieve the level of productivity that is required for it to be competitive in the world market, *if* a way cannot be found for it to substitute benign production practices for its present dependence on injurious ones. This is the case, because the American public will not tolerate the continued poisoning of its land, water and air.

Third, the development and implementation of programs with the capacity to make rural America prosper and become a healthy, pleasant place in which to live is going to require new and additional data and information, some creative thinking based on correct and relevant knowledge of economic and social conditions in rural areas, and a fund of objective research that focuses on the effectiveness of various institutions and governmental programs in the development process. Some of this information, knowledge and research is currently available. But more is needed, particularly more that is relevant to the development process. This information, this knowledge and this research will be forthcoming, we are convinced, if: (1) funding for this kind of work is increased, and (2) social scientists and educators in this area come to believe that there is market for their work—that their research products will be used. Social scientists have long known of the need for work in this area, and have, on limited budgets, done some good work. But they have also known that program support for rural development has in most years been minimal to nonexistent. Most of what they have received from Washington, D.C., is rhetoric.

Will the needed research products be forthcoming in the three critical areas described above, if funding support in these areas is increased substantially? We are convinced that the answer to this question is, yes. Our answer is based on some hard knowledge. First, we have a good research establishment in place in the United States comprised of (1) the USDA component, (2) the land grant universities and their experiment stations component, (3) numerous nonprofit institutions (e.g., private universities and endowed research institutes) engaged in research related to food and agriculture), and (4) commercial enterprises engaged in research related to food and agriculture. This research establishment is not perfect; there is much duplication of work and some recognized areas of weakness—notably in basic science and environmental innovation. But it is probably better in total than that of any other nation. And it is in place and functioning.

Second, we have a cadre of excellent basic scientists, agricultural scientists and social scientists who have either worked directly in the areas under consideration or in related areas. These men and women have for a long time worked within the confines of stagnant to declining budgets. Hence their work has not, on balance, been as productive as it could have been. With an expansion in their research budgets, however, they would quickly move into new and promising areas of research. They would also begin training new research workers to expand their areas of work.

In sum, we have a research establishment with a long tradition of work in agriculture. We also have in place the trained research personnel to manage and conduct new and promising research projects, once the money is there to support them. So we are convinced that we have a research establishment in the United States with the capacity to support a commercial agriculture that is both competitive in world markets and less dependent on toxic, injurious production practices, and with the capacity to undergird a major effort to convert rural America into a prosperous community with the social amenities demanded by prosperous Americans.

A successful research effort along the lines described above would have beneficial impacts on many different people in many different ways. The commercial farmer looking for ways to lower his unit costs of production would find them in the new and improved technologies emanating from the various research stations across the nation. The part-time farmer looking for more effective ways to market his specialty crops could benefit from marketing studies that focused on the problems of small volume enterprises. People worried about pollution of the environment would find hope in new biological techniques developed to control pests which could be substituted for toxic chemicals. Local community leaders seeking to attract new industries to their area could gain valuable knowledge about what it takes in the way of infrastructure to entice new industries into an essentially rural community. Food processors would be the beneficiaries of new and improved technologies that would reduce their unit costs of processing and yield products with greater consumer appeal. Consumers would gain knowledge about the nutritional content of different foods, and thus be able to choose a diet that promotes good health. People who work with animals, and consumers of animal products, would benefit from measures designed to control animal diseases. Citizens and political leaders would, on the basis of social science research, come to better understand the costs and benefits of different government programs for the farm and rural sectors, hence make more wise political decisions. In short, the economic and social welfare of people in almost every walk of life in modern America is dependent upon an effective and productive research and development system that focusses on the food, farm and rural areas.

The National Interest

Professor Daniel Bromley of the University of Wisconsin, in a 1989 lecture argued as follows:

> Between 1980 and 1988 the federal government provided $24 billion of assistance to rural areas. During this same period *direct* cash payments to farmers totaled $75 billion, with the overall costs of the farm programs totaling more than $115 billion. . . . In 1980 the rural unemployment rate was only 7 percent above the rate in urban areas, but by 1986 it was 40 percent higher than the urban rate of unemployment. Today, it remains approximately 15 percent above the unemployment rate in urban areas. . . .[1]
>
> The myth persists that agricultural (or farm) policy is rural policy—and that is an insult to the intelligence of rural people who know better. Indeed, some suggest that there are really four myths dominating agricultural policy. The first myth is that rural areas are depressed economically because the agriculture and natural resource sectors are depressed. The second myth is that a strong rural development policy follows automatically from a strong farm policy. Thirdly, there is the myth that rural economies benefit from low-cost unskilled labor. Finally, there is the myth that public services are cheaper in rural areas than they are in urban areas. These myths persist because they serve the interests of those who drive farm policy, and who benefit from channeling federal budgetary largess through farmers as opposed to other means of assisting rural America.
>
> I suggest that these myths—and the problems they disguise—will not be confronted until we adopt an explicit process whose purpose it would be to craft a coherent domestic economic policy, of which rural policy must be an integral part.

This entire volume supports Bromley's argument. We have tried in Chapter 6 to craft a set of policy reforms which do, in fact, constitute a positive rural policy as a integral part of a domestic economic policy for America. Our policy proposals will, we believe, create an economic and social milieu in which: (1) commercial farmers can prosper and compete in the world market without continued larger subsidies; (2) part-time farmers can thrive, become more productive and become an important part of rural America; (3) soil and water resources will be protected from pollution and degradation; (4) nonfarm people living in poverty will gain new skills and become productive citizens; (5) the farming industry will be made a safer place in which to work, and migrant farm workers will be guaranteed their legal and economic rights; (6) new industries will be attracted to rural areas providing new job opportunities and increased real incomes; (7) consumers will be assured of a plentiful, safe, healthful food supply at reasonable prices, and vulnerable groups in society will be protected by specific food programs designed to meet their needs; and (8) Americans will be attracted to the increased recreational possibilities ranging from wilderness areas, to an expanded and improved national park system, to a greatly expanded system of greenbelts, parks and outdoor activities located near metropolitan areas.

But more is involved than these specific initiatives. The increased number of jobs and the increased incomes of rural residents that flow from the initiatives enumerated above should have some important secondary effects. The out-migration of people from rural areas should be slowed, and in time be reversed. The hemorrhaging of small towns in America should be stopped. With these developments and a widespread increase in real incomes, social services should improve: health services, educational programs, and services of all kinds (food stores and restaurants, plumbing and electrical services, farm machinery and auto repair, and farm input and marketing services) in small towns should stop their decline, turn around and begin to improve both in terms of quality and quantity. In this improved economic and social setting small towns once again should become good places in which to live. As a result people in both urban and rural areas would begin to think about living in small towns in retirement, as a place to raise children, and as a good alternative to crowded crime-ridden large metropolitan areas. Small towns once again could become viable community centers.

We do not suggest that all this comes free, or without cost. But we do suggest that some of the money costs to the federal government could be met from monies saved from the elimination of the existing price and income support programs. We recognize further that the incomes of commercial farmers could for a period of time fall by the amount of the lost income subsidy, and in turn, land values for the commodities most affected could fall. Asset values capitalized to artificial levels from the receipt of income subsidies from the government must of course decline when the income subsidy is removed.

The money costs of our rural policy for America, we argue, are manageable, if the savings effected from the elimination of the existing, costly price and income support programs are used to supplement funds for our policy proposals for rural America. The future of our policy proposals thus rests to an important degree on the willingness of the president working with the Congress to greatly reduce or eliminate the continuing income subsidy to commercial farmers.

The politics of our policy reforms will be discussed in a later chapter, but here we wish to make two important points with respect to commercial farming in the United States. First, our proposals do not leave commercial farmers in an exposed, naked position in the world market. Our proposals provide commercial farmers with a safety net to protect them from any sharp deterioration in the terms of trade and from severe adverse crop growing conditions, if they wish to avail themselves of those protective measures. Second, commercial farmers in the United States are blessed and supported by a favorable climate, bountiful physical resources, an excellent marketing and distribution system, a strong research and educational system which we propose to make even stronger, and a credit system that has been tailored to their needs. In this favorable economic and physical environment, and with the safety net that our proposals provide, there is no reason why good businessmen, which modern commercial farmers must be, cannot survive and prosper.

The rural America that we foresee in the future, if it is to prosper, has numerous components: a prosperous commercial farm sector, a viable part-time farming sector, light industries of all kinds, forests, wildlife, parks and outdoor activities of all kinds, high quality health care, educational and governmental services, and small towns with a full complement of the service trades and distributive outlets. A rural policy as a part of a total domestic policy must recognize the importance of each of these components and be supportive of all of them—not just one component, commercial farming. These components complement one another, and interact to build a prosperous whole—a rural America in which people, once again, will want to live.

Notes

1. All of the data in this paragraph can be found in Deavers 1989. If the unemployment percentages seem strange, note that they are *ratios* of rural to urban unemployment.

References

Abel, Daft and Earley. 1990, January. *The Case for Planting Flexibility: An Oilseed Perspective*. Prepared for the Oilseed Council of America.

Bromley, Daniel. 1989, November 18. Lecture: "Is There a Coherent Rural Policy Environment in the United States?" The Luther Pickrel Agricultural Policy Seminar. Minneapolis, Minnesota.

Deavers, Kenneth L. 1989, Second Quarter. "Rural America: Lagging Growth and High Poverty—Do We Care?" *Choices*.

Hager, George. 1990, January. "The 'White House Effect' Opens a Long- Locked Political Door." *Congressional Quarterly Weekly Report*. 48(3): 139–44.

New York Times. 1991, March 27. "5.5 Million Children in U.S. Are Hungry, a Study Finds." P. A-12.

Stinson, Thomas. 1986. *Governing the Heartland: Can Rural Governments Survive the Farm Crisis?* Report of the Subcommittee on Intergovernmental Relations of the Committee on Governmental Affairs, U.S. Senate. Washington, D.C.: U.S. Government Printing Office.

U.S. Department of Agriculture. 1990. *1991 Budget Summary*. Washington, D.C.: USDA.

8 The International Consequences of the Proposed Policy

The policy reforms we have outlined were developed with explicit attention to the international competitive environment in which U.S. agriculture increasingly operates. This trade dependency, discussed in Chapter 3, has increased in the post–World War II period with each passing year. Today, U.S. agriculture is heavily reliant on foreign demand to support U.S. farm incomes, especially in the grains and oilseed sectors (see Runge and Halbach 1990). Other sectors, such as U.S. sugar, peanut, tobacco, wool, and dairy production, have been protected from international competition through trade barriers. These barriers include quotas, tariffs, and other restraints which shield producers from competition in foreign markets.

In this chapter, we consider the implications of the policy reforms developed in Chapter 6 for the international competitive position of these various agricultural sectors. Four main elements of our policy reforms will have important effects on this international competitive posture. First, our reform of domestic price and income supports will have the overall effect of opening much of U.S. agriculture to the world market by reducing the protective shield provided by current price and income support programs. It bears emphasis that the combined safety net program proposed for the grains, cotton and rice, as well as for oilseeds and dairy, in which income is stabilized through payments geared to an index of farm prices paid and received, is also accompanied by an insurance scheme and government stabilization purchases, so that U.S. producers are not thrown into a merciless free market. Yet by freeing base acreage over time so that a wider variety of crops can be grown, and by eliminating direct support of agricultural prices in favor of a safety net targeted to income stability, the consequence of our policy reforms would be to allow world prices to dictate planting and marketing decisions to a much greater extent. And by eliminating production controls (except for environmental set-asides and one-year emergency diversions) the productive capacity of American agriculture would be fully harnessed to compete in foreign markets, rather than hobbled by efforts to brake U.S. production.

In the past, the United States has used its production control programs to reduce output when world markets were glutted, and to increase output when they were in short supply. This has made it "stock manager" to the world, and has opened U.S. producers to greater levels of instability in farm prices and incomes than anywhere else in the developed world. While we propose to retain a stock management scheme of direct government sales and purchases, the Cochrane-Runge plan removes the government from telling farmers what they cannot grow, and eliminates artificial price incentives that tell farmers how to reap the highest subsidies. By allowing the acreage planted to respond to market conditions, we expect farmers to market *more* crops. The only restrictions on planted acreage would be those based on the vulnerability of some land to environmental damages. If the secretary of agriculture opts for one year diversions in the face of huge surpluses, they will go unpaid, relying instead on market prices to rise.

A second major component of our reforms relates specifically to the border measures which now shield the sugar, peanut, tobacco, wool, beef, and dairy sectors, and the export subsidies used to dispose of U.S. surpluses. As argued in Chapter 6, border measures barring other countries from gaining import access to U.S. markets should be converted from the current panoply of quotas and nontariff barriers to an equivalent system of tariffs for all agricultural products. We would then reduce these tariffs by 25 percent in reference to world market prices over a period of five years. Subsequent reductions would require multilateral negotiations.

The reasoning behind this trade reform is two-fold. First, it is in the general interest of American agriculture, the American consumer, and especially poor countries seeking markets in North America, to lower U.S. trade barriers *whether or not* other countries follow suit (Paarlberg 1988). These trade barriers have protected inefficient producers in the United States and denied market access to poor farmers in other countries. However, we reason that the United States should use this 25 percent reduction to gain leverage on our trading partners, pushing them to make trade reform a multilateral process. While the benefits of more open trade are almost always in favor of large trading economies like the United States, these benefits are magnified when other countries follow suit.

Again, we emphasize that such a conversion would not mean a surrender of the shield offered by these measures, but would change its form from quotas to tariffs, allowing negotiated reductions in the level of tariff protection over time in tandem with other nations. After a 25 percent reduction, further reductions would occur in both bilateral and multilateral contexts, specifically under the follow-up to the Uruguay Round of multilateral trade negotiations of the General Agreement on Tariffs and

Trade (GATT). Export subsidies, whether direct (as under the Export Enhancement Program) or indirect (such as marketing loans for U.S. cotton, rice, and soybeans), would be eliminated.

A third element in our reforms involves U.S. development assistance policy, such as the Food for Peace program, which affects market conditions in recipient countries. Because these programs have operated as a vent for U.S. surpluses directed to strategically favored countries, rather than as targeted programs of support to poorer nations, they have failed to achieve many of their stated objectives. By focusing food aid where it is most needed, and cooperating more fully with multilateral aid agencies, U.S. assistance could do far more good for the foreign poor, and far less damage as a disincentive to production for foreign farmers. Ultimately, such assistance can quicken the rate of economic growth in poorer nations, leading to higher levels of demand for commercial U.S. exports. Such successful market development was, in fact, one of the major motivations behind the original Food for Peace programs.

By working closely with the World Bank, the Food and Agriculture Organization (FAO) of the U.N., and private voluntary agencies such as CARE, the United States can focus this food aid where it is truly needed. In this way, it can serve to "prime the pump" of increased economic activity in poor countries, leading them to become better *paying* customers for U.S. exports (both agricultural and manufacturing) over time. This would be in marked contrast with current policies, in which surpluses are often dumped for political reasons into countries (such as Egypt), depressing local prices and actually *lowering* the level of hard currency purchases from U.S. farmers in the long run.

A fourth element of our policy reforms with implications for international trade is the reserve program proposed to stabilize prices in times of extreme shortage or surplus. In Chapter 6, we gave special emphasis to the fact that the objective of this program will be to stabilize prices at long-run world market levels, not at some higher level for domestic producers. By maintaining reserve stocks, the U.S. government can contribute to a more stable international regime of prices, simply because our agricultural production continues to loom so large on world markets.

Even though more open international trade in agriculture will tend to stabilize world prices, as surpluses and shortfalls in various parts of the world are allowed more readily to offset each other, there may still be weather events or political crises that call for stabilization exercises. We doubt that the international trading system could maintain a free-standing grain reserve. But as one of the world's largest exporters, the United States is in a position to help at the margin to alleviate panic buying or selling when serious shortfalls or surpluses occur, through direct sales and purchases of grains and oilseeds.

Overall, the objective of these four elements of policy is not "free trade." We believe that free trade is primarily a textbook concept, of minor academic interest to real world farmers, traders, and policymakers. We do not have free trade in agriculture today, have not had it in the recent past, and will probably never see it in the future. Yet, we believe that by opening U.S. agriculture to world market conditions, reducing barriers to import access, eliminating export subsidies, and lessening distortions and instabilities caused by U.S. development assistance and reserve policies, our reforms can help to generate a more favorable climate of both domestic and international commerce. In this sense, ours is a classically "liberal" trade policy. Moving multilaterally to a more open global trading environment will expand global agricultural trade, but will not eliminate an income safety net in domestic U.S. agriculture. It will somewhat reduce the shield of border protection, but substantial reductions will only occur in tandem with other nations over time. It will not "unilaterally disarm" U.S. farmers in world markets. And it will strengthen the ability of farmers both at home and in poorer nations to respond to market conditions, increasing rates of economic growth and development.

This will be advantageous to most sectors of the U.S. economy, including U.S. agriculture. Especially in the coarse grains and oilseed sectors, which are export dependent and internationally competitive, gains in trade will result. At the same time, phased adjustments away from certain crops are likely in less competitive, highly protected sectors, such as sugar. However, producers of these protected commodities will not face wrenching, all-at-once economic changes. As we will show, such liberalization can proceed systematically and in tandem with other nations. In addition to the advantages to U.S. agricultural producers, our policy reforms will benefit U.S. consumers, by allowing lower cost producers access to U.S. markets over time.

In the sections of this chapter to follow, we will discuss in greater detail the specific ways in which our policy reforms will contribute to a more open international trading regime. First, we will focus on the impact of these policies on the institutional agenda for U.S. multilateral trade policies—in the GATT, the International Monetary Fund (IMF), the World Bank and U.N. agencies. Second, we will focus on the impacts of the changes on bilateral relationships with key trading groups: the European Community, Japan, the "Cairns Group," the poorer nations of the Third World, and the former USSR/Eastern Europe. Finally, we will examine a generally unexplored aspect of U.S. agricultural trade policy: the competitiveness implications of the environmental regulatory agenda we have set forth.

Multilateral Trade Policy Impacts

U.S. trade policy in agriculture occurs on three main fronts: multilateral, bilateral, and the "home front" with Congress.[1] The multilateral front of trade policy is represented by institutions to which the majority of trading nations belong. These institutions include the General Agreement on Tariffs and Trade (GATT), headquartered in Geneva, Switzerland, and a variety of other international bodies which were created, like GATT, in the wake of World War II in order to bring greater stability to global economic and political affairs. Besides GATT, the two other major multilateral institutions with responsibility for economic affairs are the International Monetary Fund (IMF) and the International Bank for Reconstruction and Development (IBRD) or World Bank, both headquartered in Washington, D.C. The IMF is responsible for coordinating monetary and exchange rate policies, and has increasingly served as a critic of the economic policies of developing countries. The IMF has imposed a variety of conditions on these countries in return for granting various forms of assistance. The World Bank has been the primary multilateral lending institution since World War II. Apart from these institutions are a variety of other multilateral groups, of which the most important in economic terms is the Organization for Economic Cooperation and Development (OECD), headquartered in Paris, and the United Nations (U.N.) agencies. The OECD is composed of the world's high income developed countries, including Western Europe, Japan, the United States, and Canada. It provides a forum for evaluation of economic and social policies, and has recently concentrated especially on the environmental consequences of agricultural policies. The key U.N. agencies affecting agriculture are the Food and Agriculture Organization (FAO), headquartered in Rome, together with the World Food Program, and the U.N. Development Agency (UNDP), headquartered in New York. All U.N. signatories participate in these agencies. FAO provides support and assistance projects to developing countries, and conducts policy analysis and some scientific work. It is also responsible for the "Codex Alimentarius," the international book of rules on the health and safety of food and alimentary products. The World Food Program and UNDP both focus on development assistance, especially in poor food-deficit countries.

This complex structure of institutions provides the basis for continuing discussion of global economic issues, supplemented by periodic economic summit meetings. At economic summits, discussions in places like GATT, the IMF, or OECD are elevated for a few days or weeks from the back corridors of governments to the front pages of the world's newspapers as presidents and prime ministers strike agreements to cooperate on one or another issue of the day. The majority of the work conducted by the international civil servants employed by these agencies is, however, seldom front page news, especially when it involves agriculture. Yet agricultural (and environmental) policy is of increasing significance to all of these institutions.

The GATT is the least known and most directly trade-oriented of the group, but has emerged as a center of discussion, and controversy, concerning the reform of agricultural policies. Founded in 1947, as a weaker form of what was originally to have been a full-fledged International Trade Organization (ITO), the GATT was created less than equal with the IMF and World Bank largely because of fears in the U.S. Congress that it would undermine congressional authority over U.S. trade policy (Jackson 1969, 1989). These fears are a continuing theme, to which we will return in Chapter 10. The GATT today is composed of over 100 nations (the "contracting parties"), who under the rules of the GATT Articles agree to regulate trade so as to reduce the overall level of protection. The essential features of the GATT articles are the reciprocal recognition of rights of access to foreign markets (embodied in "Most-Favored Nation" status), the nondiscriminatory treatment of other GATT nations' exports, and the removal of trade-distorting policies such as export subsidies and import barriers. One specific principle in GATT has been the substitution of tariffs for nontariff barriers, and the gradual reduction of these tariffs over time through agreements to "bind" tariffs on certain goods so that they will go no higher, and eventually to reduce them so as to increase market access to foreign producers.

These principles have been extended since 1947 to cover an ever-larger share of world trade, and are an important reason why this trade has expanded so rapidly in the postwar period. The GATT has conducted eight major rounds of trade negotiations since its inception, the most recent of which is the most important and ambitious, the "Uruguay Round." Named for Punta del Este, Uruguay, where the negotiating round began in late 1986, the Uruguay Round was the first to attempt to bring two major sectors of the world economy under the discipline of GATT rules. These sectors were trade in services and trade in agriculture. While agricultural trade has been a continuing and frustrating focus of the GATT talks, the 1986–90 Uruguay Round was the first time that a broad consensus was reached that agricultural policies around the world were badly in need of reform (see Runge 1988).

In July, 1987, the Reagan administration put forward a sweeping proposal calling on all of GATT's contracting parties to eliminate trade distorting agricultural policies including domestic price and income supports with trade-distorting effects. In their place, the United States proposed an income "safety net," that would protect farmers from wide swings in income levels. This was linked to a domestic reform proposal (discussed in Chapter 3) advocated by Senators Boren (D-OK) and Boschwitz (R-MN) which called for "decoupling" income support payments from specific crops, and paying farmers instead through direct income supplements that would decline over time.

The U.S. proposal in GATT was attacked by the European Community and Japan as "unrealistic," while the domestic decoupling proposal was characterized by U.S. opponents as "welfare." Yet, the impetus in both the United States and European Community has been to move toward substantial reductions in the level of payments to farmers, and toward forms of domestic "decoupling." The "0-92" and flexible base provisions of the 1985 and 1990 farm bills are clear evidence of this trend in the United States. In the EC, a plan introduced by the Irish agriculture minister, Ray MacSharry, in 1991 may well mark the beginning of decoupling in the European Community. The "MacSharry Plan" calls for reductions in farm payments except those paid directly (rather than through crop subsidies). It would reduce payments to the largest producers, and redirects them to smaller farmers and environmental set-asides. In these respects, it follows the proposals outlined in the Cochrane-Runge plan. Hence, while "decoupling" has proven untenable in the form proposed by Boren and Boschwitz, it has been achieved in piecemeal form in the 1990 farm bill, and appears to be the general trend in both the United States and EC.

In December, 1990, the Uruguay Round was nearly aborted when the United States and EC failed to come to terms over agricultural trade. The December meeting, in Brussels, was intended as the "final synthesis" of the Uruguay Round, but was scheduled before the MacSharry Plan had been introduced. In February, 1991, the GATT talks were restarted, and may not ultimately conclude until 1993.

We will not try to predict the final outcome of the restarted GATT negotiation in the agricultural area. But, if the end result is a world trading system for agricultural products that is more open than that in existence in 1992, then how might the pattern of trade be changed? We get a glimpse of how trade in agricultural products might change under a more open system in Table 8.1. The baseline numbers for 1991, 1996, and 1997–2000 in Table 8.1 are based on the same assumptions as for the baseline employed in the econometric analysis in Chapter 9 (for a review of the many assumptions involved turn to a discussion of the baseline in Chapter 9). The trade policy assumptions of the GATT scenario are as follows:

1. Between 1992 and 1996 export subsidies for all agricultural exporters are reduced by 50 percent from the 1986–1988 average.

2. Import restrictions are converted to tariffs, and these tariffs are

reduced between 1992 and 1996 by 33 percent from the 1986–1988 tariff equivalents for the commodities involved.

3. Internal supports, as measured by an Aggregate Measure of Support (AMS), are reduced by 33 percent from the 1986–1988 average over the period 1992–1996.[2]

The estimates of agricultural exports presented in Table 8.1 indicate that a more open world trading system works to the advantage of the United States: the export market for the United States expands for all the commodities shown in Table 8.1 except sugar under the assumed GATT scenario. On the other hand, the export market contracts for all six commodities shown in Table 8.1 for the European Community. Japan goes from a nearly self-sufficient trade position for rice under the baseline to that of a large importer under the GATT scenario. As would be expected the export market for sugar widens for the tropical areas of the world under the GATT scenario. Australia experiences a widening of its export markets under the GATT scenario for four of the six commodities shown in Table 8.1. Clearly the pattern of world trade in agricultural products would shift under a more open system of trade, and for the most part the United States would benefit from those shifts.

Serious questions remain, however, over the willingness of some sectors in both the United States and EC to reduce border protection even a little; the estimates from Table 8.1 suggest why the EC is reluctant to move in the direction of a more open world trading system. And the politics of trade have taken on an additional layer of complexity as regional trading blocs have grown in strength. In the EC, the process of market integration under the Single European Act, scheduled for completion and often referred to simply as "1992," may lead to new pressures for domestic protection. In North America, the extension of the 1989 Free Trade Agreement with Canada to include Mexico has raised fears over "cheap labor" and unregulated competition. Organized labor, textiles, the sugar lobby and parts of the dairy industry have all lobbied against continuing the U.S./Canada/Mexico negotiation as well as the GATT talks. On the other side, feed grains and oilseeds, together with groups with broader interests in trade reform such as financial services, have lobbied in favor of continued negotiations.

The Cochrane-Runge agenda is basically consistent with the push for more open trade, although, as we have emphasized, it is not an unvarnished "free trade" proposal. First, the safety net scheme developed in Chapter 6 is a substantial move away from the production-distorting price and income supports for individual commodities that have characterized U.S. agriculture for over fifty years. While it is intended to provide basic income security to

Table 8.1. Exports for selected commodities, by countries, under the baseline and GATT scenarios, 1991–2000

	1991	1996		1997–2000 average	
	Baseline level	Baseline level	GATT (change)	Baseline level	GATT (change)
			(1,000 metric tons)		
Net wheat exports					
United States	39,240	43,940	570	48,420	528
European Community	18,540	19,710	−480	21,370	−623
Japan	−5,490	−6,070	−230	−6,420	−253
Canada	19,100	21,830	−210	23,320	−265
Australia	11,720	13,330	40	14,120	183
Developing	−73,560	−84,980	110	−93,520	203
CPEs[a]	−16,430	−15,770	100	−15,670	60
Rest of world	6,880	8,010	100	8,380	168
Net feed-grain exports					
United States	63,383	72,165	2,780	81,766	3,436
European Community	1,088	4,333	−3,918	6,056	−4,787
Japan	−21,896	−23,401	−215	−24,278	−216
Canada	4,337	4,471	186	4,184	319
Australia	2,314	2,730	66	2,713	35
Thailand	1,202	1,305	15	1,274	10
Developing	−37,625	−48,610	632	−56,722	788
CPEs[a]	−22,574	−23,615	132	−24,978	95
Rest of world	9,771	10,622	322	9,985	321
Net rice exports					
United States	2,400	2,076	476	1,976	706
European Community	−306	−390	−34	−444	−24
Japan	−11	58	−830	230	−1,229
Thailand	5,541	6,447	82	6,973	90
Pakistan	916	970	62	1,002	119
India	−387	−189	42	−182	73
Indonesia	−97	71	44	−6	57
Rest of world	−8,056	−9,043	158	−9,549	207
Net soybean exports					
United States	17,222	20,862	225	23,010	183
European Community	−12,265	−14,264	−359	−15,276	−406
Japan	−4,898	−5,412	61	−5,589	109
Argentina	3,022	3,187	8	3,212	22
Brazil	2,892	3,037	65	2,999	95
Developing	−7,351	−8,956	1	−9,938	7
CPEs[a]	−1,525	−1,789	−4	−1,900	−13
Rest of world	2,903	3,335	3	3,482	4

Table 8.1. (*continued*)

	1991	1996		1997–2000 average	
	Baseline level	Baseline level	GATT (change)	Baseline level	GATT (change)
			(1,000 metric tons)		
Net raw sugar exports					
United States	−842	−266	−550	−153	−549
European Community	3,259	2,934	−720	2,993	−728
Japan	−1,814	−1,855	−10	−1,857	−13
Australia	3,098	3,097	108	3,134	111
Brazil	1,085	1,646	584	1,442	654
Thailand	2,755	2,627	118	2,668	122
Rest of world	−7,541	−8,183	470	−8,227	404
Net beef exports					
United States	−415	−150	193	29	160
European Community	−17	−185	−666	−398	−700
Japan	−540	−962	56	−1,094	49
Canada	−30	−13	13	−9	23
Australia	971	960	14	1,013	27
New Zealand	369	412	6	427	19
Argentina	405	311	12	288	20
Brazil	322	262	11	257	16
Eastern Europe	249	234	42	226	52
Rest of world	−1,314	−869	319	−740	334

[a] Centrally Planned Economy (CPE)

Note: For the baseline scenario columns, positive numbers indicate that the country or group of countries is a net exporter; negative numbers indicate net importers. For the GATT scenario columns, a positive number indicates an increase in exports over the baseline or a reduction in imports; a negative number indicates a reduction in exports or an increase in imports.

commercial farmers, its overall impact on both production and trade is entirely consistent with the reduced protectionism advocated by the United States in GATT. The primary objective, as we have emphasized, is income *stability*, not income enhancement.

Secondly, the grain reserves program we have proposed has as its objective the stabilization of commodities prices at or near long-run world market price levels, not at an artificially supported domestic price level. By allowing domestic and world prices to seek similar levels, the reserves program is also consistent with the liberal U.S. trade position in GATT.

A third component of our proposed reforms is the conversion of quotas and other nontariff import barriers affecting all agricultural products (including but not limited to dairy, beef, peanuts, tobacco, sugar, wool and mohair) into tariff-equivalent levels of border protection. This "tariffication" has been a major element in U.S. trade negotiating strategy. It bears emphasis that the conversion of quotas to tariffs is to be followed by a unilateral 25 percent reduction, over five years, in this protection. This demonstrates our seriousness about providing other countries (especially poor developing countries) greater market access. It also allows these tariffs to be fixed ("bound") and negotiated bilaterally or downward as mutual agreements with our trading partners are worked out in GATT.

We propose to "bind" these tariffs after an initial 25 percent cut over five years, and to reduce them *only* as part of a negotiated agreement with other GATT contracting parties, either acting multilaterally or in bilateral agreements such as those reached in 1988 over beef and oranges with Japan. (In this agreement, the United States and Japan agreed to replace nontariff barriers with fixed tariff protection in Japan declining from 70 to 50 percent on beef and oranges from 1993 onwards.) This process is not one in which U.S. producers of commodities that rely on border measures would find themselves subject to wrenching adjustments. Instead, a systematic and orderly process of mutually negotiated reductions would occur.

A fourth aspect of our proposed reforms with important international consequences for the U.S. role in GATT is the elimination of export subsidies, including both the Export Enhancement Program (EEP) and the "marketing loans" currently applied to U.S. cotton, rice, and soybeans. The EEP is clearly a distortion of international trade, and its benefits to U.S. exporters have been modest, at best. Robert Paarlberg (1990a) concluded that the program's overall benefits have been far outweighed by the costs to taxpayers, and that lower U.S. support levels, together with exchange rate adjustments, are far more effective mechanisms of export market expansion than subsidy payments under EEP. The marketing loans, described in Chapter 3, are in reality the mirror image of the European Community's export restitution: a payment which effectively covers the difference between domestic supported prices and world market prices. Since the United States has complained continually about the EC restitution payments in GATT, it would be a progressive step in the direction of more liberal trade to eliminate marketing loans from U.S. policy, hopefully in tandem with negotiated reductions in EC levels of subsidy. Even without such EC actions, however, U.S. cotton, rice, and soybeans would continue to be more globally competitive if based on the policies proposed in our reforms than through continued payment of these disguised export subsidies. By separating the income stabilization safety net from specific commodity price supports, our program would allow most U.S. commodities to be priced at a level sufficient to expand market shares.

While GATT has received the lion's share of attention in agricultural circles in recent years, what about other multilateral institutions?

The IMF and World Bank are two other multilateral agencies that would be affected by various parts of our reform package. Even though the IMF and World Bank function separately, it is best to think of them, together with GATT, as forming a three-legged institutional foundation for international economic affairs. Monetary policy, development assistance, and rules for trade are their respective areas of coverage. As a result of a specific set of negotiations in the Uruguay Round of GATT (the so-called "Functioning of the GATT System" negotiations), both the IMF and World Bank have agreed to tie their policies more closely to GATT in the years ahead, pushing continually for more liberal international trade. The explanation for this is that less developed countries, the primary focus of IMF and World Bank policy, will be some of the most important beneficiaries of domestic agricultural policy reforms in the developed countries. Because less developed countries (LDC's) are the primary focus of World Bank lending and the debt and monetary policy advice provided by the IMF, the involvement of these institutions in trade reform is likely to enhance the willingness of the countries of Latin America, Africa and Asia to pursue more open development and trade strategies.

In this context, several elements of our reform package are likely to have important implications for the LDC's. First is the aforementioned conversion of quotas and other nontariff barriers to tariffs in the sugar, peanut, tobacco, wool, beef, dairy, and other protected sectors, and their reduction by an initial amount of 25 percent over five years. Below, we shall consider some quantitative estimates of the benefits likely to occur for poorer nations seeking access to the U.S. market in these and other commodities. A second aspect of our package with particular effects on the poor nations of the world is the revamping of U.S. development assistance policy. As we have noted, by converting U.S. food aid from a vent for surplus to a true program of emergency relief and poverty alleviation in those countries most in need, our reforms will help to accelerate rates of growth and thus to increase the demand in these nations for exported U.S. production.

We have emphasized that the mechanism by which this aid should be broadened in focus is to cooperate more fully with multilateral aid agencies, reducing the role of the U.S. Agency for International Development (AID) in the food aid area. Clearly, such a change in emphasis will mean that the United States cannot be allowed to be in arrears in its payments to the U.N. as it has been in the last decade. By reductions in the U.S. AID budget, funds should be made available to pay our dues in the U.N., maintain our contributions to the World Bank, and alter our emphasis from one of bilateral food aid flowing to a few strategically placed countries to one based on provision of critically short commodities.

A final element in our package with implications for international organizations is the reserve program designed to stabilize prices in times of extreme shortage and surplus. Because of the inordinate contribution of U.S. production to world trade in grains and oilseeds, U.S. actions to stabilize the prices of these commodities around the concept of "long-run world market prices" are likely to effect the level of world prices themselves, at least periodically. As a result, policy decisions taken in USDA affecting the level and release of reserves cannot be wholly unilateral, and must recognize that the reserves, and international price stability, are a form of "public good," shared by all trading nations (Runge, von Witzke, and Thompson 1987). We would argue that periodic consultative meetings of the Board responsible for grain reserve operations should be undertaken with representatives of the Organization for Economic Cooperation and Development (OECD), as well as with LDC representatives in GATT, the World Bank, IMF, and FAO in Rome. The objective would be to assure that U.S. reserves policy is consistent with (or at least not inconsistent with) the stabilization objectives of other exporting and importing countries In general, so long as the U.S. reserve helps in avoiding wild swings in world commodities prices, it is likely to be helpful to both exporters and importers alike, although some price movement is clearly both necessary and beneficial as global supply and demand shift over time (see Newberry and Stiglitz 1981).

Bilateral Trade Policy Relations

Having considered the broad implications of our proposals for multilateral bodies, it is important to evaluate more specifically the impacts on a variety of key trading partners. These include the European Community (EC), Japan, the "Cairns Group" of exporting nations, the LDC's and the former USSR/Eastern Europe.

THE EUROPEAN COMMUNITY

The European Community, in our view, is most likely to feel the pinch from our proposed set of policy reforms (see Moyer and Josling 1990). This "pinch" will come as competitively-priced U.S. exports force the Community to pay higher and higher subsidies to retain markets, or to reduce these subsidies. In the long run, the EC can be expected to recognize that it is less competitive than the United States as an exporter of grains and oilseeds, and that its money would be better targeted to smaller farms. But this recognition can be speeded along by the market-oriented policies we have proposed for the United States. By reducing the overall level of support for U.S. program crops, and especially by eliminating acreage set-asides except for environmental reasons or in times of extremely high stock levels, our policies will no longer allow the EC to benefit from the U.S. role as stock manager to the world (see Chapter 3). In addition, reduction in the level of border protection through tariffication and the initial 25 percent cut in these tariffs will likely put indirect pressure on several EC price support regimes, such as the sugar price program, which is even more protectionist than that of the United States.

On the other hand, several of our proposed reforms are likely to benefit the EC, at least indirectly. Greater market access in the dairy sector, for example, might increase U.S. imports of European cheeses. The elimination of the Export Enhancement Program (EEP) of export subsidies would reduce the head-to-head subsidy wars that the United States has conducted with the EC in contested markets. However, as we have emphasized, the overall impact of our policies is likely to increase U.S. market share in the oilseeds and feed grains (corn, sorghum) markets, as well as in fruits such as oranges and grapefruit and also in various livestock markets.

In general, the impact of our reform package on the EC will depend on the *mutual* accommodations made by both the EC and United States. Although we believe that our policies will be beneficial *regardless* of the European response and should be undertaken under any circumstances,[3] the interaction of the two groups' agricultural policies will obviously determine the final result. In a series of pathbreaking papers, Johnson, Mahé, and Roe (1989, 1990) have constructed simulations of politically acceptable trade compromises between the EC and United States. By using a world trade model coupled with different scenarios of coordinated (and uncoordinated) trade and/or agricultural policies in the EC and United States, these authors estimate the impacts on various special interest groups likely to be affected by such changes. By determining the political clout (or "policy preference weighting") of each interest group (e.g., sugar growers, dairy producers), it is possible to suggest which coordinated policy scenarios are "feasible" in both an economic and political sense.

Using the policies in effect in 1986, this work shows that net social gains (i.e., real income gains to the two societies) from more open trade of the sort we have prescribed are greatest when *both* the United States and EC undertake such reforms. Moreover, the results support the intuitive point emphasized above that total "free trade" is politically infeasible. The result underlines the consistency and mutually reinforcing character of policies in the United States and EC which eliminate direct price supports in favor of income stabilization payments, while also ending punitive and expensive export subsidies.

JAPAN

A second trading partner which has been a difficult adversary in agricultural trade is Japan. Despite much contentiousness, Japan stands as the most important single market for U.S. agricultural exports (see Paarlberg 1990b). Unlike the general *merchandise* or manufacturing trade deficit which the United States chronically runs with Japan, in agriculture it is the *United States* which runs the surplus, and Japan which is chronically in deficit. Japan has been more open to granting the United States access to its agricultural markets than it has in the industrial or service sectors (although the rice market, for reasons discussed below, is an important exception). In general, the Japanese acknowledge that U.S. agriculture (unlike U.S. industry) has an inherent comparative advantage over Japanese farmers. Unfortunately, it is precisely this fact which is often held up in trade negotiations such as GATT as a justification for the protection and high levels of subsidy Japanese farmers receive. Without such protection, Japan contends, its dependence on other countries would be so great (or conversely, its self-sufficiency so limited) that it would be subject to the gale winds of international markets and politics. An often-cited example of such a threat to its "food security" is the 1973 embargo on the export of soybeans imposed by then President Nixon in the face of a short U.S. crop, which drove Japanese soybean (and soy sauce) prices sky high in a few weeks.

The consequence is that Japan has one of the most protected agricultural sectors in the world. The Australian Bureau of Agricultural and Resource Economics, in a 1988 study, noted that between 1955 and 1980–82, the tariff-equivalent level of Japanese agricultural protection increased from 18 to 210 percent, or over 10-fold (Riethmuller 1988). The domestic market for rice, in particular, is politically sacrosanct, because rice is both a staple and a national symbol of sustenance (Wailes, et. al. 1991). In addition, Japanese rural interests continue to play a highly disproportionate political role in the Japanese diet, or national legislature, because of the way legislative seats are apportioned.

Yet despite the popular image of protectionist Japan, the Japanese market for U.S. agricultural exports is large and growing. In fiscal year 1989 Japan imported $8.2 billion worth of U.S. farm products accounting for more than a fifth of the value of total U.S. farm exports, more than all of Western Europe, more than twice as much as the former Soviet Union, and more than all of Africa and Latin America combined (Paarlberg 1990b). In contrast to this $8.2 billion export market for the United States, Japan sent only $200 million of farm products to the United States in 1989. Over the last 40 years, as the Japanese food basket has shifted from rice to include more meat, U.S. exports of not only poultry, pork and beef but also of feed ingredients have boomed. Animal protein consumption in Japan increased from 27 grams daily in 1965 to 41 grams by 1985. During the first *six months* of 1989, after the 1988 deal with the United States in which market access for beef and oranges was opened, U.S. beef exports expanded 45 percent (Paarlberg 1990b). And as the agreement to expand beef and oranges imported to Japan takes effect, further increases in markets for these U.S. commodities are anticipated.

The reforms we have proposed will allow a continuation of both market expansion and export development with Japan. We believe this is especially true in the oilseeds sector, where we expect U.S. production to increase in response to a more flexible whole farm base. By allowing U.S. production to be unrestrained by the acreage reduction programs, we would also expect increases in U.S. beef exports in response to strong demand in Japan. Finally, tariffication, which has already occurred in the limited cases of beef and oranges, can be a more general basis for trade reforms with Japan, opening additional markets, perhaps even rice, to U.S. exporters.

THE "CAIRNS GROUP" OF AGRICULTURAL EXPORTERS AND THE DEVELOPING COUNTRIES

A third group of general international significance for U.S. agriculture has come to be known as the "Cairns Group" of agricultural exporting nations. Formed during the run-up to the 1986–90 Uruguay Round in GATT, and named for the town in Australia where an important early meeting was held, the Cairns countries are led by Australia, New Zealand and Canada, but also include Brazil, Argentina, Chile, Colombia, Uruguay, Hungary, the Philippines, Indonesia, Thailand, Malaysia, and Fiji. Apart from the old Commonwealth countries, these nations have one or both feet in the developing country camp. The Cairns Group has been a relatively consistent voice for the long term reform of agricultural trade, as well as for greater market access by LDC's to developed country markets. It has also served as an important coalition forcing the United States and EC to continue bargaining in GATT, and has been especially vocal in its opposition to U.S. and EC export subsidies.

What do the Cairns Group of exporting countries, as well as other developing countries outside the Cairns coalition, have to gain from the specific proposals enumerated under the Cochrane/Runge plan? We believe the answer is: "a great deal." These gains extend beyond net exporters of agricultural commodities, and include many food importing countries as well. Yet it would be a mistake to suppose that the Cairns Group and all other developing countries see eye to eye. Evidence of these differences emerged relatively early in the Uruguay Round, when a Food Importing Group (FIGs) was formed in GATT to differentiate the needs of these countries from the main agricultural exporting countries, most of whom had joined the Cairns Group. In a proposal spelling out the position of the net-importers, the FIGs countries called on the other contracting parties in GATT to "alleviate the burden of increased prices on the import bill and balance of payments situation of net food importing developing countries," and to "enhance the capacity of these countries to increase agricultural production" (General Agreement on Tariffs and Trade 1989). Specifically, the proposal cited a variety of studies showing major losses to food importers from trade policy reform due to the increased prices widely forecast to result from trade reform. Given such losses, the FIGs argued for compensation in the form of concessional food sales, export credits and grants, improved market access, increased food aid, and reduced levels of debt servicing.

The differences in GATT between food importers and food exporters were linked in turn to debt servicing questions. Lower world commodities prices due to export subsidy competition between the United States and EC were a primary reason for debt-servicing problems in net exporting countries such as Argentina and Brazil, but the situation of the net importing countries was opposite. Because alleviation of export subsidies and internal reforms in the North were expected to *raise* world prices, the food bill of net importers would increase, making debt service even more difficult. As the FIGs statements argued

> The rise in import prices of food will exacerbate the debt servicing problems of net food importing developing countries and therefore we propose that international financial organizations should take the increase in import prices of food fully into account in negotiating structural adjustment programs; specifically these programs should be made more flexible (GATT, p. 3).

The overall interest of developing countries in trade reform thus have two main axes: North/South and South/South. From a North/South perspective, developing countries have argued for increased market access to the industrialized countries, whether they were net food importers or exporters. But along the South/South axis, the critical issue of debt servicing divided those countries that would gain from rising international commodities prices (net exporters) from those who asserted that would lose (net importers). This South/South division turns critically on the estimated impacts of the trade reform process on prices and net welfare.

Several recent studies which have attempted to simulate the effects of a more open world trading system support the view that more liberal trade in agricultural commodities along the lines we have proposed will tend to raise the level of commodities' prices worldwide. For Cairns Group countries that are already net exporters, such as Australia and Canada, this will be an unambiguous gain. But even for importers, a sufficiently high increase in prices will stimulate domestic production, in some cases converting net importers into net exporters. Since the beneficiaries of these changes are typically poorer farmers, the distributional impact will be skewed in favor of the least-well-off.

There is also evidence that more open agricultural trade, in and of itself, would reduce the fluctuations in commodities prices on world markets. In combination with the grain and oilseed reserves program we have proposed, the risks posed by these fluctuations to governments (especially those who are periodic buyers of emergency supplies) and to farmers in developing countries would be reduced. When the revamped priorities for food aid we have proposed are added, focusing on poor countries with true emergency needs, the overall positive effects on poorer nations are likely to be substantial. If general trade liberalization is slow to occur, there is evidence that even partial opening of access to U.S. markets could have very substantial positive effects on some LDC countries, with minimal disruptions for U.S. producers.

Consider the case of U.S. sugar policy. In a recent empirical analysis of U.S. sugar programs in the Caribbean Basin, Messina and Seale (1990) indicate that if U.S. sugar quotas were relaxed by roughly 25 percent so as to return them to the levels of 1983/84, the gains would be so great as to exceed those provided by virtually all of the development aid currently granted to Caribbean Basin recipients. While this may seem large, in fact it would increase U.S. domestic sugar supplies by only a few percent. The results of this study suggest that declines in prices received by U.S. sugar growers would therefore be relatively modest—falling from 22.45 cents to 20.72 cents, or about 2 cents per pound in the United States. These revenue impacts on domestic sugar growers would still put them ahead of their total revenues in 1981, although fewer acres are likely to remain in sugar if our proposed reforms are adopted. Total annual sugar exports from Caribbean basin countries, meanwhile, would increase by 8.9 percent to the U.S. market, representing a 2.5 percent increase in overall exports, of which sugar forms an important part. This increase would be worth $135 million in constant dollars (Messina and Seale 1990).

In a recent empirical study, Anderson and Tyers (1990) conducted a dynamic simulation study of world food markets. The model employed a procedure to "solve" for prices and quantities which clear the world market under a variety of different assumptions concerning trade and domestic policies. The baseline of the model was taken from projecting current policies through to the year 2000, with alternative policies then compared with this baseline. Their model was global in coverage, including 30 countries or country groups, and included the cross effects in both production and consumption for grains, livestock, and sugar. Using this model they show that "virtually all developing countries could benefit from global liberalization of food markets and that the vast majority of the world's poor would be better off" (Anderson and Tyers 1990, p. 3). This differs from predictions of major losses, especially to net food importing developing countries, if global prices rose following liberalization. What accounts for this difference in view? The result turns critically on how realistically the reform process is described.

Four elements are introduced in the Anderson and Tyers work that provide this greater realism. First, while it is generally acknowledged that rising world prices of agricultural commodities would cause unambiguous improvements in the terms of trade in food exporting countries; it is less often emphasized that some net food importing countries would expand production, and become net exporters over time. Second, this production expansion is likely to be driven by induced innovations in developing countries' technology and institutions. By shifting domestic supply curves out, welfare gains can exceed the losses resulting from worsened terms of trade. Third, if developing countries which have insulated consumers by subsidizing domestic food prices, encouraging import-dependency, instead allowed world price increases to be reflected domestically, the elimination of these distortions could more than offset the losses due to worsening terms of trade. This effect is amplified if induced innovations lead to the above-mentioned supply response and increased exports. Fourth, even if a country remained a net food importer and had no domestic food subsidies, if it protected its nonfood sector (e.g., through overvalued exchange rates) then eliminating these *nonfood* distortions would raise the *relative* price of food, with the same effects possible as in the first three cases above. In short, by acknowledging that increased output, induced innovations leading to higher productivity, and distortions in existing food and nonfood sectors characterize the dynamic process of adjustment to trade reform, a different picture emerges of its impacts on food importing countries. Negative impacts are not certain *a priori*, and must be determined empirically.

Empirical estimates of these impacts were made for two scenarios: complete liberalization in just the North; and liberalization in both North and South. While we question whether complete liberalization is likely to occur, it provides an analytic point of reference against which to compare policy alternatives. We also have reservations (stated elsewhere in Cochrane 1980; Runge and Myers 1985) over the use of net welfare measures, although the equivalent variation measure used by Anderson and Tyers has superior properties when compared to traditional surplus measures. In the two scenarios, productivity increases were first held constant, then allowed to respond to increased prices. Food markets included in the model were grains, meats, dairy products and sugar, accounting for about half of world food trade. The estimates for 1990 show what would have occurred in equilibrium if distortions in the North or in both North and South were eliminated. The effects of subsidized food imports in developing countries were captured by lowering the relative internal food price consistent with the 1988 calculations of Krueger, Schiff, and Valdes.

Table 8.2, row 1 shows that if the North liberalized alone, international food prices would have risen in 1985 dollars by 24 percent compared to the reference level. Net economic welfare in developing countries increased by $11 billion. If productivity growth was induced in response to these price increases, prices would rise by 26 percent and net economic welfare in developing countries increase by $17 billion. If *both the North and South liberalized, the effect on world food prices would be a negligible −1 percent,*

Table 8.2. Effects on International Food Prices and Economic Welfare of Liberalizing Food Markets, 1900

	International food price change	Change in net economic welfare		
		Industrial countries	Developing countries	Global total
	(%)	(1985 US$ billion per year)		
North:				
Liberalization of industrial country food policies with:				
•exogenous productivity growth	24	40	11	50
•price-responsive productivity growth	26	47	17	62
North/South:				
Liberalization of policies affecting food markets in industrial and developing countries with:				
•exogenous productivity growth	−1	62	28	90
•price-responsive productivity growth	−1	73	33	106

Source: Anderson and Tyers, 1990, p. 22.
Note: Economic welfare changes here apply only to agents in the food sector, as measured by equivalent variations in income of consumers and changes in producer surplus, in net government revenue from the food sector and in net profits from food stock holding. The global total includes the (small) effect on net economic welfare of Eastern Europe and the former USSR.

since the actions have offsetting effects. But welfare increases in developing countries would be $28 billion assuming no productivity response, and $33 billion with it, about twice the level that would occur if the North liberalized alone.

A final dimension of these changes is shown in Table 8.3, which estimated the impacts of liberalization on the stability of international agricultural prices. When either the North or South insulated their producers from international prices, they in effect "exported" domestic price instability into the international economy. This has been described as a form of "free riding," in which the international public good of price stability is eroded through protection by either producers or consumers (Runge, von Witzke and Thompson 1987). Anderson and Tyers calculated that if the North liberalized, variation in international prices would be reduced by about one-third (from a coefficient of 0.34 to 0.23) and that if a North/South liberalization occurred, by about two-thirds (from 0.34 to 0.11).

Despite the fact that total liberalization of the sort described in this model is unlikely, the implications of Anderson and Tyers' estimates are important to the international case for more open trade that we have presented. First, they suggest that the losses due to trade liberalization predicted by net food importers such as the FIGs group are probably overestimates of the welfare impacts of declining terms of trade. Second, the results emphasize that distortionary policies in developing countries, if eliminated, would actually increase the welfare gains of liberalization in a joint North/South action. Third, the price stabilization effects of trade policy reform suggest that liberalization may be a better mechanism to achieve such stability than international commodity agreements, which have often been justified as stabilization programs.

The Anderson and Tyers study also undermines arguments by apologists for the international price-depressing effects of the EC's Common Agricultural Policy, who have asserted that such effects are beneficial to such importing countries. The estimated negative effects of food policies on the economic welfare of developing countries is so large (as much as $17 billion in 1985 dollars) "as to effectively erode about half of the official development assistance received by developing countries from the OECD" (Anderson and Tyers, 1990, p. 16).

EASTERN EUROPE

A final part of the world likely to be affected by some aspects of our reform proposal will be the former Soviet Union and Eastern Europe. Here, the impacts are much more difficult to estimate, for several reasons. First,

Table 8.3. Effects of removing policy distortions to food markets in industrial and developing countries on the instability of international food markets prices

	Wheat	Coarse grain	Rice	Beef and sheep meat	Pork and poultry	Dairy products	Sugar	Weighted average
International Price Instability								
Reference coefficient of variation (from baseline)	0.58	0.53	0.38	0.24	0.08	0.26	0.36	0.34
Coefficient of variation in the absence of policy distortions in:								
All industrial countries	0.33	0.47	0.28	0.07	0.08	0.11	0.25	0.23
All industrial and developing countries	0.15	0.23	0.09	0.04	0.05	0.06	0.07	0.11

Source: Anderson and Tyers, 1990, p. 24.
Note: The coefficient of variation is the standard deviation divided by the mean value for 100 repeated simulations with random supply shocks.

the former USSR and Eastern Europe are in a state of rapid change, the outcome of which is difficult to predict. While they are likely to become more integrated with the world economy as a whole, this integration will be painful and likely to occur in fits and starts. Secondly, their own import needs are likely to continue to vary considerably. This variability has led U.S. commercial interests to seek long term agreements (LTAs) in order to smooth out the fitfulness of the former Eastern bloc demands. Unfortunately, they have generally failed to do so. Such sales, especially to the former USSR, had occurred more or less as the former Soviets had determined them to be needed; and when they were not, the LTAs were not honored. In addition, both the former USSR and China demanded that the Export Enhancement Program subsidies paid to others be extended to them, lowering their effective import prices.

Under our proposal, the elimination of export subsidies and more limited reliance on LTAs would be likely to make food imports to the former USSR, Eastern Europe and China more expensive. On the other hand, the increased stability in world commodities prices likely to result from other parts of our program would be beneficial. If food aid, development assistance and emergency relief are targeted to the former Eastern bloc countries when in need, it might also be useful in easing their transition to market economies.

BEYOND THE URUGUAY ROUND—THE GROWING ROLE OF NONTARIFF TRADE BARRIERS

Even if the actions proposed above were fully implemented, an important set of challenges to international agricultural trade would remain.[4] This is the growing role of environmental, health and safety regulations operating as disguised barriers to trade. The problem has gained new force as environmental policies move to the forefront of many national agendas. As noted in Chapter 6, because environmental standards have growing national constituencies, they are especially attractive candidates for disguised protectionism. International distinctions are created in the level of environmental risks generally considered tolerable because the weight attached to environmental standards tends to vary with the income levels of different countries. Incentives are created to move restricted products and processes into areas of lax regulation, notably developing countries, while denying import access to countries that may not subscribe to the regulatory policies of the developed countries. Without multilateral action, environmental standards become sources of trade tension. These tensions have occurred both in GATT and the U.S./Canada/Mexico trade agreement.

The environmental reforms we have proposed must be developed and implemented with this international perspective clearly in mind. Otherwise, reforms in the United States can serve as disguised protectionism. These issues have been brought to the forefront of international agriculture by a number of recent developments.

On January 1, 1989, the European Community (EC) announced a ban on all beef imports from the United States containing hormones used to help increase cattle growth. Citing health risks, the EC action touched off a cycle of retaliation worth hundreds of millions of dollars. This apparently isolated example of health regulations acting as trade barriers is part of an emerging pattern especially important to trade between developed and developing nations. In September, 1989, the European Commission also took up discussions of further rules to restrict imports of cattle or dairy products produced with the bovine growth hormone BST (bovine somatotropin). BST is also at the center of domestic controversies over the safety of food supplies in the United States and Canada.

In a related development former Senator Pete Wilson (R-CA) introduced federal legislation in December, 1989 that would ban companies from exporting pesticides that are illegal in the United States. This legislation was incorporated as an amendment to the 1990 farm bill, but ultimately withdrawn in committee. It was justified as a way of breaking the "circle of poison" resulting from the import of foreign products treated with chemicals banned in the United States. While ostensibly aimed at the "circle of poison," the legislation was largely prompted by the Western Growers Association of Irvine, California. Wilson stated that "export of dangerous pesticides creates a competitive inequity between foreign and American farmers and growers." A spokesperson for the growers argued that "we are under extreme pressure from foreign farmers," noting hundreds of growers who have gone out of business because of competition with Mexico and other countries where "they can use whatever [chemicals] they want in most cases."

These examples are part of an emerging pattern in which environmental and health risks are increasingly traded among nations along with goods and services. These risks are the opposite of services—they are environmental and health disservices traded across national borders. They arise directly from the transfer of technology, and will increasingly affect international investment flows, trade and development, and the relative competitiveness of national industries and agriculture (Nolan and Runge 1989). The examples cited above demonstrate that environmental regulations are not purely domestic policy issues. As Ingo Walter of New York University has written, "The fact of national sovereignty in environmental policy, when coupled with its economic consequences, leads directly to repercussions on international economic relations" (Walter 1982).

There has been longstanding recognition of the possibility for conflicts between national environmental policy and more open international trade. The GATT Articles explicitly recognize the possibility that domestic health, safety and environmental policies might override general attempts to lower trade barriers (Jackson 1969). GATT law emphasizes that any restrictions imposed on foreign practices for environmental or health reasons must also reflect a domestic commitment, so that exceptions allowed under GATT cannot be misused as a disguised form of protection. Yet the proposed "circle of poison" ban shows that GATT's attempts to balance the objectives of more open trade with national sovereignty over environmental and health measures have not successfully defused the problem.

Indeed, although tariff barriers, especially in the manufacturing sector, have fallen several-fold since 1947, nontariff barriers have become an increasingly seductive means of protection. Recognizing this problem, in 1971 a special commission (the Williams Commission) sought to identify key areas of potential trade conflict, and to recommend policies to prevent the spread of nontariff protectionism. In that year the Williams Commission recommended that "serious efforts be made to harmonize environmental quality standards to the greatest possible extent," but the goal has been far easier to state than to achieve. Writing in the early 1980s, Rubin and Graham (1982) noted that developed countries were moving along a far faster track of environmental regulations than other parts of the world. As they emphasized, a strong political constituency had emerged in the developed countries for environmental standards. Less obvious was the fact that this constituency could also be turned to the purpose of protectionism. "In the United States, and perhaps elsewhere," they wrote, "hard political battles to establish environmental standards have recently been fought and won. Proponents of these standards will fight equally hard to prevent their modification to accommodate an international consensus" (Rubin and Graham 1982).

At roughly the same time, the Tokyo Round of Multilateral Trade Negotiations promulgated a "Standards Code" that has tried (also largely without success) to grapple with the balance between health, safety and environmental standards and trade liberalization.[5] This 1979 code supplemented the GATT rules that require "national treatment" (no less favorable to importers than to domestic parties) and prohibited the "nullification or impairment" of trade concessions through the back-door device of nontariff barriers (Jackson 1969). The purpose of the Code was to prevent any product, technical, health, safety or environmental standard from creating "unnecessary obstacles to international trade" (Rubin and Graham 1982).

Despite an additional decade of discussions, including substantial attention to both technical standards and nontariff barriers in the Uruguay Round, it is still unclear when and where such standards constitute an "unnecessary obstacle to international trade." If anything, the temptation to use environmental and health standards to deny access to home markets is stronger now than in the 1980s. As the European Community moves towards its goal of market integration, it will have strong incentives to create common regulations for internal purposes, but to impose restrictions vis-à-vis the rest of the world. A similar propensity may occur as a result of harmonization under the U.S./Canada free trade agreement. Even if *national* standards can be harmonized, moreover, there is every reason to expect subnational jurisdictions to utilize various health and environmental standards to protect certain markets.

Underlying the development of these trade tensions are fundamental differences in the views of developed and developing countries (the "North" and "South") concerning the appropriate level and extent of environmental regulation. Differences in the domestic policy response to these problems are well represented in the food systems of the North and South.

In the developed countries of North America and Western Europe, the "food problem" arises not from too little food, but generally too much. As predicted by Engels' Law, the incomes of developed countries have increased, and the share of this income spent on food has fallen in proportion to other goods and services. This characteristic makes food an "inferior good" in economic jargon. In contrast, environmental quality and health concerns have grown in importance with increasing income levels. They are what economists call "superior goods," in the sense that they play a larger role in the national budget as national incomes increase (see Runge 1987).

In low-income developing countries, while the share of national resources devoted to food and agriculture remains large (creating substantial markets for yield-increasing products), environmental quality and occupational health risks are widely perceived as concerns of the rich. Even if environmental and health risks are acknowledged, the income levels of most developing countries do not permit a structure of environmental regulation comparable to that in the North. This two-tiered structure of international environmental regulation, with stricter regulatory regimes in developed countries paired with lax or nonexistent regulations in developing countries, increases the North-South flow of environmental risks. A kind of "environmental arbitrage" results, in which profits are gained by exploiting the differential in regulations, as investments flow to low regulation areas. This environmental arbitrage results from conscious policy choices that reveal differences in the value attached to environmental quality by rich and poor countries. As these paths of institutional innovation increasingly diverge, so will the differential impact of environmental constraints on producers in the North and competitors in the South such as Argentina and Brazil (Runge et al. 1988).

The competitiveness implications of these trends are not lost on northern producers. They have been quick to see the trade relevance of environmental and health standards. Growing consumer concerns with the health and environmental impacts of agriculture create a natural (and much larger) constituency for nontariff barriers to trade, justified in the name of health and safety. As between countries in the North, obvious differences in values also exist, although the regulatory gap is less yawning.

Given the tensions separating North and South, and the lesser differences between countries in the North, it would appear that a single set of standards is unlikely to be successful. In principle, the United States should seek to raise the level of environmental protection throughout the world. But the means must be through multilateral rather than unilateral action. The GATT Subsidies Code adopted during the Tokyo Round is at least a necessary starting point, but some mechanism must be found to accommodate differences in national priorities linked to levels of economic development and cultural factors.

In view of differences in levels of economic development and national priorities, it is clear that standards cannot be wholly uniform. However, it bears emphasis that both the GATT articles (Article XX) and U.S. trade law allow the United States to maintain the highest standards in its own domestic markets. Jeffrey James (1982) suggests that despite valid arguments for improved health and environmental regulations in the South, "it does not follow from this that countries of the Third World should adopt either the same *number* or the same *level* of standards as developed countries." James suggests what may be called *intermediate* standards, "in the same sense and for the same basic reason as that which underlies the widespread advocacy of inter-mediate technology in the Third World." This does not imply a "downgrading" of U.S. regulations, but an "upgrading" of LDC norms, together with recognition that the social costs of regulation are relative to national income.

Under GATT law, these distinctions are recognized as "Special and Differential Treatment" of lower income countries. While "S&D" often creates serious longrun distortions, the terms under which it is granted, as James emphasizes, may actually reduce current regulatory differentials by raising norms in the South, thus improving Third World environmental policies. While this may not satisfy all competing producers in the North, it can contribute to reductions in overall trade tension while improving environmental quality in the South.

The key is to recognize the inherently international character of environmental quality and health—issues which are similar in nature to human rights. Only the force of international standards defining the duties of nations, corporations and individuals, can hope to resolve these difficult issues.

Because of the emphasis we have given to environmental, health and safety issues in the United States, it is important to emphasize that we would extend these benefits in the process of trade to other nations. We are *not* arguing that U.S. standards should be reduced to some lower common denominator. But neither should they become an artifice of protectionism. The key is to raise international standards, to U.S. levels wherever possible, and vigorously to enforce environmental protection at home, without using it as an excuse for trade protectionism abroad.

Notes

1. The "home front" will be discussed in detail in Chapter 10.
2. Table 8.1, the statement of assumptions, and the discussion that follows of possible changes in exports for selected agricultural commodities under the GATT scenario are based upon materials in the report by the Center for Agricultural and Rural Development (1991).
3. See Paarlberg (1988).
4. This section draws on C. Ford Runge (1990).
5. Code of Conduct for Preventing Technical Barriers to Trade, General Agreement on Tariffs and Trade, Multilateral Trade Negotiations, Doc. MTN/NTM/W1192/Rev. 5, cited in Rubin and Graham (1982).

References

Anderson, Kym and Rod Tyers. 1990, July. "Welfare Gains to Developing Countries from Food Trade Liberalization Following the Uruguay Round," Department of Economics and Centre for International Economic Studies, University of Adelaide, Adelaide, Australia.

Center for Agricultural and Rural Development. 1991, January. *Implications of a GATT Agreement for World Commodity Markets, 1991–2000.* GATT Research Paper 91-GATT1. Ames, Iowa: Iowa State University.

Cochrane, W. W. 1980. "Some Nonconformist Thoughts on Welfare Economics and Commodity Stabilization Policy." *American Journal of Agricultural Economics* 62: 508–11.

General Agreement on Tarifs and Trade. 1989. "Ways to Take Account of the Negative Effects of the Agriculture Reform Process on Net Food Importing Developing Countries by Group W/74," in conjunction with MTN. GNG/NG5/W/74. Submitted to the Negotiating Group on Agriculture, Geneva,

Switzerland, October 25, 1989.

Jackson, John H. 1969. *World Trade and the Law of GATT (A Legal Analysis of the General Agreement on Trade and Tariffs)*. Indianapolis: Bobbs-Merrill.

Jackson, John H. 1989. *The World Trading System: Law and Policy of International Economic Relations*. Cambridge: The MIT Press.

James, Jeffery. 1982. "Product Standards in Developing Countries." In Frances Stewart and Jeffery James, eds., *The Economics of New Technology in Developing Countries*. Boulder, Colo.: Westview Press.

Johnson, Martin, Terry Roe, and Louis Mahé. 1989. *The GATT Negotiations and US/EC Agricultural Policies Solutions to Non-Cooperative Games*. St. Paul, University of Minnesota: Economic Development Center. Bulletin 89-2.

_____. 1990. "Political Economy of Policy Reform in the United States and European Community." *Background Papers for Report on the Task Force in the Aggregate Measure of Support: Potential Use by GATT for Agriculture*. Working Paper 90-1. St. Paul: International Agricultural Trade Research Consortium.

Krueger, A. O., M. Schiff, and A. Valdes. 1988, September. "Measuring the Impact of Sector-specific and Economy-wide Policies on Agricultural Incentives in LDCs." *World Bank Economic Review* 2(2): 255–72.

Messina, William A., Jr. and Seale, James L., Jr. 1990, March. *U.S. Sugar Policy: A Welfare Analysis of Policy Options Under Pending Caribbean Basin Expansion Act Legislation*. Staff Paper 382. Gainesville, Fla., University of Florida: Food and Resource Economics Department.

Moyer, H. Wayne and Timothy E. Josling. 1990. *Agricultural Policy Reform: Politics and Process in the EC and the U.S.A.* London: Harvester Wheatsheaf.

Newberry, David M. G. and Joesph E. Stiglitz. 1981. *The Theory of Commodity Price Stabilization: A Study in the Economics of Risk*. Oxford: Clarendon Press.

Nolan, Richard and C. Ford Runge. 1989. *Trade in Disservices: Environmental and Health Damages in International Trade*. Staff paper 89-8. St. Paul: University of Minnesota, Department of Agricultural and Applied Economics.

Paarlberg, Robert L. 1988. *Fixing Farm Trade: Policy Options for the U.S.* New York: Council on Foreign Relations.

_____. 1990a, Second Quarter. "The Mysterious Popularity of EEP." *Choices*.

_____. 1990b. "The Upside Down World of U.S.-Japanese Agricultural Trade." *Washington Quarterly*. Autumn: 131–42.

Riethmuller, Paul. 1988. *Japanese Agricultural Policies. A Time of Change*. Canberra: Australian Bureau of Agricultural and Resource Economics.

Rubin, Seymour J. and Thomas R. Graham, eds. 1982. *Environment and Trade: The Relation of International Trade and Environmental Policy*. Totowa, NJ: Pinter.

Runge, C. Ford. 1987. "Induced Innovation in Agricultural and Environmental Quality." In Tim T. Phipps, Pierre R. Crosson and Kent A. Price, eds., *Agriculture and the Environment, the National Center for Food and Agricultural Policy, Annual Policy Review 1986*. Washington, D.C.: Resources for the Future.

_____. 1988, Fall. "The Assault on Agricultural Protectionism." *Foreign Affairs*. 67(1): 133–50.

_____. 1990, Spring. "Trade Protectionism and Environmental Regulations: The New Nontariff Barriers." *Northwestern Journal of International Law and*

Business. 11(1): 47–61.

Runge, C. Ford and Daniel Halbach. 1990. "Export Demand, U.S. Farm Income and Land Prices, 1949–1985." *Land Economics.* 60-2.

Runge, C. Ford and Robert J. Myers. 1985. "Shifting Foundations of Agricultural Policy Analysis: Welfare Economics when Risk Markets are Incomplete." *American Journal of Agricultural Economics* 67:5 (December): 1010–16.

Runge, C. Ford, Harald von Witzke, and Shelley Thompson. 1987. "Liberal Agricultural Trade as a Public Good: Free Trade Versus Free Riding Under GATT." Staff Paper 87-11. St. Paul: University of Minnesota, Department of Agricultural and Applied Economics.

Runge, C. Ford, James P. Houck, and Daniel W. Halbach. 1988. "Implications of Environmental Regulations for Competitiveness in Agricultural Trade." In John D. Sutton, ed., *Agricultural Trade and Natural Resources: Discovering the Critical Links.* Boulder and London: Lynne Rienner Publishers.

Wailes, E. J., S. Ito, and G. L. Cramer. 1991. *Japan's Rice Market: Policies and Prospects for Liberalization.* University of Arkansas. Agricultural Experiment Station Report Series 319. Fayetteville, Ark.

Walter, Ingo. 1982. "International Economic Repercussions of Environmental Policy: An Economist's Perspective." In Seymour J. Rubin and Thomas R. Graham, eds., *Environment and Trade: The Relation of International Trade and Environmental Policy.* Totowa, N.J.: Pinter.

9 Quantitative Estimates of the Proposed Policy

To appraise, hence judge, the acceptability of the proposals outlined in Chapter 6, quantitative measures of the impacts of those proposals are a necessity. With the assistance of the Food and Agricultural Policy Research Institute (FAPRI) we present such measures for the United States in this chapter.[1] The quantitative estimates presented in this chapter do not, however, measure the impacts of our rural development and environmental proposals; they are limited to the impacts on the commercial farming sector. Estimates of the impact of the Cochrane-Runge policy proposals for such variables as commodity prices, agricultural production, farm income, and government outlays for the projected years 1992 through 1996 were developed using the FAPRI econometric policy model. It is important to recognize that these estimates *are not forecasts*; they are projections based on certain assumptions, which will be spelled out as we proceed.

The FAPRI Model

A general description of the FAPRI econometric policy model in non-technical language has been provided by the Institute. It reads as follows:

> The FAPRI annual agricultural policy model has components for each of the major commodities. These include *livestock*: beef, pork, and poultry, and for *crops*: feed grains (corn, sorghum, oats and barley), soybeans, wheat, rice, and cotton. The econometric models for the commodity components include behavioral relationships for production, stocks, exports, imports, final consumption and, if appropriate, consumption of the commodities as intermediate products. Each commodity model can be operated on a "stand alone basis" or integrated into a larger system with other commodity components. . . .
>
> The commodity components are linked for the policy analysis. . . . These linkages between the commodity markets are designed to reflect the

simultaneity of price determination processes in U.S. agriculture. For example, livestock prices condition the demand for feed grains while feed grain prices, in turn, influence investment and production decisions for livestock and correspondingly, livestock prices. These linkages across commodity markets are especially important for policy evaluation. For example, government policies for the major commodity markets in the U.S. are only for crops. Thus, to evaluate fully the policies, linkages to the livestock markets must be included.

In addition to the commodity components, the FAPRI policy model has farm income and government components. The farm income component utilizes output for the major commodity components, along with simplified information on the specialized commodities and farm expenses, to generate estimates of gross farm income, net farm income, and other sector-wide performance measures. The government component estimates costs by commodity program and total budget exposure. In addition, this component calculates additional information reflecting the extent of government intervention in agriculture.

The dimensions of the FAPRI model are, by necessity, relatively large. First, the model resides on an extensive set of predetermined or exogenous variables. These variables reflect the U.S. domestic economy, the world economy, climatic conditions, and other determinants of prices in agricultural commodity markets. These conditioning or predetermined variables are presently over 1,100 in number. The number of endogenous variables or variables determined by the model is 325; 130 for livestock, 110 for crops, with the remainder for farm income and government cost. The model has 250 behavioral equations and 75 identities.(FAPRI 1985)

The FAPRI policy model employed to measure the impacts of the Cochrane-Runge policy proposals was estimated from annual data for the period 1967–86.

There are a large number of structural parameters in the FAPRI policy model. A complete review of these parameters is not within the purview of the present discussion. However, selected parameters that were employed in the simulation of the Cochrane-Runge proposals are presented in Table 9.1. From that table it may be observed that the short-run export elasticities measured at the mean for the period 1967–1987 are inelastic in most cases in the FAPRI model. This is not surprising. Short-run export elasticities for agricultural products generally have an absolute value of less than one, while longer-term elasticities are near one. Selected domestic retail demand elasticities utilized in the model are also presented in Table 9.1.

In order for the FAPRI projections of key farm variables under various policy alternatives, including the Cochrane-Runge proposals, to be meaningful, or have program significance, those projections are compared year by year with a set of baseline projections. Baseline projections in the FAPRI analysis thus become a standard of comparison for the analyses. The

Table 9.1. Representative short-run structural elasticities from the FAPRI agricultural policy model

Commodity	Feed		Food		Exports		Stocks		Total	Acreage response elasticity[d]
	Elasticity	Share[a] (%)	Elasticity	Share (%)	Elasticity	Share (%)	Elasticity	Share(%)		
Corn	−.19	41	−.08	3	−.27	17	−.61	31	−.32	.35
Wheat	−1.00	7	−.02	20	−.40	35	−.28	35	−.31	.49
Soybeans	−.85[b]	50			−.53	31	−.55	15	−.67	.30
Soymeal	−.10	77			−.88	23			−.28	
Rice	−.03	8	−.07	28	−1.06	39	−.69	22	−.46	.38
Cotton	−.05[c]	39			−.93	30	−.25	31	−.38	.27

Short-run export demand own and cross price elasticities

Commodity	Corn	Wheat	soybeans	Soybean meal	Soybean oil	Rice	Cotton
Corn	−.27			.03			
Wheat		−.40				.07	
Soybeans			−.53	.43	.22		
Rice						−1.06	
Cotton							−.93

Retail meat price and income effects[e]

Commodity	Beef	Pork	Chicken	Income
Beef	−.35	.13	.15	.60
Pork	.07	−.79	.40	.42
Chicken	.51	.44	−.67	.35

[a]Shares are computed at the average 1985–1989 level for the indicated variables.
[b]Bean crush demand
[c]Cotton mill demand
[d]Foreign supply elasticities for major competitors, corn: Thailand, .30; Argentina, .27; and wheat: Australia, .12; Canada, .54; Argentina, .38. soybeans: Brazil, .08; Argentina, 1.10.
[e]Diagonal price effects and income effects are flexibilities. Off diagonal effects are retail cross elasticities of price transmission.

baseline projections must therefore be an analytically acceptable standard comparable to, say, sea level for measuring the height of land forms.

The set of baseline projections employed in the analysis of the Cochrane-Runge policy proposals is called the July 1990 FAPRI Baseline, and was the baseline employed in policy analyses by FAPRI in the second half of 1990. The macro-economic assumptions undergirding the July 1990 Baseline are presented in Table 9.2. It will be observed that those assumptions do not reflect developments emanating from the "Gulf Crisis" in the second half of 1990; the assumptions also reflect neither deep depression nor great prosperity. There is however a dip in GNP in 1990 and slow economic growth thereafter.

The baseline projections must also take into account the relevant farm program provisions. When this analysis was undertaken in October 1990, the 1990 farm bill was still being debated, and many of the specific program provisions of the 1990 Act were still unknown. Thus, the farm program provisions utilized in the July 1990 Baseline, the baseline employed in this analysis, are the 1989 provisions of the 1985 Act. However, the 1990 program changes were not sufficient to alter the baseline projections significantly. The specific program provisions utilized in the July 1990 Baseline may be reviewed in Table 9.3.

Cochrane-Runge Program Changes

The Cochrane-Runge proposals involve six program changes from the traditional farm programs of the late 1980s the impacts of which are

Table 9.2. Macro-economic projections on which the July, 1990, baseline projections are based

Variable/Year	1988	1989	1990	1991	1992	1993	1994	1995	1996
					(%)				
Real GNP (change)	4.4	3.0	1.9	2.2	2.4	2.7	2.7	2.5	2.5
Rate of inflation	3.3	4.1	4.2	4.0	4.3	4.3	4.4	4.4	4.3
Unemployment rate	5.5	5.3	5.6	5.8	5.6	5.3	5.0	4.9	4.8
3-month T-bill rate	6.7	8.1	7.9	8.1	8.3	8.4	8.2	7.9	7.7
MERM exchange rate (change)	−5.8	4.3	−3.5	−3.3	−2.6	−2.3	−2.1	−1.8	−2.1
					(Billion $)				
Federal budget surplus	−146	−149	−159	−134	−113	−94	−79	−64	−53
Current account	−127	−106	−99	−109	−118	−124	−121	−136	—

Table 9.3. Farm program provisions for the FAPRI July, 1990, baseline

Variable/Year	89/90	90/91	91/92	92/93	93/94	94/95	95/96
				($ per bushel)			
Target price							
Corn	2.84	2.75	2.75	2.75	2.75	2.75	2.75
Sorghum	2.69	2.61	2.61	2.61	2.61	2.61	2.61
Barley	2.43	2.36	2.36	2.36	2.36	2.36	2.36
Oats	1.50	1.45	1.45	1.45	1.45	1.45	1.45
Wheat	4.10	4.00	4.00	4.00	4.00	4.00	4.00
Rice ($/cwt.)	10.80	10.71	10.71	10.71	10.71	10.71	10.71
Cotton (¢/lb.)	0.734	0.729	0.729	0.729	0.729	0.729	0.729
Loan rates							
Corn	1.65	1.57	1.49	1.42	1.44	1.39	1.37
Sorghum	1.57	1.49	1.41	1.35	1.37	1.32	1.30
Barley	1.34	1.28	1.21	1.15	1.17	1.13	1.12
Oats	0.85	0.81	0.77	0.73	0.74	0.72	0.71
Soybeans	4.53	4.50	4.50	4.50	4.50	4.50	4.50
Wheat	2.06	1.95	1.86	1.95	2.01	1.94	1.94
Rice ($/cwt.)	6.50	6.50	6.50	6.50	6.50	6.50	6.50
Cotton (¢/lb.)	0.500	0.503	0.530	0.542	0.532	0.539	0.544
ARP Program				*(%)*			
Corn	10.0	10.0	5.0	7.5	7.5	7.5	7.5
Sorghum	10.0	10.0	5.0	7.5	7.5	7.5	7.5
Barley	10.0	10.0	5.0	7.5	7.5	7.5	7.5
Oats	5.0	5.0	5.0	5.0	5.0	5.0	5.0
Wheat	10.0	5.0	5.0	5.0	5.0	5.0	5.0
Rice	25.0	20.0	15.0	15.0	20.0	20.0	20.0
Cotton	25.0	12.5	10.0	10.0	10.0	10.0	10.0
Other idled area conservation reserve	29.6	34.2	34.2	*(million acres)* 40.0	40.0	40.0	40.0
CRP rental rate				*($ per acre)*			
new enrollment	49.91	51.00	51.00	—	—	—	—
Average	48.70	49.06	49.06	49.30	49.30	49.30	49.30
Export enhancement program expenditures	566	566	566	*(million $)* 566	566	566	566
Calendar year	1990	1991	1992	1993	1994	1995	1996
Dairy Support Prices				*($ per hundredweight)*			
Milk	10.10	9.60	9.60	9.60	9.60	9.60	9.60
Butter	105.20	89.19	84.36	84.36	84.36	84.36	84.36
Nonfat dry milk	83.17	83.85	86.51	86.51	86.51	86.51	86.51
Cheese	111.00	106.45	106.57	106.57	106.57	106.57	106.57

estimated by the FAPRI policy model, and then compared with the baseline estimates. Those program changes involve:

1. The elimination of all price supporting actions, target prices, and deficiency payments for wheat, feed grains, rice, cotton, oilseeds, and dairy.

2. The elimination of acreage set-asides for the period under consideration, 1992–96.

3. The expansion of the Conservation Reserve to 45 million acres by 1996.

4. The institution of a Stabilization Payments Program in which payments would be made to producers up to a maximum of $20,000 per producer and a total of $7 billion per year when the terms of trade turned against farmers. Milk producers as well as crop farmers are included in the Stabilization Payments Program.

5. The institution of a grain reserve program with the authority to acquire stocks up to 75 million metric tons, and with the objective of stabilizing grain prices at or approaching the "long-run" world price of the grains through the purchase, sale, and donation of those grains. The authority to engage in price stabilization operations is also extended to include soybeans.

6. The elimination of export subsidy programs and reduction by 25 percent of import duties over a five-year period.

A price triggering mechanism was proposed and described in Chapter 6 for implementing the Stabilization Payments Program. It was proposed that the farming areas of the United States be divided into six regions and that indices of prices received by farmers and prices paid by farmers be constructed by the U.S. Department of Agriculture for each of those regions. According to the formula proposed in Chapter 6 when the percentage increase in the index of prices paid exceeded the percentage increase in the index of prices received, for the year in question for the region involved, stabilization payments would be made to producers up to $20,000 per farm in that region. But neither the authors (Cochrane-Runge) nor FAPRI had the time or the money to construct reliable indices of prices received and prices paid for six farming regions of the United States while this book was being written. Thus the policy analysis conducted by FAPRI of the Cochrane-Runge proposals involves the relationship of prices received and prices paid for United States as a single unit. The index numbers involved in the proposed price triggering mechanism for the nation as a whole are presented in Table 9.4. It will be observed that the price triggering mechanism calls for the making of stabilization payments to crop farmers in each of the projected five years and the making of payments to dairy farmers in all but one of the five years.

IMPACTS ON THE CROP SECTOR

The preliminaries are now complete. We can now begin to look at the projections produced by the FAPRI model of the Cochrane-Runge (C/R) policy proposals, and compare those projections with the baseline. Looking first at the impact on planted acreage (Table 9.5), we observe that planted acreages for wheat, corn, sorghum, barley, and wheat increase under the C/R proposals over those in the baseline. This results from the fact that acreages held idle under annual control programs of the Act of 1985 are released under the C/R proposals. These released acres thus become free to be (1) planted to crops, or (2) go into the CRP, or (3) simply vanish from farm program records, perhaps as pasture or some other nonintensive use. The FAPRI model suggests that some 12 million of those released

Table 9.4. Price index trigger system employed in the Cochrane/Runge proposals

Price indices	1992	1993	1994	1995	1996
			(1910-14 = 100)		
Price paid index					
C&S, int, taxes, & wages	1288.2	1323.4	1360.9	1409.3	1458.7
3-Year moving average	1255.5	1288.4	1324.2	1364.5	1409.6
% change from year ago	1.84%	2.62%	2.78%	3.05%	3.30%
Prices received index					
Crops	460.8	462.8	477.9	487.2	495.4
3-Year moving average	490.4	473.3	467.2	475.9	486.8
% change from year ago	−4.90%	−3.48%	−1.30%	1.88%	2.28%
Make stabilization payment for crops?	YES	YES	YES	YES	YES
			(1980 = 100)		
Prices paid index					
Dairy producers	115.0	118.4	122.2	125.2	128.9
3-Year moving average	116.8	116.7	118.5	121.9	125.4
% change from year ago	−3.4%	−0.1%	1.6%	2.9%	2.9%
Prices received index					
Dairy products	88.4	91.7	95.0	96.8	99.7
3-year moving average	99.0	93.3	91.7	94.5	97.2
% change from year ago	−4.8%	−5.8%	−1.7%	3.1%	2.8%
Make stabilization payment for dairy?	YES	YES	YES	NO	YES

Table 9.5. Impacts of the Cochrane/Runge proposals on areas planted

Variable/Year	92/93	93/94	94/95	95/96	96/97	5-Yr avg
			(million acres)			
Wheat						
Baseline	76.0	77.2	77.5	77.8	78.2	77.3
C/R Proposal	79.6	79.7	79.1	78.9	78.8	79.2
Difference	3.6	2.5	1.6	1.1	0.7	1.9
% Difference	4.7%	3.3%	2.1%	1.4%	0.9%	2.4%
Corn						
Baseline	75.1	75.7	75.3	75.0	75.0	75.2
C/R Proposal	76.9	77.0	76.8	76.6	76.4	76.7
Difference	1.7	1.3	1.5	1.6	1.5	1.5
% Difference	2.3%	1.7%	2.0%	2.1%	1.9%	2.0%
Soybeans						
Baseline	57.8	57.9	59.9	61.5	61.9	59.8
C/R Proposal	61.7	61.7	62.5	63.1	63.3	62.5
Difference	3.9	3.8	2.6	1.6	1.4	2.7
% Difference	6.7%	6.5%	4.3%	2.6%	2.3%	4.4%
Sorghum						
Baseline	11.5	12.0	12.0	11.9	12.1	11.9
C/R Proposal	13.2	13.0	13.1	12.9	12.8	13.0
Difference	1.7	1.0	1.1	1.1	0.7	1.1
% Difference	14.3%	8.7%	9.2%	8.9%	5.5%	9.3%
Barley						
Baseline	8.4	9.3	9.3	9.4	9.6	9.2
C/R Proposal	9.9	9.9	10.1	10.1	10.1	10.0
Difference	1.5	0.7	0.8	0.7	0.5	0.8
% Difference	17.6%	7.1%	8.4%	7.4%	4.8%	8.9%
Oats						
Baseline	10.9	10.6	10.5	10.5	10.5	10.6
C/R Proposal	9.7	9.7	9.6	9.6	9.5	9.6
Difference	−1.2	−0.9	−0.9	−0.9	−1.0	−1.0
% Difference	−11.3%	−8.4%	−8.6%	−8.7%	−9.6%	−9.3%
Cotton						
Baseline	12.7	12.5	12.4	12.5	12.2	12.5
C/R Proposal	13.2	13.3	13.0	13.0	12.8	13.0
Difference	0.5	0.7	0.6	0.5	0.6	0.6
% Difference	4.0%	5.8%	4.8%	3.9%	4.6%	4.6%
Rice						
Baseline	3.0	2.9	2.8	2.8	2.7	2.8
C/R Proposal	3.4	2.8	2.6	2.6	2.6	2.8
Difference	0.4	−0.1	−0.2	−0.2	−0.1	0.0
% Difference	12.6%	−2.1%	−6.4%	−7.4%	−3.2%	−1.1%

acres were planted to crops in the first year 1992–93 (this figure is the sum of the difference numbers in Table 9.5, or as shown as an aggregate in Table 9.8).

In the four years following 92/93 in the projection this total acreage planted in the baseline increases significantly—increasing by about 7 million acres. Over the same period the total acreage planted in the Cochrane-Runge proposals declines moderately, with the result that the total acreage planted under the C/R proposals exceeds that of the baseline by only some 4 million acres by 96/97 (see Table 9.8). With respect to individual crops the largest increases in planted acreage in 1992–93 in the C/R proposal occurs for soybeans, 3.9 million acres, and wheat, 3.6 million acres (see Table 9.5). The large increase in soybean acreage and the small increase in corn acreage, 1.7 million acres, occurs because returns to soybeans are greater than for corn in 1992–93. The planted acreage projections for cotton and rice are somewhat more questionable than the projections for the other crops, since the equations for these two commodities in the model lack the desired number of historical observations free of price support. But the main point to take away from Tables 9.5 and 9.8 is that the planted acreage increases for all crops except oats under the C/R proposals as annual acreage control measures are eliminated for the period under consideration.

Production of all crops increases with the exception of rice (see Table 9.6). But production per crop increases by a smaller percentage than for planted acreages, reflecting decreases in average yields as the area planted to crops expands to include less productive acres.

With the elimination of annual acreage controls and price supporting operations under the C/R proposals farm commodity prices fall sharply in 1992–93 relative to the baseline. This results from the increased production of all crops except oats (see Table 9.6), and the release of stocks of grain held by CCC—some 9 million metric tons (see Table 9.9). But this brings into play the proposed Grain Stabilization Program which was designed to deal with sharp, short-run price movements. In this instance the Grain Stabilization Program acquires, or takes over, the 9 million metric tons (MT's) of grain released by the CCC and acquires through purchase 16.2 million MT's of grain for a total acquisition of 25.4 million MT's of grain in 1992–93 (see Table 9.9). The commodity breakdown of grain acquisitions in 1992–93 may be reviewed in Table 9.9. The Program also acquires .4 million MT's of soybeans. These operations moderate the price declines in 1992–93 under the C/R proposals relative to the baseline (see Table 9.7). The price declines for wheat are limited to 4.7 percent, for corn to 3.2 percent, for cotton to 2.5 percent, and rice to .4 percent. The largest price decline in 1992–93 occurs for soybeans; the price of soybeans declines by 12.6 percent.

During the remaining four years, 1993–96, some grain is purchased each year by the Grain Stabilization Program to buoy commodity prices, but in much smaller amounts than during 1992–93. By the year 1996–97 the Grain Stabilization Program has acquired grain stocks totalling 39.9 million MT's

Table 9.6. Impacts of the Cochrane/Runge proposals on crop production

Variable/Year	92/93	93/94	94/95	95/96	96/97	5-Yr avg
			(million bushels)			
Wheat						
Baseline	2,519	2,600	2,630	2,662	2,692	2,621
C/R Proposal	2,621	2,654	2,650	2,661	2,694	2,656
Difference	102	54	20	−1	3	36
% Difference	4.0%	2.1%	0.8%	0.0%	0.1%	1.4%
Corn						
Baseline	8,446	8,678	8,814	8,950	9,132	8,804
C/R Proposal	8,610	8,792	8,953	9,104	9,273	8,946
Difference	165	113	139	154	141	143
% Difference	2.0%	1.3%	1.6%	1.7%	1.5%	1.6%
Soybean						
Baseline	1,954	1,979	2,052	2,116	2,147	2,050
C/R Proposal	2,050	2,072	2,116	2,155	2,183	2,115
Difference	96	94	63	39	35	66
% Difference	4.9%	4.7%	3.1%	1.9%	1.6%	3.2%
Sorghum						
Baseline	690	730	741	744	776	736
C/R Proposal	786	787	805	806	814	800
Difference	96	58	64	62	38	63
% Difference	13.9%	7.9%	8.6%	8.3%	4.9%	8.6%
Barley						
Baseline	440	487	494	505	521	489
C/R Proposal	512	519	533	539	544	529
Difference	72	32	39	34	23	40
% Difference	16.3%	6.6%	7.8%	6.8%	4.5%	8.2%
Oats						
Baseline	379	365	365	372	378	372
C/R Proposal	373	379	371	377	372	374
Difference	−6	14	6	5	−6	2
% Difference	−1.6%	3.8%	1.6%	1.3%	−1.6%	0.6%
Cotton			*(million bales)*			
Baseline	15.85	15.79	15.76	16.15	15.91	15.89
C/R Proposal	15.90	16.07	16.00	16.42	16.34	16.15
Difference	0.05	0.28	0.25	0.27	0.43	0.26
% Difference	0.3%	1.8%	1.6%	1.7%	2.7%	1.6%
Rice			*(million cwt)*			
Baseline	168.6	163.2	162.8	164.0	159.4	163.6
C/R Proposal	186.0	160.2	153.9	153.6	155.0	161.7
Difference	17.4	−3.0	−9.0	−10.5	−4.4	−1.9
% Difference	10.3%	−1.8%	−5.5%	−6.4%	−2.8%	−1.2%

(see Table 9.9). The amount of grain purchased each year for each commodity and in total can be easily computed by subtracting the stocknumber in the line, C/R Proposal, of year one (say 92/93) from year two (say 93/94). With this level of grain acquisitions, and the small acquisitions of soybeans, commodity prices for the grains, soybeans, cotton, and rice increase modestly over the period 1992–96 under the C/R proposals (see Table 9.7). In sum, under the Cochrane-Runge policy proposals farm prices do not fall disastrously; in fact they remain only a few percentage points below the baseline prices. Stated more generally, the government assisted farm market economy proposed by Cochrane and Runge results in stable commodity prices only slightly lower than the baseline prices.

The Grain Stabilization Program operates over the period 1992–96 as was intended in Cochrane-Runge proposals. It acquires stocks when grain prices fall sharply in the short run. But it does not seek to push grain prices above the long-run world level as measured by the baseline. In achieving its price stabilization objective it acquires only about 40 million MT's of grain over the five-year period, far short of the maximum level of stock holdings suggested in Chapter 6 of some 75 million MT's. Further, since the FAPRI model assumes average weather, and has no major wars or international food crises built into it, the model does not call for any stock releases in the period 1992–96. But history suggests that over the five-year period 1992–96 some areas of the world would experience war or drought or floods with the consequent food shortages in which the United States would be called upon to provide food relief. Thus, for the period in question the Grain Stabilization Program would almost certainly have released some stocks as donations, and perhaps sold some grain in the event of an international crisis. The workings of the FAPRI model illustrate the price stabilizing role of the Grain Stabilization Program, but not its role in providing grain stocks in famine or international crisis situations, since none are built into the model.

IMPACTS ON THE DAIRY AND LIVESTOCK SECTORS

The impacts of the Cochrane-Runge proposals on milk supply, use, and prices may be reviewed in Table 9.10. Relative to the baseline total milk production increases modestly as does fluid product use and manufactured use. These latter developments would appear to be the result of modest declines in both the manufacturing and fluid prices of milk. This general, but modest, decline in the price of milk occurs because under the C/R proposals the government no longer purchases manufactured dairy products to support the price of milk. But it is important to note once again that declines in milk prices are modest as the farm economy moves in the direction of a less restricted market.

Table 9.7. Impacts of the Cochrane/Runge proposals on market prices

Variable/Year	92/93	93/94	94/95	95/96	96/97	5-Yr avg
			($ per bushel)			
Wheat						
Baseline	3.30	3.38	3.46	3.52	3.55	3.44
C/R Proposal	3.15	3.17	3.21	3.40	3.37	3.26
Difference	−0.15	−0.21	−0.25	−0.13	−0.18	−0.19
% Difference	−4.7%	−6.2%	−7.4%	−3.6%	−5.2%	−5.4%
Corn						
Baseline	2.25	2.31	2.31	2.36	2.37	2.32
C/R Proposal	2.18	2.24	2.21	2.24	2.24	2.22
Difference	−0.07	−0.07	−0.10	−0.12	−0.13	−0.10
% Difference	−3.2%	−3.2%	−4.2%	−5.0%	−5.6%	−4.3%
Soybean						
Baseline	5.67	6.26	6.44	6.14	6.30	6.16
C/R Proposal	4.95	5.50	5.62	5.66	5.98	5.54
Difference	−0.71	−0.76	−0.82	−0.48	−0.32	−0.62
% Difference	−12.6%	−12.2%	−12.8%	−7.8%	−5.1%	−10.1%
Sorghum						
Baseline	2.16	2.17	2.15	2.23	2.20	2.18
C/R Proposal	1.96	2.04	1.98	2.02	2.02	2.01
Difference	−0.19	−0.13	−0.16	−0.21	−0.18	−0.17
% Difference	−9.0%	−5.9%	−7.7%	−9.3%	−8.0%	−8.0%
Barley						
Baseline	2.29	2.30	2.33	2.37	2.37	2.33
C/R Proposal	2.04	2.10	2.11	2.17	2.18	2.12
Difference	−0.25	−0.20	−0.22	−0.20	−0.19	−0.21
% Difference	−10.9%	−8.7%	−9.6%	−8.5%	−7.8%	−9.1%
Oats						
Baseline	1.43	1.47	1.52	1.55	1.55	1.50
C/R Proposal	1.41	1.40	1.43	1.46	1.50	1.44
Difference	−0.02	−0.07	−0.09	−0.09	−0.06	−0.07
% Difference	−1.3%	−5.1%	−5.9%	−5.8%	−3.8%	−4.4%
Cotton			*(¢ per pound)*			
Baseline	60.88	63.28	67.77	69.20	70.96	66.42
C/R Proposal	59.37	61.53	65.14	66.09	67.41	63.91
Difference	−1.51	−1.75	−2.64	−3.11	−3.54	−2.51
% Difference	−2.5%	−2.8%	−3.9%	−4.5%	−5.0%	−3.8%
Rice			*($ per cwt)*			
Baseline	6.69	6.86	7.12	7.36	7.50	7.11
C/R Proposal	6.66	7.00	7.49	7.95	7.73	7.37
Difference	−0.03	0.14	0.37	0.59	0.23	0.26
% Difference	−0.4%	2.0%	5.1%	8.0%	3.1%	3.7%

The impacts of the Cochrane-Runge proposals on livestock production and prices may be reviewed in Table 9.11. The C/R proposals result in modest increases in the production of beef, pork, and broilers over the period 1992–96 relative to the baseline. These modest increases in production cause the prices of these livestock products to decline modestly throughout the entire five-year period. Once again the movement in the direction of a government assisted market economy does not create any severe industry disruptions.

THE AGGREGATE EFFECTS

The net effect of the Cochrane-Runge proposals on the farm economy may be seen in Table 9.12, which compares net farm income under the C/R proposals with that in the baseline. Relative to the baseline projections, net farm income dips sharply, or by nearly 16 percent, in 1992–93 under the C/R proposals, and then improves both relatively and absolutely over the remaining four years. The sharp fall in net farm income in 1992–93 under the C/R proposals relative to the baseline is due to three things: (1) reduced

Table 9.8. Impacts of the Cochrane/Runge proposals on key aggregates

Variable/Year	92/93	93/94	94/95	95/96	96/97	5-Yr avg
			(million acres)			
Total area planted						
Baseline	264.6	267.1	268.8	270.6	271.4	268.5
C/R Proposal	276.8	276.3	275.9	276.0	275.6	276.1
Difference	12.1	9.2	7.2	5.4	4.2	7.6
% Difference	4.6%	3.4%	2.7%	2.0%	1.6%	2.8%
Total area idled						
Baseline[a]	61.1	58.2	57.1	56.6	55.3	57.7
C/R Proposal	40.0	41.3	42.5	43.8	45.0	42.5
Difference	−21.1	−16.9	−14.6	−12.8	−10.3	−15.1
% Difference	−34.5%	−29.1%	−25.5%	−22.6%	−18.5%	−26.2%
Value of exports			*(billion $)*			
Baseline	20.85	22.21	23.37	24.07	25.13	23.13
C/R Proposal	19.94	21.19	22.23	23.33	24.30	22.20
Difference	−0.91	−1.01	−1.14	−0.74	−0.83	−0.93
% Difference	−4.4%	−4.6%	−4.9%	−3.1%	−3.3%	−4.0%
Volume of exports			*(million metric tons)*			
Baseline	134.74	137.56	141.61	145.89	150.58	142.08
C/R Proposal	136.60	139.17	143.97	147.98	152.46	144.04
Difference	1.86	1.61	2.36	2.09	1.89	1.96
% Difference	1.4%	1.2%	1.7%	1.4%	1.3%	1.4%

[a]Assumes 40 million acres are in the Conservation Reserve every year. Total area idled includes set-aside acres, 0/92 acres and CRP acres.

Table 9.9. Impacts of the Cochrane/Runge proposals on government-
owned stocks

Variable/Year	92/93	93/94	94/95	95/96	96/97	5-Yr avg
			(million metric tons)			
Wheat						
Baseline	4.1	4.1	4.1	4.1	4.1	4.1
C/R Proposal	8.8	12.2	12.9	13.6	14.0	12.3
Difference	4.8	8.2	8.8	9.5	9.9	8.2
% Difference	116.7%	200.0%	216.7%	233.3%	243.3%	202.0%
Corn						
Baseline	3.8	3.8	3.8	3.8	3.8	3.8
C/R Proposal	14.6	17.1	19.7	21.6	23.5	19.3
Difference	10.8	13.3	15.9	17.8	19.7	15.5
% Difference	283.3%	350.0%	416.7%	466.7%	516.7%	406.7%
Sorghum						
Baseline	1.3	0.6	0.0	0.0	0.0	0.4
C/R Proposal	1.3	1.3	1.3	1.3	1.3	1.3
Difference	0.0	0.6	1.3	1.3	1.3	0.9
% Difference	0.0%	100.0%	—	—	—	—
Rice						
Baseline	0.0	0.0	0.0	0.0	0.0	0.0
C/R Proposal	0.7	1.1	1.1	1.1	1.1	1.0
Difference	0.7	1.1	1.1	1.1	1.1	1.0
% Difference	—	—	—	—	—	—
Total grains						
Baseline	9.2	8.5	7.9	7.9	7.9	8.3
C/R Proposal	25.4	31.8	35.0	37.6	39.9	33.9
Difference	16.2	23.3	27.1	29.7	32.0	25.7
% Difference	177.2%	272.9%	343.7%	376.4%	405.8%	310.3%
Soybeans						
Baseline	0.0	0.0	0.0	0.0	0.0	0.0
C/R Proposal	0.4	1.6	1.6	1.6	1.6	1.4
Difference	0.4	1.6	1.6	1.6	1.6	1.4
% Difference	—	—	—	—	—	—

government payments, (2) lower crop and livestock receipts, and (3) a negative change in the value of inventory. The gap in net farm income between the baseline and the C/R proposals, however, narrows through time as production expenses under the C/R proposals decline relative to the baseline, and the change in the value of farm inventories becomes relatively less unfavorable. Thus, although it cannot be argued that the C/R proposals improve the net income position of commercial agriculture, it can be argued that aggregate net farm income trends upward under the proposed market conditions and at a lower level of government payments to farmers (see Table 9.12).

Table 9.10. Impacts of the Cochrane/Runge proposals on milk supply, use, and prices

Variable/Year	1992	1993	1994	1995	1996	5-Yr avg
Milk cows			*(thousand head)*			
Baseline	10,021	10,000	9,979	9,960	9,945	9,981
C/R Proposal	9,981	9,945	9,925	9,912	9,904	9,934
Difference[a]	(40)	(55)	(54)	(47)	(42)	(47)
% Difference	−0.40%	−0.55%	−0.54%	−0.48%	−0.42%	−0.48%
Production/cow			*(million pounds MEU)*			
Baseline	15,235	15,472	15,718	15,978	16,257	15,732
C/R Proposal	15,151	15,431	15,693	15,953	16,235	15,693
Difference[a]	(84)	(41)	(25)	(25)	(22)	(39)
% Difference	−0.55%	−0.26%	−0.16%	−0.16%	−0.13%	−0.25%
Milk production						
Baseline	152,664	154,719	156,850	159,139	161,684	157,011
C/R Proposal	151,222	153,464	155,756	158,134	160,793	155,874
Difference[a]	(1,442)	(1,255)	(1,094)	(1,005)	(892)	(1,138)
% Difference	−0.94%	0.81%	0.70%	0.63%	−0.55%	−0.72%
Fluid product use						
Baseline	58,214	59,002	59,576	60,099	61,144	59,607
C/R Proposal	58,363	59,057	59,667	60,292	61,290	59,734
Difference	149	55	91	193	147	127
% Difference	0.26%	0.09%	0.15%	0.32%	0.24%	0.21%
Manufactured use						
Baseline	88,747	89,953	91,471	93,175	94,617	91,593
C/R Proposal	87,135	88,627	90,278	91,972	93,576	90,318
Difference[a]	(1,612)	(1,327)	(1,193)	(1,203)	(1,041)	(1,275)
% Difference	−1.82%	−1.47%	−1.30%	−1.29%	−1.10%	−1.39%
Manu. grade price			*($/Cwt)*			
Baseline	11.09	11.24	11.62	11.87	12.17	11.60
C/R Proposal	10.71	11.15	11.55	11.82	12.16	11.48
Difference	−0.37	−0.08	−0.06	−0.05	−0.01	−0.12
% Difference	−3.37%	−0.75%	−0.53%	−0.42%	−0.09%	−1.00%
Fluid price						
Baseline	12.47	12.62	12.99	13.24	13.53	12.97
C/R Proposal	11.71	12.15	12.55	12.82	13.16	12.48
Difference	−0.76	−0.47	−0.44	−0.42	−0.30	−0.49
% Difference	−6.10%	−3.71%	−3.37%	−3.18%	−2.78%	−3.80%
All milk price						
Baseline	12.12	12.27	12.65	12.91	13.21	12.63
C/R Proposal	11.54	11.97	12.40	12.64	13.02	12.31
Difference	−0.58	−0.31	−0.25	−0.27	−0.19	−0.32
% Difference	−4.76%	−2.49%	−1.99%	−2.09%	−1.45%	−2.52%

[a]A number in parentheses indicates the C/R proposed value to be less than the baseline value.

The question of government payments to farmers under the Cochrane-Runge proposals needs to be discussed at this point. Stabilization payments to farmers up to $7 billion a year were proposed in Chapter 6 when the

Table 9.11. Impacts of the Cochrane/Runge proposals on livestock produc-
            tion and prices

Variable/Year	1992	1993	1994	1995	1996	5-Yr avg
Beef			*(million pounds)*			
Baseline	23,664	24,048	24,366	24,186	24,015	24,056
C/R Proposal	23,708	24,208	24,489	24,463	24,289	24,231
Difference	44	160	123	277	274	176
% Difference	0.19%	0.67%	0.51%	1.14%	1.14%	0.73%
Pork						
Baseline	16,688	16,370	16,122	15,947	16,367	16,299
C/R Proposal	16,733	16,411	16,379	16,150	16,509	16,436
Difference	44	41	257	203	142	138
% Difference	0.27%	0.25%	1.59%	1.27%	0.87%	0.84%
Broiler						
Baseline	19,691	20,140	20,601	21,127	21,682	20,648
C/R Proposal	19,796	20,269	20,769	21,283	21,821	20,788
Difference	105	129	168	156	139	139
% Difference	0.53%	0.64%	0.82%	0.74%	0.64%	0.68%
Total						
Baseline	60,043	60,558	61,089	61,259	62,064	61,003
C/R Proposal	60,237	60,888	61,638	61,896	62,619	61,455
Difference	193	330	549	636	555	453
% Difference	0.32%	0.55%	0.90%	1.04%	0.89%	0.74%
Omaha fed steer			*($/cwt.)*			
Baseline	$72.26	$69.47	$69.45	$71.44	$72.79	$71.08
C/R Proposal	$71.42	$67.97	$68.25	$69.33	$70.71	$69.54
Difference[a]	($0.84)	($1.50)	($1.21)	($2.11)	($2.07)	($1.54)
% Difference	−1.16%	−2.16%	−1.74%	−2.95%	−2.85%	−2.17%
Kansas City feeder						
Baseline	$80.77	$77.77	$77.64	$77.69	$79.77	$78.73
C/R Proposal	$79.73	$76.50	$76.78	$76.30	$77.98	$77.46
Difference[a]	($1.04)	($1.27)	($0.85)	($1.39)	($1.79)	($1.27)
% Difference	−1.29%	−1.63%	−1.10%	−1.79%	−2.24%	−1.61%
Barrow & Gilt						
Baseline	$40.92	$46.24	$52.31	$55.81	$50.26	$49.11
C/R Proposal	$40.40	$45.58	$49.62	$53.16	$48.30	$47.41
Difference[a]	($0.52)	($0.65)	($2.69)	($2.64)	($1.96)	($1.69)
% Difference	−1.28%	−1.41%	−5.14%	−4.73%	−3.90%	−3.45%
12-city broiler						
Baseline	$57.06	$57.85	$59.62	$60.84	$61.86	$59.45
C/R Proposal	$56.29	$57.51	$57.88	$59.82	$61.20	$58.54
Difference[a]	($0.77)	($0.34)	($1.74)	($1.03)	($0.66)	($0.91)
% Difference	−1.36%	−0.59%	−2.91%	−1.68%	−1.06%	−1.53%

[a]A number in parentheses indicates the C/R proposed value to be less than the baseline
value.

terms of trade turned against farmers. The price triggering mechanism for
making stabilization payments was discussed earlier in this chapter and
given numerical values for each of the five years in the period 1992–96. For

Table 9.12. Impacts of the Cochrane/Runge proposals on net farm income

Variable/Year	1992	1993	1994	1995	1996	5-Yr avg
			(*billion $*)			
Crop receipts						
Baseline	82.09	85.25	89.31	92.23	95.21	88.82
C/R Proposal	81.31	83.80	87.27	90.33	93.51	87.24
Difference	−0.77	−1.45	−2.04	−1.90	−1.70	−1.57
% Difference	−0.9%	−1.7%	−2.3%	−2.1%	−1.8%	−1.8%
Livestock receipts						
Baseline	83.57	84.19	87.73	90.23	90.59	87.26
C/R Proposal	81.83	83.03	86.29	88.43	89.28	85.77
Difference	−1.74	−1.17	−1.44	−1.80	−1.31	−1.49
% Difference	−2.1%	−1.4%	−1.6%	−2.0%	−1.4%	−1.7%
Government payments						
Baseline	9.02	8.16	7.15	6.48	5.99	7.36
C/R Proposal	7.00	7.00	5.00	5.00	5.00	5.80
Difference	−2.02	−1.16	−2.15	−1.48	−0.99	−1.56
% Difference	−22.4%	−14.2%	−30.0%	−22.8%	−16.5%	−21.2%
Other income						
Baseline	16.63	17.12	17.89	18.57	19.12	17.87
C/R Proposal	16.36	16.81	17.44	18.05	18.62	17.46
Difference	−0.27	−0.31	−0.45	−0.52	−0.50	−0.41
% Difference	1.6%	−1.8%	−2.5%	−2.8%	−2.6%	−2.3%
Production expenses						
Baseline	149.54	154.25	159.41	164.09	169.19	159.30
C/R Proposal	150.03	153.59	158.30	162.02	166.90	158.17
Difference	0.50	−0.67	−1.11	−2.07	−2.29	−1.13
% Difference	0.3%	−0.4%	−0.7%	−1.3%	−1.4%	−0.7%
Value of inventory change						
Baseline	0.32	1.11	0.65	0.47	−0.70	0.37
C/R Proposal	−0.96	0.87	0.23	0.30	−0.71	−0.05
Difference	−1.28	−0.25	−0.42	−0.17	−0.01	−0.43
% Difference	−398.0%	−22.3%	−64.4%	−35.9%	−1.3%	−114.5%
Net farm income						
Baseline	42.09	41.59	43.33	43.89	41.02	42.38
C/R Proposal	35.51	37.92	37.93	40.09	38.81	38.05
Difference	−6.58	−3.67	−5.39	−3.80	−2.21	−4.33
% Difference	−15.6%	−8.8%	−12.5%	−8.7%	−5.4%	−10.2%

crops the percentage increase in the index of prices paid greatly exceeded the downward movement in the index of prices received in 1992 and 1993 under the C/R proposals thus requiring that stabilization payments be made. But the total amounts of payments to be made, it will be recalled, was to be a political decision. In this case the "political" decision was made to make payments up to the maximum of $7 billion in 1992 and 1993; that "political" decision was in fact made by Cochrane and Runge. Consequently, the government payments shown in Table 9.13 under the C/R

Table 9.13. Impacts of the Cochrane/Runge proposals on government
            outlays for price and income support

Variable/Year	FY-93	FY-94	FY-95	FY-96	FY-97	5-Yr avg
			(million $)			
Direct payments						
Baseline	8,350	7,275	6,581	6,081	5,995	6,856
C/R Proposal	7,000	7,000	5,000	5,000	5,000	5,800
Difference	−1350	−275	−1581	−1081	−995	−1056
% Difference	−16.2%	−3.8%	−24.0%	−17.8%	−16.6%	−15.4%
Stock outlays						
Baseline	421	159	153	229	159	224
C/R Proposal	—	—	—	—	—	—
Difference	—	—	—	—	—	—
% Difference	—	—	—	—	—	—
Storage and handling						
Baseline	163	149	138	127	127	141
C/R Proposal	—	—	—	—	—	—
Difference	—	—	—	—	—	—
% Difference	—	—	—	—	—	—
Other costs						
Baseline	1,701	1,673	1,683	1,723	1,714	1,699
C/R Proposal[a]	488	488	488	488	488	488
Difference	−1213	−1185	−1195	−1235	−1226	−1211
% Difference	−71.3%	−70.8%	−71.0%	−71.7%	−71.5%	−71.3%
Total CCC outlays						
Baseline	10,635	9,255	8,555	8,161	7,995	8,920
C/R Proposal	7,488	7,488	5,488	5,488	5,488	6,288
Difference	−3147	−1767	−3067	−2673	−2507	−2632
% Difference	−29.6%	−19.1%	−35.9%	−32.8%	−31.4%	−29.5%

[a]Includes program costs for wool and mohair, honey, peanuts, tobacco, and operating
expenses for CCC and a reduced ASCS.

proposal are $7 billion for the fiscal years 1993 and 1994. These payments
keep net farm income from falling significantly in those two years.

The domestic terms of trade continue to turn against farmers in 1994,
1995, and 1996 under the C/R proposal, with the percentage increase in the
index of prices paid exceeding the movement in prices received in each of
those years. But the difference in the percentage movement of the two
indices is greatly reduced in those three years, indicating that the terms of
trade are becoming less unfavorable to farmers with each passing year. The
"political" decision was thus made by the authors to reduce the total
government outlay for stabilization payments to $5 billion in each of the
fiscal years 1995, 1996, and 1997 (see Table 9.13). Our reasoning was that
the net incomes of commercial farmers were being held within reasonable
limits by payments totalling $5 billion per year, and the $2 billion saved

could be employed more effectively in rural development or environmental or educational programs. Given the fact of limited resources the choice of a policy and pursuit of that policy boils down to making a judgement about the best use of those limited resources. The authors made the judgmental decision in this case; in the context of government it would be a political judgmental decision.

Total government outlays, as well as the principal components of those outlays for farm income support under the baseline and under the C/R proposals are presented in Table 9.13. Government outlays under the baseline exceed those under the C/R proposal by an average of $2.6 billion per year. The larger government outlays under the baseline are primarily the result of (1) larger payments to farmers and (2) various CCC and ASCS expenditures (e.g., stock acquisitions for price support, storage and handling, and operating expenses).

Government outlays for the Grain Stabilization Program are not listed in Table 9.13 (Government Outlays for Price and Income Programs) because the objectives of the Grain Storage Program are broader than farm price and income support. The Grain Stabilization Program, as proposed has three broad objectives: (1) to protect American farmers against sharp, short-run price declines in the grains and oilseeds; (2) to protect American consumers against upward spiralling food costs in periods of domestic or international crises; and (3) to enable the United States to take the lead in dealing with famines and critical food shortages around the world. Thus, we argue that costs of the Grain Stabilization Program should not be charged against the farm price and income programs. The management decisions of the Grain Stabilization Program, like those of the Federal Reserve System, or the national oil reserve, have important implications for farm income. But they also have income implications for other sectors of the economy at home and abroad, hence their costs of operation are chargeable to the maintenance of a healthy general economy. The Grain Stabilization Program is not just another farm program; it is a vital program piece of a national policy to maintain a stable, prosperous economy.

The government costs of initiating the Grain Stabilization Program in the period 1992–96 are presented in Table 9.14. Grain acquisition costs plus handling and storage charges average $1.1 billion per year, as total grain stocks are built up to a level of some 40 million MT's. No grain sales or donations are indicated in Table 9.14, since the events (e.g., a famine, or a war) that would give rise to grain sales or donations are not built into the FAPRI model. Since the operating objective of the Grain Stabilization Program is to hold actual grain market prices at or near the long-run level of world grain prices, it should, if donations by the federal government are

Table 9.14. Impacts of the Cochrane/Runge proposals on the grain
stabilization program

Variable/Year	FY-93	FY-94	FY-95	FY-96	FY-97	5-Yr avg
			(million $)			
Acquisitions or sales	1,651	937	301	253	219	672
Handing and storage	257	425	502	540	574	460
Total	1,908	1,362	803	793	793	1,132

excluded, come close to breaking even over time in terms of profits and
losses.

INTERPRETING THE RESULTS

Reflecting on the forest of numbers presented in Tables 9.2 through
9.14 several general points, or general conclusions, would seem in order.
First, the Cochrane-Runge proposals represent considerably less government involvement in the farm economy, and considerably less control over
individual farm business decisions than the programs of the 1985 Act, but
achieve very similar price, quantity, and income consequences (see summary
Table 9.15). The C/R proposals substitute two broadly conceived stabilization programs for a set of detailed commodity-specific programs. This latter,
or traditional, approach has reached stifling proportions, and the 1990 farm
legislation, despite some positive features, represents more of the same.

Net farm income under the C/R proposals averages, for the 1992–96
period, $4.3 billion below the baseline. But these reductions come with an
estimated savings of $2.6 billion per year to the government for farm
income support (see Table 9.15). By the end of the 1992–96 period the net
farm income gap is closed to within $2.2 billion (see Table 9.12). In other
words, the C/R proposals creates a government assisted market, with almost
no control over individual management decision making, at only a small loss
in farm income and a significant savings in government outlays.

Second, to gain the advantages of the Cochrane/Runge proposals, the
managers of the Grain Stabilization Program must understand the triple
objectives of the Program and be skilled stock managers, and the decision
makers in the Stabilization Payments Program must exercise restraint in
setting the size of payments once the price triggering mechanism calls for
the making of payments. Failure to exercise this discipline will cause the
Commodity Stabilization Program to become just another price enhancing
program, and the Payments Stabilization Program to become just another
deficiency payments program. But if the managers of the two Stabilization
programs fully understand and recognize the stabilization objectives of the

Table 9.15. Summary of major changes under the Cochrane/Runge proposal

	Five-year averages		
	Baseline	C/R	Change from baseline
	($/bushel)		
Farm Prices			
Corn	2.32	2.22	−0.10
Soybeans	6.16	5.54	−0.62
Wheat	3.44	3.26	−0.18
	(million acres)		
Acreage			
15 crops planted	268.5	276.1	7.6
Total idled	57.7	42.5	−15.2
	(million metric tons)		
Government-owned stocks			
Total grains[a]	8.3	33.9	25.6
Soybeans	0.0	1.4	1.4
	(billion $)		
Net farm income	42.4	38.0	−4.2
Government outlays	8.9	6.3	−2.6

[a]Includes wheat, corn, sorghum, and rice

programs and have a national perspective, as opposed to a specific commodity objective, then the advantages of the programs are attainable. This is the case because the mechanics of the proposals were conceived to achieve long-run price stability and to provide an income safety net for all farmers—not to push farm prices and incomes above long-run market levels.

Third, the FAPRI policy model does not take into account two important aspects of the Cochrane-Runge proposals: (1) the regional payment program with a regional price triggering mechanism, and (2) the distribution of payments by size of farm. The fact that stabilization payments to farmers in one region might be large, up to say the limit of $20,000 per farm, and small to nonexistent in another region, depending upon the terms of trade in each region, could not be introduced into the FAPRI model. The failure to introduce the regional price triggering mechanism into the FAPRI model probably resulted in an overstatement of total program costs and payments to farmers under the C/R proposal. And the effects of the $20,000 payment cap per farm in the C/R proposal on the distribution of payments could not be estimated by the FAPRI model. The low payment cap of $20,000 could, for example, result in some medium-sized farmers in a given region receiving the same total payment as a very large farmer.

The regional reapportionment and the farm redistribution effects of the Payment Stabilization Program of the C/R proposals are not estimated in the FAPRI model and given quantitative content. But a driving force behind the policy reforms proposed by Cochrane and Runge was and is the inequitable distribution of government largesse under the traditional farm commodity programs. Thus, we argue that the logic of the C/R proposals suggests that there would be important reapportionment and redistribution effects from those proposals in which payments in regions with favorable terms of trade would decline, and payment assistance to individual farmers would become less skewed in the direction of large, wealthy farmers.

Fourth and finally, a review of the data in this chapter—farm prices, farm income, stabilization payments, stocks acquisitions—suggests that the five year period 92/93 through 96/97 modelled by FAPRI of the Cochrane-Runge policy proposals was too short from a purely analytical viewpoint. The fact that grain stocks accumulation occurred over the entire period, although at a declining rate, and that stabilization payments were made over the entire period, although at a declining rate, suggests that the farm economy had not in this simulation completed its transition from a price-income supported sector to a stabilized sector at some concept of a long-run equilibrium. The declining trend in the difference between net farm income in the baseline and in the Cochrane-Runge proposals in Table 9.12 suggests that if the FAPRI simulation had been run over a longer period, say 10 years, that an equilibrium situation might have been reached.

At the inception of the Cochrane-Runge proposals in 92/93 some 21 million acres of land previously idled under government program were suddenly turned loose. Of this total, land in crops under the Cochrane-Runge proposals increased by 12 million acres relative to the baseline, and 9 million acres were abandoned, turned into pasture or put in some nonintensive use. In other words, the total productive farm plant was increased by 12 million acres in one year. Somehow this expanded farm plant, plus 9 million metric tons of government held stocks of grain, had to be assimilated into the farm economy in a politically acceptable manner, and the price-income supported farm sector transformed into a market oriented sector in long-run equilibrium. The FAPRI five-year simulation takes us part way. Now we will sketch a long-run scenario that could produce that equilibrium solution.

• At the inception of the Cochrane-Runge proposals the release of acres from the government acreage reserve plus the release of government owned grain stocks could have caused crop prices to plummet. But that did not happen.

• The acquisition of stocks under the Cochrane-Runge Grain Reserve Program moderated the decline in crop prices. Nonetheless crop prices fell between 3 and 10 percent.

• After the initial expansion in crop acreage, the total acres planted to crops held almost constant over the five-year period 92/93 through 96/97. At the lower level of crop prices there was no inducement to expand total crop acreage.

• Production in the major crops increased modestly over the period 92/93 through 96/97 as yields increased.

• But the market for the grains expanded over the five-year period as exports increased importantly and the feeding of grain to livestock increased at the lower grain prices. This development resulted in the significant increases in planted acreages of wheat, soybeans, sorghum, and barley under the baseline, and a steady increase in the grains and soybeans prices under the Cochrane-Runge proposals.

• Concurrently production expenses were increasing under the Cochrane-Runge proposals, but not as rapidly as in the baseline. Lower capital costs resulting from lower land values and lower livestock production costs resulting from the lower prices of feed were dampening the upward movement of production costs under the Cochrane-Runge proposals.

• As a result, net farm income under the Cochrane-Runge proposals was only $2.2 billion less than the baseline income in 96/97 compared with a difference of $6.6 billion in 92/93, and all this with a reduction in total stabilization payments from $7 billion to $5 billion per year.

• What was happening over the period 92/93 through 96/97 was an expansion in the total market for crops, which reduced, or absorbed, the excess production capacity of the farm plant brought about by the addition of 12 million acres of cropland in 92/93 under the Cochrane-Runge proposals.

• If the trends described above were to continue through a second five-year period where the total market for the crops was growing faster than production under the Cochrane-Runge proposals then a point in time should be reached, possibly at or near the end of the second five-year period when the farm economy was in long-run equilibrium and *continuous* acquisitions of grain stocks and the making of stabilization payments was no longer necessary.

• The characteristics of this market oriented farm economy in long-run equilibrium stated in relation to the baseline could be as follows:

1. Crop prices are modestly lower.
2. The livestock industry is more prosperous.

3. Land prices are somewhat lower.
4. Total net farm income is modestly lower.
5. There is greater freedom to farm on the part of individual operators.
6. The farming industry is not permanently subsidized, but still provides farmers with a safety net.

The above scenario is an analytical possibility over a ten-year period *granted* the benign macro-economic assumptions and the average weather conditions built into the FAPRI model. And it may be a useful description of what could happen *if* the national and world economies remained on an even keel over a ten-year period, while the American farm economy moved from a price-income supported one to a market-oriented one in long-run equilibrium under the Cochrane-Runge proposals. But *if* widespread crop failure and famine occurred in the Far East in say, Year 6, the accumulated grain stocks shown in Table 9.9 could easily disappear in one year. Or *if* the national economy should falter and become severely depressed in the 1990s the decline in the total amount of stabilization payments projected in the above scenario would never have occurred.

The FAPRI simulation of the Cochrane-Runge proposals represents a special case with very special assumptions. The quantitative estimates illustrate how two of the safety net programs proposed by Cochrane and Runge—the income stabilization program and the grain reserve program—could come into play to soften the transition from a price-income supported farm economy to a market-oriented economy in long-run equilibrium in a non-bumpy world of continuous economic prosperity and average weather.

Notes

1. The Institute, FAPRI, is based, in a joint arrangement, at the Center for National Food and Agricultural Policy at the University of Missouri–Columbia and the Center for Trade and Agricultural Policy at Iowa State University. FAPRI conducts analyses, or impact studies of alternative farm policies on its economic policy model. It conducts analyses of alternative farm policies on its own initiative, for various private groups and organizations and for governmental agencies, such as the House and Senate Agricultural Committees of the Congress. Inquiries regarding the analytical studies of FAPRI should be directed to Abner W. Womack of the Department of Agricultural Economics, University of Missouri–Columbia.

References

FAPRI. 1985. *Options for the 1985 Farm Bill: An Analysis and Evaluation*. FAPRI Staff Report #1-85. Columbia: University of Missouri, Center for Food and Agricultural Policy.

10 The Politics of the Proposed Policy

Linkages to the National Economy

Our goal in this volume has been to propose a set of policies for the food, farm and rural sectors that are an integral part of a positive national economic and social policy. Our approach is that of dealing with the needs and problems of the food, farm and rural sectors, recognizing their linkages to other sectors of the national economy and society. For example, the food produced on the farm must be processed and distributed to mostly urban consumers in a safe and appealing form and at affordable prices; farmers, nonfarm rural residents and urban people all have a stake in protecting and conserving the land base and the limited water supply in rural areas, and in providing green belts, forest preserves and parks of all kinds for society to enjoy; businessmen looking for places to locate manufacturing plants are interested in the literacy and training of potential workers, as well as social amenities, in rural areas; and the economic future of many rural areas is absolutely dependent on local industrial development.

The linkages between and among the food, farm and rural sectors and the rest of the national economy and society go on and on. But to an important degree these linkages have either been ignored or given superficial consideration in the past. We have tried in our policy proposals to correct this state of affairs. We have tried to support and strengthen those linkages essential to a smoothly operating national economy and a stable, healthy rural society.

We believe further that there could be strong support for our set of proposals from many and diverse groups in the national electorate, *if* those groups came to understand the nature and importance of their linkages to the food, farm and rural sectors, and that such understanding could be converted into political support and action given the appropriate leadership. The linkages between the many and diverse groups in the national society and parts of the food, farm and rural sectors must lead to a convergence of interests for the people involved. It is our thesis that this convergence of interests can be converted into political support for our policy proposals on the part of the many and diverse groups in society, if the appropriate leadership is forthcoming. As we shall develop later, there are all kinds of people in American society who have an interest in what goes on in rural areas. But that interest has been turned off by the continuing and narrow struggle over price and income support for commercial farmers.

This belief in the potential widespread political support for the policy reforms proposed in Chapter 6 is grounded in the internal consistency of those reforms with the policy decision principles developed in Chapter 2. The first decision principle was the *Majority Rule* principle. Under that principle it was argued that a successful policy for the food, farm and rural sectors must have the majority support of all members of American society; not just the commercial farm sector. The set of policy reforms purposed in Chapter 6 was designed to benefit *all* of American society. Majority support for this package of reforms can be forthcoming if the diverse groups in society, which would benefit from the legislative acceptance of these reforms, were informed and marshalled by the appropriate leadership. The latent majority support is there waiting to be activated.

The second decision principle was *Protection for the Minority*. The policy reform package takes account of this principle in two ways. The reform package does not leave the minority, commercial farmers, unprotected from economic and physical forces beyond their control; it provides a safety net comprised of four parts to protect them against those adverse forces. The reforms further provide farmers with much greater "freedom to farm" than was the case under previous commodity programs. This is a reform that has been high on the agenda of commercial farmers for years.

The third decision principle was *The Duty of Government to Assist the Poor and the Downtrodden to Become Productive Members of Society*. The policy reform package is strongly supportive of this principle. It is recommended that the food assistance programs be continued, and that special measures be developed to reach the homeless, the elderly and children who are in need. And much of the rural development program is aimed at the poor and the downtrodden. It provides small grants to the poor to assist them in completing their education and obtaining job training, an employment service to help them find jobs, housing assistance, and low-interest loans to rural municipalities to repair or build needed service facilities (e.g., schools, health clinics). The eradication of poverty in rural areas is a dominant thrust of the policy proposals set forth in Chapter 6.

The fourth decision principle was *Government Responsibility for the Economic Health of the Nation*. The entire policy reform package is directed to the goal of a strong and stable farm economy in the context of a strong and growing national economy. The following provisions of that package—greater production flexibility on individual farms; pricing policies designed to encourage agricultural exports; a grain stabilization program; support for an expanding part-time farming sector; a revived and productive rural nonfarm sector based on a better educated and a better trained work force; increased protection for the important natural resources, land, water and forests, of the nation; a strengthened research component; and a population that is healthier as the result of improved nutrition at all levels of society—are designed to increase resource productivity, human and physical, of the nation and thereby enable it to grow on a sustained basis. There are no quick fixes in our set of policy reforms; but they do provide the basis of sustained economic growth.

Our argument is then the following: the policy reforms proposed in Chapter 6 are consistent with and are supportive of our interpretation of the basic values of American society. Given the fact that those policy reforms are consistent with and supportive of these basic values, it should be possible to build the political support to enact them into law. The building of the political coalition to enact them into law awaits, however, the leadership with the skill and the interest to do so.

The Existing Legislative Process

There is another side to the politics of reform; it is the existing legislative process. In this process close working relationships are forged between the powerful farm commodity lobbying associations and their congressional representative counterparts. The commodity associations help elect the congressional representatives, and the congressional representatives help pass the legislation sought by, or kill the legislation opposed by, the commodity associations which helped elect the representatives in the first place. The commodity associations will vigorously oppose any efforts to eliminate or reform the existing commodity programs, which have been constructed piece by piece by the associations representing their members, the large commercial farmers. Thus, on the basis of past legislative history, it is virtually certain that if our proposals were introduced into Congress in the form of legislation, such legislation would be "quietly killed" in the agricultural committees to which it was assigned. The powerful farm commodity lobbying associations, working with their congressional representatives on those committees, would do the killing. That has been the fate of every important piece of reform legislation dealing with commercial agriculture since the end of World War II.

Three different administrations attempted major reforms of American farm policy between 1948 and 1962, but each reform package was defeated in Congress (the broad outlines of those proposed policy reforms are presented on pages 42–47 in Chapter 3).[1] The Brannan Plan, named for Secretary of Agriculture Charles Brannan (who proposed it), was introduced into Congress in April 1949 and by late summer of that year had gone down to defeat. The specific causes of its defeat are numerous, but two stand out above all others: (1) the large commercial farmers were dead set against the income payments provisions and the payment limitations provisions of the Plan and working through their farm representative in the Congress they forged a powerful coalition to oppose it, and (2) the way the Plan was developed and introduced into the Congress, it became a highly partisan issue, and the Republicans in the Congress closed ranks and fought it vigorously and successfully. Certain provisions of the Brannan Plan eventually were enacted into law, but by 1950 the Plan as a coherent reform package was dead.

Secretary of Agriculture Ezra Taft Benson was an ardent advocate of the free market, and he tried during the Eisenhower administration to move farm policy in that direction. In 1954 the Eisenhower administration, with the backing of the American Farm Bureau Federation, asked Congress to approve a system of flexible price support in which the level of price support would decline as stocks in government hands increased. The administration won a limited victory, in which the secretary was given the authority to lower the level of price support modestly. But the Congress would not give the secretary the authority to lower price supports for the important crops—wheat, cotton and corn—to levels approaching that of a free market, and thereby shut off the avalanche of production in that period. Democrats and Republicans alike in the Congress could not see the sense of lowering the price support level in a period of overproduction and falling farm prices and incomes. Thus, Secretary Benson was forced to accept a form of voluntary production controls under the new name of the Soil Bank in 1956.

The Kennedy-Freeman administration understood full well the general nature and persistence of the excess capacity problem of America's agriculture. But it believed that this problem could be solved: first by expanding the demand for farm products through a series of programs and, second, by adjusting supplies to that expanded demand at a set of prices (determined by Congress to be fair to producers and consumers alike) through the imposition of a system of tough, mandatory production controls. The administration introduced legislation into Congress in 1961 and 1962 along these lines, and each time it was defeated. Commercial farmers and their congressional allies were in no mood to accept mandatory production controls, when they (the farmers) were already being paid to take land out of production on a voluntary basis. And powerful members of Congress were unwilling to give the administration the authority to operate production control programs in a manner that would effectively control production. Thus, the policy reform package of the Kennedy-Freeman administration, which involved a major planning effort on both the demand and supply sides, was soundly defeated in Congress.

Although the specifics of each of these three situations were different, commercial farmers and their congressional allies were successful in each case in holding on to the main features of their traditional price and income support programs, and in defeating the policy reform package of each administration. This was achieved in the legislative process by the effective working relationships between the commercial farm lobbying associations and their representative counterparts on the agricultural committees, and the trading of votes among farm state representatives and between rural and urban representatives.

It is our thesis that this need not have been the case *if* the president in each case had provided more leadership and expended more political capital in support of the administration's farm policy reform package. The president in each situation was supportive of the reform effort, but for different reasons he did not provide the strong leadership that the effort required.

President Truman, the one president with a farm background, was so engaged in international affairs—the Marshall Plan, the fall of China, the cold war and the Korean War—that he had little time, and perhaps energy, to devote to the enactment of the Brannan Plan. Further, his election victory in 1948 was a close one, thus he did not have an overwhelming mandate to effect economic reforms.

President Eisenhower won big in 1952 and had a strong mandate to govern. Further, he was sympathetic to the free market philosophy of his secretary of agriculture. But he had little interest in agriculture or policy reforms for that sector. Thus, he provided little leadership and expended little political capital in the battle with Congress to win the passage of legislation to give the secretary of agriculture the authority to "flex" price supports downward to levels required to resolve the excess production capacity problem. President Eisenhower turned the task of winning passage of their reform package over to Secretary Benson, and he (Benson) did not have sufficient political clout to carry the day.

President Kennedy, like President Truman, won in a squeaker and did not have a strong mandate to govern. And like President Eisenhower, his interest in agriculture was minimal. But most important, once the Kennedy White House learned that farmers would accept mandatory production controls only at farm product price levels that would raise food prices significantly, presidential support for the reform package eroded away. Consequently, the price support incentives acceptable to the Kennedy administration in the policy reform package introduced into Congress simply were not acceptable to commercial farmers (were not high enough to win their support) under a strict regime of mandatory production controls. Thus, the reform package of 1961 died in committee and the legislation that passed in 1962 was shorn of its mandatory features except for wheat, and the mandatory control provisions for wheat were defeated in referendum in 1963.

The historical experience is clear; it is extremely difficult to pass farm legislation that seeks to effect major reforms in commodity price and income support programs. Certainly it cannot be done without strong presidential leadership and support, and that was not forthcoming in the three efforts made between 1948 and 1962. Since that time one administration after another has taken the easy way out. Each has pretty much let the Congress write the "farm legislation," and sought to check congressional excesses with respect to program costs through the threat of the veto.

The result has been piece after piece of "farm legislation" that deals almost exclusively with the specific needs and problems of commercial farmers in which the major outlines of the legislation have changed very little, but in which incremental changes are made, sometimes yearly, sometimes every five years, to take account of the needs of a particular farm group in a particular producing area. There is one important exception to the above generalization. That exception is the development of the food assistance programs for the urban poor, which came about as a compromise between the declining number of farm representatives and the increasing number of urban representatives to, in effect, save the "farm programs." A bargain was struck between the farmers' representatives and the urban representatives in which the price of maintaining the farm commodity programs was a huge increase in the size of the food assistance programs.

The legislative process of the federal government of the United States, as in most western, industrialized democracies, is rigged to enable special interest groups of a particular area, or a particular industry, or a particular farm commodity to gain important benefits for their constituents by spreading the cost to everyone else in the national society. How does this legislative process work? The representative of one special interest group, say the producers of peanuts, will in the usual case not have, or control, enough votes to achieve his legislative goal, say some generous loan rate for peanuts. So he will make a deal, with the help of his lobbying friends, with other legislators for their votes in support of his loan rate proposal for which he will in turn vote in support of one of their legislative efforts. These vote trading arrangements, sometimes called logrolling are, of course, not limited to agriculture. They go on all the time for every thing of any conceivable value to the constituents of congressmen in our democracy. But we are interested here in the food, farm and rural sectors, and the congressional representatives of commercial farmers, and their lobbying associates, have developed the logrolling process to a fine art.

As Tullock and Hillman point out, this political structure and legislative process is extremely hard to break through (Tullock and Hillman 1989). What fails to fit the needs or wishes of the farmers' congressional representatives and their lobbying associates simply dies in committee. But historically there have been breakthroughs. These have occurred when a strong president has gone over the heads of the legislators and taken his case directly to the people, to the voters. On occasion a strong president has pushed legislation of national importance through a reluctant Congress by appealing directly to the people and marshalling their support. It can be done, and it has been done.

The Presidential Formula

How can a strong president break through the special-interest, legislative bargaining process and pass farm policy reform legislation? That is the question. First, to be strong in the political sense the president must have been elected by a solid majority of the voters; he must have a recognized mandate to govern. Second, the president must be knowledgeable about the problems and conditions of agriculture and rural America and have a desire to do something about them (the knowledge may be first hand, or the product of good staff work). Third, the president must be willing to spend some of his political capital to marshal the many and diverse groups of people who have a legitimate interest in the food they eat, the business of farming and rural America, and resource use and conservation, and then use the political power so derived to break the stranglehold of the special interest in the legislative process. We will return to the role of the strong president in obtaining the passage of farm policy reform legislation later in this chapter, but the central idea to grasp is this: the strong president becomes stronger and derives the political muscle to pass farm policy legislation by "leap-frogging" the congressional bargaining process and going straight to the people, the voters, who have a legitimate interest in the results that will flow from the legislative reforms.

The question may be asked: Where do we find such a president? They don't come along often, but they do come along. The two Roosevelts come to mind. Theodore Roosevelt, a Republican, felt deeply about the need to protect and conserve our natural resources and he had the political strength to take action in this direction; the Forest Service was created and new policies came into being to promote and control irrigation development, land reclamation and the use of hydroelectric power during his administrations. Franklin D. Roosevelt, a Democrat, had a similar concern about the need to protect and conserve our natural resources, and a driving interest to improve the economic lot of farm people. Thus he and his lieutenants conceived and pushed through all manner of government programs to protect and conserve our natural resources and to assist farmers economically as well as improve their quality of life. These included the Farm Credit Act of 1933, the Agricultural Adjustment Administration, the Civilian Conservation Corps (CCC), the Soil Conservation Service, the Taylor Grazing Act, the Tennessee Valley Authority, the Farm Security Administration, the Rural Electrification Administration (REA), and a whole series of food distribution agencies. Franklin D. Roosevelt used the great power of the presidential office to marshal the political power to push reform legislation through a Congress, often as opposed to reform as the Congress of 1992, and just as controlled by special interest groups. But President Roosevelt had a deep interest in rural America, and he had the will to use the power of the presidency to push legislation through the thicket of special interests in the Congress. The result was a set of policies and programs with the capacity to deal with the resource conservation needs of his day and the economic problems of farmers and rural America in the 1930s.

We do not have in the early 1990s the crisis of a Great Depression to motivate a president, but we do have environmental problems in both urban and rural America that have reached crisis proportions; we have rural communities in many parts of the nation that are dying; and we have a set of farm commodity programs designed decades ago for an agriculture of a completely different structure from that in existence today, which is providing substantial income subsidies to the already rich farmers and doing little or nothing to help small and part-time farmers. These problems prompted the writing of this book, and could and should prompt a president to take the leadership in developing and pushing to fruition policy reforms for the food, farm and rural sectors.

But we also have a Congress structured to provide benefits to the special interests which work with, or control, the congressional representatives with the same legislative interests. In this context the policy reforms which we propose will emerge from the Congress when, and only when, a strong president gets behind them and marshals the overall political power to break the stranglehold of the special interests in the legislative process.

The Groups Involved

Who are the people in the national society who have an interest in the policy reforms that we have proposed? And what coalition, we argue, must be marshalled by a strong president to effectuate those reforms? We would include ten groups. Certain of these groups are very homogeneous, but others are heterogeneous. And, of course, some analysts might include groups of people that we have left out, and omit groups that we have included. In our judgement the following groups of people would have sufficient interest in the reforms proposed in Chapter 6 to constitute a latent political force, which if marshalled by a strong president, could provide the political power to enact these or similar reforms into legislation. These groups are:

1. Farmers and their families who are dissatisfied with the present thrust of farm programs.
2. Rural leaders (religious leaders, bankers, educators, some local politicians, and some farmers) who see their communities dying.
3. Nonfarm people who are concerned about the costs of existing commodity programs.
4. Urban and rural people concerned about the environment.
5. People concerned about the quality and safety of their food.
6. Minority groups and others subject to discrimination (Blacks, Hispanics and Native Americans).
7. The elderly, ranging from the economically well-off who seek environmentally safe places to retire, to the poor who need food and housing assistance.
8. Professional social workers, and many social scientists.
9. Members of society who are highly motivated to improve economic and social conditions of the poor.
10. The poor themselves, both urban and rural, who do not fit in to any of the groups listed above.

The first group really divides into two subgroups. The first subgroup is made up of farmers who believe that the government should not intervene in the economy—that it is wrong for the government to take programmatic actions to control production and support farm prices and incomes. This belief may stem from economic reasoning that a free market provides the best form of economic organization, or it may stem from moral or religious teachings. But the policy conclusion is the same. Government should get out of the business of managing or supporting or directing the farm economy. This sub-group of farmers could be most helpful in eliminating the traditional commodity programs, but farmers in this group might find it difficult to support many of the other proposals set forth in Chapter 6.

Farmers in the second sub-group are not necessarily opposed to government intervention in the farm economy, but they are most unhappy with the direction that intervention has taken. These are the conservation minded farmers—farmers who have been active in soil conservation work for years, who now are a part of the Low-Input Sustainable Agricultural Movement, or who may have taken the final step into organic farming. These farmers would like to see less emphasis on government programming of price and income support, which induces farmers to make heavy use of chemical fertilizers and toxic pesticides, and greater emphasis on research, extension, and economic incentives which (a) encourage farmers to cut back on farm chemical usage and (b) encourages farmers to adopt low-input, sustainable agricultural practices. As of 1992 this is a relatively small group of farmers, comprising no more than 5 to 10 percent of all farmers. But it is a rapidly growing group. And important to this discussion, it is a group which would support the policy reforms proposed in Chapter 6 with verve and vigor. What farmers in this group need is a president and a secretary of agriculture to lead them.

The second group, rural leaders, is a heterogenous group. Many of the people in this group are already politically active: religious leaders through their church affiliation, bankers through their banking associations, educators through their educational organizations and farmers through their farm organizations. But their focus on the needs of rural communities is often lost in the wider agendas of their respective associations and organizations. What these people need to support their efforts is the belief and the conviction that someone is listening to them, and that there is a reasonable chance that their efforts will have a pay-off in the form of more prosperous and viable rural communities. A president with a strong message on the need to improve the rural environment and promote rural development can be instrumental in helping these rural leaders gain the belief and the conviction that positive things are going to happen in their communities. The result should then be a redoubling of the efforts of these rural leaders to enact the kinds of reforms proposed in this volume. This form of political support is essential to our reform agenda, because it points out to congressional representatives from nonmetropolitan areas that they must consider the needs of constituents other than those of large commercial farmers in their districts.

The third group, those concerned with farm program costs, breaks down neatly into two subgroups. The first subgroup is concerned with getting government out of agriculture and cutting program expenditures to the bone; the second subgroup is generally sympathetic to some form of assistance for agriculture, but feels that the making of payments (and sometimes very large payments) to large and often rich farmers is wrong and should be stopped. The authors do not know how the numbers break down between these subgroups in our society, and we recognize that our reform agenda is not likely to appeal to the severe program cost cutters. But we believe that our policy proposals are tailor-made for those members of society who believe that agriculture and rural America need some form of constructive assistance, but that the commodity programs, as they now stand, are highly skewed to those already most advantaged with large landholdings. To those people who object to this inequity, the president can and should make a strong appeal for support. These are likely to be urban people, subject to some of the false images discussed in Chapter 2, but who believe intuitively that constructive reforms are needed in agriculture and rural America, not a cost-cutting spree across the board. A president with an appreciation of the needs of agriculture and rural America could, through a strong and informative message to these kinds of people, convert them into a powerful political force.

The fourth group, those with environmental concerns, has the potential for becoming one of, if not the most, potent political force in support of our policy proposals. This is a growing group; it is homogeneous in terms of interest; and the members tend to be politically active. The members of this group do not need to be mobilized; they are already mobilized. What they need is leadership at the national level. A president with a strong environmental message could turn the membership of this group into an army of political workers: letter writers, door-to-door canvassers and campaign contributors. All these people need is some political guidance from a strong president.

The fifth group, people with food quality and safety concerns, is a heterogeneous, disorganized group. Yet the people in this group are deeply concerned about food quality and food safety for themselves and their families, and have learned over the past several decades that their state of health depends to a large degree on what they eat. As consumers of food they are barraged by advertisements about what they should and should not eat, and they see their government, at all levels, influenced by commodity and business interests. Thus, they are often in a quandary about what they should and should not eat. It is not likely that the members of this group could be mobilized into a potent political force, as in the case of the environmental group. Nonetheless, a president who could convince consumers of food, by word and deed, that he was initiating programs designed to guarantee their safety, and to provide them with objective dietary information, would certainly go a long way toward building an electorate supportive of general reforms in the agricultural and rural sectors. This is a wide and amorphous group, but a president who could build trust on the part of members of this group with respect to their special interest, food safety, would certainly build trust and support for related program initiatives.

The sixth group, disadvantaged racial minorities, is already highly organized. Each minority has very specific and highly visible goals: civil rights, language protection, and treaty rights and land restoration. The problem here is to convince each group that the package of policy reforms outlined in Chapter 6 has important benefits for their peoples: food assistance, job training and actual jobs in rural areas, and housing assistance in rural areas. A president who is able to convince members of these minority groups that the above benefits would flow to them, if they supported his package of reforms for the food, farm and rural sectors, would add another and powerful contributing force to the enactment of those reforms. The leadership task here is a formidable one, because these minority peoples have been lied to and defrauded so often. But a president who gains their confidence also gains lasting and powerful political support.

The seventh group, the elderly, have become a potent force in American politics. In fact, the elderly probably constitute the largest and most cohesive interest group on the American political scene. The two goals of the highest priority for this group unquestionably are: (1) improved retirement benefits and (2) health care. But related to health care, and because many of the elderly have low incomes, the twin objective of food assistance and food safety also command high priority. Improvements in the environment and the increased viability of small towns also are important to the elderly as a means of improving their quality of life. Thus a latent, but powerful political force, in the form of the elderly exists to be marshalled in support of the policy reforms proposed in Chapter 6. A strong and politically skilled president, knowledgeable of the needs of the elderly on one hand and the needs of the food, farm and rural sectors on the other, should be able to weld them together and mobilize major political support for our policy reforms.

The eighth group, professional social workers and social scientists, does not constitute a large group in relative terms. But this group contains opinion makers and leaders, who have an important role to play in molding public opinion in support of policy changes and the enactment of legislation. These are the people who write letters to the editor, appear on public affairs programs and provide the data and the information for the president and his staff in developing a campaign of support for a policy change or the enactment of legislation. The support of this group is crucial to developing an effective campaign in support of the policy reforms proposed in Chapter 6. And the important point for this argument is that for the most part they fall on the pro-side of these reforms, because they are well aware of the inequities in the traditional commodity programs, the sad state of much of rural America, the actual and potential destruction of the environment and the food assistance needs of the poor and the homeless. Thus, once these professionals come to believe that the president is serious about dealing with the problems noted above, they will fall in behind him and give him strong support. They will now know that their knowledge and their efforts will be put to effective use.

The ninth group, those highly motivated to improve the economic and social conditions of the poor, constitute a heterogeneous group, and many of its members constitute a part of the previous groups (e.g., the environmental group, the professional social workers). Further, we have no idea how large this group may be or how important it is in the national electorate. But members of this amorphous group are highly motivated and will go the extra mile in support of their beliefs. And since the beliefs of many, if not most, "do-gooders" coincide with the policy reforms proposed in this volume, it is logical to conclude that members of this group constitute a built-in constituency in support of those reforms. In fact, an unfriendly critic of these reforms might say that they were proposed by a couple of "do-gooders." In any event, highly motivated members of society desirous of improving the economic and social conditions of the poor are certain to give unstintingly of their time and resources in support of our policy reforms.

The tenth group, the poor themselves, as it says in the book of Matthew "are always with you" (Matthew 26:11). And never was this more true than in the United States in the late 1980s and early 1990s. And it would also appear to be a group that is growing in size. Unfortunately, the typical member of this large group is poorly informed, rarely votes and falls outside the mainstream of American politics. But the poor are not totally unrepresented in the American political process. The plight of these people gets told, or is reported, by a diverse group of "volunteer representatives." These "volunteer representatives" include: investigative news reporters, church men and women who work with the poor, foundations that report on their health status and living conditions, and various public officials (big city mayors, state welfare officials, and a few congressmen). These "volunteer representatives" keep the needs and problems of the poor in the public's eye even when the poor are unable to do it for themselves. And it is to these "volunteer representatives" of the poor with their reports, testimonies and documentaries that a strong president should turn for support in enacting the policy reforms for the food, farm and rural sectors. In asking for their support, he could detail the many, many ways that these reforms could help the poor: food assistance, housing assistance, job training and jobs themselves. A skillful president could create a whole new dimension of political support from these "volunteer representatives" and their clients, the poor.

These then are the groups that can be marshalled in support of the proposed policy reforms by a strong and skilled president. Certain of them are large in size and cohesive in membership, others are heterogeneous and unknown in size. Some are already politically active in our areas of concern (e.g., the environmental groups), others constitute a latent political force. But all require the effective leadership that a strong president can provide. And one thing is certain, the policy reforms proposed here will die in congressional committee as the results of pressures from existing commodity associations of large farmers, unless the groups described above are mobilized in an effective manner in support of the reforms.

The Mechanics of the Operation

The question needs to be asked: How does the president operate to enact a set of policy reforms into legislation? Or stated differently what steps must a president take to move a set of program ideas—in this case new program ideas for the food, farm and rural sectors—into legislation? We suggest that four basic steps are involved; of course, there are a large number of actions in each step.

First, the president must appoint a secretary of agriculture, and a secretary of interior as well, sympathetic to the policy reforms proposed here. These two Cabinet members with their staffs must convert these policy proposals into workable program proposals and then into a comprehensive legislative package. After all the program details have been worked out and the budget requirements agreed upon, the package is then submitted to the president for his approval.

Second, the president will submit the proposed legislative package to Congress once his staff has reviewed it and approved it. But in submitting it to Congress the president must have worked out arrangements with the leadership in the two Houses whereby the package is broken down and parts of it assigned to committees that are at least moderately sympathetic to the proposals. By this strategy, if parts of the package are killed in hostile committees, those parts can be added to the legislative packages on the floor of the House and the Senate, if some parts of the proposed legislation make it through committees that are friendly to it. The arrangements that the president makes with leaders of the House and Senate regarding the handling of a bill in the legislative process is all important in guiding it through the legislative maze.

Third, the president must seek out and gain the active support of influential senators and representatives for this piece of legislation. Their active support is required in a number of ways: to initially sponsor the legislation, to speak for it and protect it in committee sessions, to speak for it and support it on the floor of the Senate and the House, to travel around the country to give speeches in its behalf, and help the president marshal support for it in the critical legislative process. The president is the central figure in this process, but he must have help. Influential senators and representatives can provide that help.

Fourth, the president, by speeches, news conferences, the issuance of special or technical reports, and letters and phone calls must marshal the ten groups that we have described and convert them into an effective political force in support of this legislative proposal for the food, farm and rural sectors. This political force will take the form of letters and phone calls to their elected representatives, meeting and conferences in support of the legislation, news stories and paid advertisements of all kinds. The president must lead his troops, the political activists in the ten groups, and demonstrate to the congressional legislators that the support for this legislative package far out-weights the opposition which the entrenched interests can muster.

In all this the president is the central figure providing leadership, intellectual guidance and political strategy in a complex political process. To gain the passage of a controversial piece of reform legislation he must bring together many and diverse people and groups in which these people and groups give generously of their time and resources as well as risk their reputations. Reform legislation of the type under consideration here does not get enacted into law because a few people think that it is a good idea. The entrenched interests have rendered any major reforms to farm legislation "dead on arrival" to the Congress since the end of World War II. The policy reforms proposed in Chapter 6 for the food, farm and rural sectors will gain passage into law only by a step-by-step process, directed by a strong president along the lines outlined in this section.

The Strong President in Modern America

Can the modern American society produce the kind of strong president extolled in these pages? And, if it can, will such a strong president have any more interest in dealing constructively with the problems of the food, farm and rural sectors than recently elected presidents? The cool, cynic of modern urban America will give the answer of "no" to both questions.

We hope this is not the case. And, we believe, it need not be the case.

There are some hopeful stirrings on the American political scene. The news media, at least the printed news media, has shown some remorse over the way it covered the 1988 presidential election, giving too much emphasis to the sensational and too little attention to the issues. Some writers and editors have promised to do better in the future. The politicians themselves are beginning to worry about the insane methods of campaign fund raising of which they are a part. There appears to be some serious talk about curbing the worst excesses of campaign fund raising. And in states like California, where the elected politicians have refused to deal with tough economic and social problems, the people are taking government in their own hands through the petition and referendum initiative. Whether this latter kind of political action leads to good government the authors are not sure, but certainly it illustrates how the people can and will act where the elected politicians will not deal with difficult issues.

This latter form of political action is suggestive further of the means whereby the nation can produce presidents with the capacity and the will to push to enactment the kind of policy reform package under discussion in this volume. The people in the ten groups identified in this chapter through their organizations *plus* many, many other groups of people—professional groups, business groups, labor groups, women's groups, peace groups and on and on—must force candidates for political office to take stands on the important issues of the day. If the people in the groups care enough and become involved enough, they can succeed in forcing the candidates to discuss the issues and ultimately take stands on those issues. The negative weapons of such organizations of concerned people include the withholding of endorsements and the withholding of campaign contributions. The positive weapons include the sponsoring of public lectures and debates, the issuance of reports and "white papers" on the issues involved and the position of the candidates on those issues, and, of course, paid newspaper and T.V. advertisements.

The point we wish to make is the following—if the people of America are willing to select their president on the basis of the images flashed on the T.V. screen in 30-second sound bites, then they are going to get for a president the type of leader that the image makers want. But if they are willing to give of themselves in the electoral process through the activities of their organizations, then they can make a difference with respect to who is nominated and who is elected. The power of the people to make a difference in legislation and political outcomes has been demonstrated in recent years by the petition and referendum initiatives in California, and in the unfortunate struggle over abortion rights.

The political role of the ten groups of people identified earlier in gaining passage of the policy reforms is thus a double one. They must through an understanding of their linkages to the food, farm and rural sectors be active in inducing and/or forcing candidates for the presidency to discuss its problems and conditions, and to take stands on the issues involved. Once a president is elected who shows a willingness to undertake policy reforms, in the food, farm and rural sectors, then those people must become the troops who help the president push those reforms through a Congress that is not likely to be cooperative in passing a piece of legislation that violates their usual vote-trading, logrolling way of doing political business.

We have identified ten groups of people, besides the large commercial farmers, who have a legitimate interest in what goes on in the food, farm, and rural sectors. If these people play an active role in the political process—in electing a president willing to push the kinds of reforms proposed in this volume and then in supporting that push once the reforms are before Congress—then chances of these reforms becoming law are good. We believe that people can make a difference. But if we continue to go down the political road of the past 20 years in which the "farm bills" are hatched in Congress, without a strong presidential input, and through the "friendly" working relationships between the elected representatives in the agricultural committees and the entrenched special interest groups, then no major reforms in the food, farm and rural sectors are going to occur.

Notes

1. For a fuller discussion of these reform efforts see Chapter 3 of Cochrane and Ryan (1976).

References

Cochrane, Willard W, and Mary F. Ryan 1976. *American Farm Policy 1948 1973*. Minneapolis: University of Minnesota Press.
Tullock, Gordon and J. Hillman. 1989, September. "Public Choice and Agriculture: An American Example." Lecture at the 9th World Congress of the International Economic Association.

11 The Closing Argument

The agricultural policy reforms that we have advanced, while composed of many complicated details, have a straightforward rationale. Current policy has become so dysfunctional that it fails to provide benefits fairly and efficiently, damages the environment and inadequately supports the commercial farm sector. It is time for a change. When reduced to its essentials, our agenda for policy reform can be stated in terms of four basic points.

First, current agricultural policies offend a basic, widely held principle: fairness. By providing the lion's share of benefits to a relatively few, large commercial farmers, existing policies skew the distribution of farm income, encourage the enlargement of farms through the cannibalization of smaller farmers, and provide almost no help to part-time operators and nonfarm rural people.

Second, current policies are strikingly inefficient, in numerous ways. While inefficiency is not a new problem in government policy, or agriculture, farm programs manifest such obvious distortions, contradictions, and lack of impact in achieving their goals that they call out for reform in the name of taxpayers who are footing the bill. Of the many government intervention schemes that bolster the U.S. economy, agriculture has become a leading candidate for the title of most serious "government failure." The impacts of this inefficiency are felt both domestically and internationally.

Third, agricultural policy has increasingly been identified with serious negative impacts on the environment. We believe that the future of the environment is so important to the American people that agricultural policy cannot give it too much attention. The environmental agenda, together with the need to refocus farm programs on broader objectives of rural development and rural people, are key elements of our reforms.

Where does this reorientation of agricultural policy leave the modern, highly efficient, commercial farmer, on whom the nation relies for the great bulk of its food and fiber? If greater fairness, efficiency, and environmental quality are the first three reasons to adopt sweeping reforms, a fourth, of equal importance, is to continue to assure the competitiveness of American commercial agriculture. It bears repeating that we do not propose to cut commercial producers loose to fend for themselves in an open marketplace. On the contrary, we provide for substantial government intervention in the commercial farm sector. This intervention takes the form of a four-part income stabilization program, including direct government payments in times of deteriorating terms of trade, a commodity stabilization program that purchases, stores, sells, and donates surplus production, an expanded crop insurance plan, and a government purchasing program for perishable commodities when market gluts occur. We believe that these will protect farm income from sharp downward swings, but will also stop the taxpayer from writing a blank check each year to large farm producers who increasingly have looked to government, rather than the market, as their primary source of support. We also propose to continue to put resources into research designed to maintain commercial agriculture as one of America's world class industries, competitively positioned to continue to capture global markets.

The reforms that we advocate are not the result of a laissez-faire philosophy, in which government is entirely removed from the food and agricultural sector. This will never happen, nor should it. There is an important role for government in agriculture, but not the role it is playing now. We propose to continue intervening to stabilize farm incomes. But we propose much more than that.

In essence, we have argued that agricultural policy cannot afford to focus primarily on 300,000 or so large commercial farms, to the exclusion of millions of other rural residents, and in spite of its environmental and social impacts. Rather than a policy to support farm incomes at all times and in direct proportion to farm size, we would stabilize farm incomes in times of trouble, and limit this to a reduced (though still ample) direct payment of $20,000 per farm and $7.0 billion overall. The result will be to distribute government income stabilization payments far more fairly. But farm income stabilization is only one of several targets. We also aim to improve the rural economy as a whole, through a variety of infrastructure improvements and aids to part-time farmers, and to launch a major program of environmental affirmative actions. The result will be a policy which is fairer, more efficient, and more protective of the environment, but which continues to assure income stability in commercial farming.

In this final chapter, we will draw together the threads of our proposal, showing how it promotes greater fairness, efficiency, and environmental quality, while maintaining a commercial farm income safety net. This is our closing and final argument, which we present to a jury of our colleagues, leaders in the Congress and administration, and the public.

Fairness

Aaron Wildavsky (1979), in a well-know study, noted that the role of
the policy analyst is to "speak truth to power." Our purpose in drawing
attention to the unfairness inherent in the design of farm programs is to
unmask claims that farm policy is focused on the small "family farm" and
to tell the truth about its actual distributive effects. We have documented
these effects in earlier chapters, showing that roughly 90 percent of farm
support payments flow to only 20 percent of producers. This truth is an
uncomfortable one, for it shatters the illusion that these programs are
keeping small farmers in business.

To whom are we speaking? Not just to the powerful farm lobbies, but
to the president and his assistants and the Congress and the overwhelming
number of urban voters who elect them. If voters knew that their hard-
earned dollars were spent in 1989 to provide payments averaging $31,718
to farmers with gross incomes averaging $500,000 or more, they might tell
their congressman to reconsider how such payments are made (USDA/ERS
1991). Even if farmers are deserving of some government assistance, there
are surely more equitable ways of providing it.

Our proposal is to revamp the way in which these payments are made.
In Chapters 3 and 4 we emphasized the basic issues that any farm income
stabilization scheme must address. We address these issues by converting
the current "bases" for various crops into a whole farm base, on which
payments are made per acre, but only in those years in which product prices
are falling at the farm gate relative to the prices that farmers must pay for
seed, fertilizer, equipment, and interest. We do *not* pay farmers come thick
or thin. In addition, we strictly cap these payments at $20,000 per farm, and
$7.0 billion overall. The effect is both to limit total spending and (because
current payment limits are abused, leading the rich to get richer) to curtail
large payments to large producers. This is the Will Rogers principle: that
money, like manure, is spent best when it is spread more evenly.

While fairness is the driving principle behind this policy, its effect will
be to slow the process of cannibalization of small farmers by the large. In
order to focus more attention on these small farmers, as well as on the
majority of rural residents who are not farmers, we provide for both a Part-
time Farming Agency and a Rural Development Agency. The Part-time
Farming Agency will make county extension offices a source of information
targeted especially to these farmers. The Rural Development Agency will
be a one-stop source of financial assistance to rural families, communities

seeking to underwrite health care facilities, day care programs, or schools, and counties attempting to maintain the quality of rural roads, bridges, and waste treatment.

The idea of fairness is also behind the reforms in the "other" programs discussed in Chapter 5. We continue existing food assistance programs to the underprivileged and provide for special programs for infants, children, and the elderly, through new community food centers, nursing homes, and other facilities, which are targeted to those segments of the population too poor or infirm to provide for themselves. Similarly, programs designed to help migrant farm labor, and to improve the safety of farm work, are meant to fill current gaps in the capacity of individuals to fend for themselves in the face of unemployment and occupational risks.

Of course, these innovations will cost money, although the amount spent per child, or per part-time farmer, or per elderly rural resident, will be likely to be very small in comparison with current program spending for large farmers. By redirecting these resources to populations most in need of food, or advice, or financial assistance, we will not only make agricultural policy more fair. We will also broaden the base of its political support, by spreading its benefits to many who now receive almost no help at all. This is why, despite the anticipated opposition of large commercial farmers, we think that a strong leader—a strong president—could carry our plan successfully with a majority of voters and members of Congress.

Efficiency

The late Arthur Okun, in a famous treatment of the trade-offs between fairness and efficiency, employed what he called the "leaky bucket" test (Okun 1976). If the objective of a program or policy is to transfer money or benefits from one group to another, it is like carrying a bucket of water. We can measure the efficiency of the transfer by how much of it leaks along the way. U.S. farm programs today are a very leaky bucket, which taxpayers fill with a portion of their income so that payments can be meted out year after year, encouraging farmers to plant crops whether or not they are in demand. The inefficiencies in this system—its leakages—are so many as to defy summary. Consider some examples, divided into domestic and international cases.

Domestically, the commodity programs have made "farming the government" more profitable than seeking new markets. While the 1990 farm bill takes certain steps away from the support of prices for specific crops, and toward a whole farm base, it still locks many farmers into continued reliance on the government for signals about what to grow.

Current policy persists in paying farmers to grow on the one hand while demanding that they take acres *out* of production with the other. We have likened this to keeping one foot on the brake and one foot on the gas simultaneously. It would be very inefficient to run a car this way, and it is a very inefficient way to run farm policy.

The "triple base" or "flex-acres" improvements made under the 1990 bill are only a small step toward our "whole farm base." In wheat country, for example, the so-called "triple base" plan reduces deficiency payments, and in return grants "flexibility" to plant other crops on wheat base acres. But it continues to mandate acreage reductions. Most wheat farmers have very few options other than wheat, for reasons of climate and soils. Hence, the 1990 farm bill gives some flexibility, but not nearly enough, in proportion to the resources and acres eligible for planting that are taken away. In the financial sector, to take another example, the Farmers Home Administration (FmHA) has long been criticized for granting "emergency loans" to virtually all comers, leading to a very high proportion of delinquencies and defaults, again at taxpayer expense. While efforts have been made to patch these leaks, they are still a serious problem, and will become worse in any future recession.

These examples illustrate why we have argued for a major overhaul in the way domestic crop support programs work as well as the termination of most FmHA programs (with the exception of the rural housing program). The inefficiencies of the current system demand a new approach, in which a straightforward income stabilization payment is made to farmers *only* in times of need, in which no one is paid *not* to produce, in which financial assistance is spread to more groups and better risks, and in which total taxpayer liabilities are kept down by strict caps on spending.

Internationally, U.S. farm programs have also contributed to inefficiency, although of a different sort. Consider the U.S. sugar program. While taxpayers do not directly pay beet sugar or cane growers, as consumers they pay as much as four times the price sugar fetches in other countries because import quotas hold domestic prices high. Efficient producers of sugar, such as the Caribbean nations, are kept out of the U.S. market so that relatively inefficient production can be maintained in the United States. This is why we have proposed the conversion of these quotas to tariffs, and the reduction of these tariffs according to a fixed schedule of 25 percent over five years, and further if other countries will agree to do the same. Sugar growers in the United States could enter their acres into a whole farm base.

Internationally, we have also called for the elimination of export subsidies. The Export Enhancement Program (EEP), discussed earlier, is a notorious case of the leaky bucket. In theory it is to create "new markets" for U.S. exports. In fact, the United States has spent billions of dollars on these subsidies, the benefits of which flow indirectly, and only marginally, to farmers. While little market creation has occurred, the level of spending on EEP, which has been more than matched by the European Community, has seriously depressed world prices. It would have been more efficient to pay farmers for their wheat directly and then to have given it away or destroyed it.

The international policy we have proposed for the United States strongly supports trade liberalization under the auspices of the General Agreement on Tariffs and Trade (GATT) and through further bilateral deals with Japan, Mexico, and our other trading partners. Since World War II, GATT has been a major force allowing more efficient allocation of global production—except in agriculture, where protectionism persists. In the manufacturing sector, the result has been to multiply the rate of world economic growth, meaning more jobs, higher incomes, and more trade than anyone thought possible at GATT's inception in 1947. We believe that a similar success is possible in agriculture, but only if countries can find a way to liberalize trade *and* maintain farm income stability. This is the purpose of our "safety net" payments to commercial farmers.

The reason that we support more liberal trade in agriculture is not that we think that "free trade" is possible, or even desirable. It is because, relative to the protectionism that exists today, a *more* open trading system in agriculture *will work to the overall advantage of U.S. farmers, because they are among the most individually efficient producers in the world*. If the farm sector and the rural communities of the United States do not continue to produce for export markets around the globe, they will lose more farmers and farms. We are a trading nation, with a strong comparative advantage in agriculture, simply because we have more efficient producers than most other countries—an efficiency based on human skills, improved, modern technologies, and bountiful natural resources. If we protect them behind walls of quotas and subsidies, however, they will lose that edge. At the same time, trade liberalization will benefit poor farmers in many developing countries who have been shut out of high income markets by policies like the sugar import quotas. While poor, many of these farmers are also efficient producers, whose earnings from expanded access to these markets would spur demand for more U.S. exports, both in and out of agriculture.

Environmental Quality

In reaching out to include a variety of groups affected by agriculture but not well covered by farm programs, we have given special emphasis to the environment. This emphasis arises directly from our experience and beliefs. We are not alone in these beliefs, however. Virtually every opinion poll of the last decade has recorded a strong and growing constituency for improved environmental quality. As the effects of modern farming practices on surface and groundwater, soil loss, wildlife, and human health have become more clear, the public has focused its attention more directly on agriculture as a source of these problems. Additions to the 1985 farm bill, continued in the 1990 act, reflected a growing recognition that agricultural and environmental policy are now, and forever, intertwined.

Unfortunately, despite changes in recent law, the U.S. Department of Agriculture has yet to commit itself fully to an environmental agenda. This commitment will involve not only the resolution of existing environmental problems, but an aggressive program of environmental affirmative actions that will *improve* water quality, *reduce* soil erosion, *expand* greenbelts and wilderness areas, *protect* wildlife, and *enhance* the quality of our food and our way of life. Just as expanding the mandate of agricultural policy to include nonfarm rural people and food and feeding programs broadens its constituency, so would an active commitment to the environment. This broadened base would further enhance the political attractiveness of the proposed reforms.

We have outlined a major set of environmental initiatives with several prominent features. We would expand and redesign the Conservation Reserve Program, with additional coverage of wetlands and a system of penalties and rewards for environmental damages and improvements on agricultural lands. The overcrowded and undermanaged national parks and forests would be expanded, with specific attention, including expanded research, given to biological diversity. Water quality would be raised to the highest priority. Green belts would be established around urban areas. Agricultural chemicals would be subjected to new review processes that are both more comprehensive, but less time-consuming, in recognition of the public's growing concern with food safety. Finally, a variety of institutional reforms will be required to implement this broad scheme, affecting numerous agencies of the federal government.

Like the issue of improved efficiency, improvements in environmental quality have not only domestic but international implications. If the United States is not willing to make environmental quality a global issue, then our own efforts to improve the environment will be frustrated by other countries' failure to do so. Perhaps the clearest case is that of food safety, since many specialty food products which Americans consume are grown or produced abroad.

Commercial Agriculture

Despite the often harsh criticism that we have directed at the design of farm programs, and the particular focus we have given to the failures resulting from concentrating so many benefits in so few hands, the commercial farm sector that reaps these benefits is not really the culprit. Naturally, interest groups arrayed around particular commodity groups, like the National Corn Growers Association or the U.S. Sugar Beet Association or the National Milk Producers Federation, are concerned with protecting whatever benefits these programs provide. It would be foolish not to.

But the real reasons that farm programs have evolved in the way they have is rooted in institutional history. Farm legislation was passed in the 1930s to prevent total ruin for a sector that accounted for nearly a third of the population. Since then, although the details have changed, the thrust of farm programs has remained the same: price and income support to farmers is provided on the basis of the number of units of product which each farmer produces. When such price and income support results in surplus production the government takes a combination of intervening actions—acreage reduction programs, foreign surplus disposal and various kinds of border protection. To complicate this chronic excess production problem, the government then spends substantial sums on research to improve overall agricultural productivity.

In this context, as fewer and fewer farmers over the last half century fed a growing population, it was inevitable that those remaining would garner more benefits in proportionate terms than at the outset. And members of Congress, ever-willing to find ways of spending taxpayers' money on their own constituents, discovered in the farm programs a way to do just that. From a rural congressman's point of view, what difference does it make that a program is unfair, inefficient or even environmentally harmful, so long as his or her vocal and powerful constituents are pleased, and everybody else remains confused by the complexity of agricultural legislation?

Yet even within the farm sector, the concentration of these benefits on a favored few—today about 300,000 of the largest producers—has led to calls for change in the name of a larger public interest in rural development and environmental quality. What is critical is that in making such changes, we do not lose sight of the fact that the talents of the American commercial farmer, and the agricultural marketing system of the United States, are the envy of the world. We would aggressively expand research for the utilization and efficiency of U.S. agriculture, as well as directing research dollars at environmental improvements in farming practices. Both agricultural productivity *and* environmental quality would be given equal emphasis. As a critical positive contributor to the U.S. balance of payments, as a key strategic sector, and as the source of our daily bread, it would be folly to undertake policies that would jeopardize American agricultural competitiveness.

Rural America

While we believe that commercial agriculture will prosper under our proposals, our larger concern is with rural America as a whole. For decades the federal government has been niggardly in its support of the nonfarm rural economy while lavishing huge expenditures on commercial farming. We believe this one-sided support is bad. First, it is unfair. Second, it ignores the potential for economic development in a sector with extensive underemployed resources. The Cochrane-Runge proposals seek to change this. Part-time farmers and nonfarm rural residents would be major beneficiaries under our proposals which include a wide range of specific programs: housing assistance, training grants, child care, an effective employment system, technical production assistance, rural credit expansion, low-interest loans to provide and improve physical infrastructure, and improved education and health care. This array of programs properly supported should make the concept of rural development come alive.

Beyond the borders of the United States, our reforms would lead to active negotiations to expand foreign markets for U.S. products, but without the crippling retaliation and beggar-thy-neighbor effects of export subsidy wars.

The authors of this book have been critical of past and present policies, but have been driven by something deeper and more important than this critical view. We hold a future vision of American agriculture and rural life in which agriculture continues to produce bountifully, but where government acts to assure that the fruits of this bounty are more fairly and efficiently distributed, in which the environmental quality of rural areas is enhanced and improved, and in which farming is again regarded as a sustainable way for families to make either a full or part-time living. This vision is within our grasp, if we are prepared, like the creators of the New Deal programs were, to seize our future, rather than to remain captured by our past. With appropriate leadership, this vision can be realized. Without it, we are condemned to a recurrent exercise in governmental waste.

References

Okun, Arthur M. 1975. *Equality and Efficiency, The Big Tradeoff*, Washington, D.C.: Brookings Institution.

U.S. Department of Agriculture/ERS. 1991. *Economic Indicators of the Farm Sector, National Financial Summary, 1989*. ECIFS 9-2. Washington, D.C.: USDA/ERS.

Wildavsky, Aaron B. 1979. *Speaking Truth to Power: The Art and Craft of Policy Analysis*. Boston: Little, Brown.

INDEX